THE LOGIC OF
DECISION AND ACTION

THE LOGIC OF
DECISION AND ACTION

Edited by

Nicholas Rescher

Essays by

Alan Ross Anderson   Nicholas Rescher
Donald Davidson   Herbert A. Simon
Georg Henrik von Wright

With Comments by

R. Ackermann   H. N. Castaneda
A. R. Anderson   R. M. Chisholm
N. D. Belnap, Jr.   E. J. Lemmon
R. Binkley   J. Robison

UNIVERSITY OF PITTSBURGH PRESS

Library of Congress Catalog Card Number: 67–18272

Manufactured in England by
Stephen Austin & Sons, Ltd., Hertford

DEDICATION

Its contributors dedicate this volume
to the memory of their fellow symposiast

E. J. LEMMON

whose premature death in the summer of 1966
robbed the discipline of philosophical logic of one
of its ablest and most promising contributors.

CONTENTS

Page

PREFACE ix

I. *The Logic of Heuristic Decision Making*
   Herbert A. Simon 1
   A. *Comments* by R. Binkley 21
   B. *Comments* by N. D. Belnap, Jr. 27
   C. *Reply* by H. A. Simon 32

II. *Semantic Foundations for the Logic of Preference*
   Nicholas Rescher 37
   A. *Comments* by A. R. Anderson 63
   B. *Comments* by R. Ackermann 71
   C. *Reply* by N. Rescher 77

III. *The Logical Form of Action Sentences*
   Donald Davidson 81
   A. *Comments* by E. J. Lemmon 96
   B. *Comments* by H. N. Castaneda 104
   C. *Comments* by R. M. Chisholm 113
   D. *Reply* by D. Davidson 115

IV. *The Logic of Action: A Sketch*
   Georg Henrik von Wright 121
   A. *Comments* by R. M. Chisholm 137
   B. *Comments* by J. Robison 140
   C. *Reply* by G. H. von Wright 144

APPENDIX I: *The Formal Analysis of Normative Systems*
   Alan Ross Anderson 147

APPENDIX II: *Aspects of Action*
   Nicholas Rescher 215

INDEX OF NAMES 221

SUBJECT INDEX 223

PREFACE

THE PAPERS collected in the body of this volume – all of them original studies – were first presented at a three-day conference on *The Logic of Decision and Action* held at the University of Pittsburgh in March 1966, under the sponsorship of its Department of Philosophy. I am happy to be able to include as an Appendix a paper by my colleague Alan Ross Anderson, which has been highly influential since its initial circulation ten years ago in mimeographed form, but which has not heretofore appeared in print.

In seeing this material through the press, I have been aided by Miss Dorothy Henle and Miss Alena Horner, and I am happy to acknowledge their assistance. I am grateful to Mr. Michael Pelon for his help in preparing the indexes.

Nicholas Rescher
Pittsburgh
June 1966

I

THE LOGIC OF HEURISTIC DECISION MAKING

Herbert A. Simon*

The task of a comprehensive theory of action is to describe or prescribe the occasions for action, the alternative courses of action (or the means of discovering them), and the choice among action alternatives. The task of a comprehensive logic of action is to describe or prescribe the rules that govern reasoning about the occasions for action, the discovery of action alternatives, and the choice of action.

Approaches to the theory of action have often taken their starting point in the modalities of common language: in the meanings of "ought" and "must" and "can."[1] But because common language is complex, flexible, and imprecise, travelers on this path have encountered formidable difficulties. To the best of my knowledge, no theory based on modalities has been developed sufficiently far to serve as a working tool for a practitioner in a field of action such as engineering or management science.

A different starting point is to ask what the practitioners actually do. How does an inventory manager decide when to reorder stock? How does an engineer design an electric motor? How does a production scheduler choose the appropriate factory employment level for the current and future months? These practitioners reason and reason to action – be it well or badly. Perhaps we shall find that they have already forged satisfactory logics of norm and action. Or perhaps, on analyzing their practice, we shall discover that the ordinary predicate calculus of declarative discourse is adequate to their purposes. By examining their reasonings, we shall perhaps be relieved entirely of the task of constructing a new logic of norm and action; at worst, we shall have to make explicit what is implicit in practice, correct it, and improve it. In any event, we may hope to find that a large part of the work has already been done for us.

For these reasons I have found the logic used by professional decision makers an excellent starting point for inquiry into the requirements of imperative and deontic logic. Particularly useful for the task are areas of

* The work reported here was supported in part by Public Health Service Research Grant MH-07722-01 from the National Institutes of Mental Health. I am indebted to Allen Newell for numerous comments and suggestions.

1 An excellent example of this approach is G. H. von Wright's *Norm and Action* (New York, The Humanities Press, 1963).

practice where the decision-making process has been imbedded in formal models: normative economics, statistical decision theory, management science, computer programming, operations research, and certain areas of modern engineering design.

In a previous paper, I reported the results of such an inquiry, concerned in the main with schemes for choosing among given action alternatives.[2] The central conclusion reached in that paper is that there is no need for a special "logic of imperatives" or "logic of action"; the basis for the conclusion is that the practitioners in the fields examined clearly get along very well without one.

> No different brand of logic is used in normative economics from that used in positive economics. On the contrary, the logic employed is the standard logic of declarative statements.
>
> Imperatives enter the normative systems through rules of correspondence that permit commands to be converted into existential statements, and existential statements into commands. The conversion process always takes place in the context of a complete model, with the command variables and environmental variables designated, the state of knowledge about the latter specified, and the causal relations among variables determined. In such a context, commands that bind one or more of the command variables can be converted to the corresponding declarative statements; while declarative statements that can be solved for command variables, but are not identities in those variables, can be converted to commands by binding the command variables with the command operator.[3]

The best-developed formal models of the decision process – those examined in Part 1 of my previous paper – are concerned largely with choice among given alternatives; the alternatives of action themselves are assumed to be known at the outset. In Part 2 of that paper, I explored in a preliminary fashion the question of whether the reasoning involved in designing possible courses of action could also be subsumed under the standard predicate calculus of declarative statements. Again, the tentative answer appeared to be affirmative. I should like to pursue that question here to a more definite conclusion, and to extend the inquiry, as well, to the reasoning involved in determining the occasions for action. The method, again, will be to point to what sophisticated practitioners actually do: to show that they reason rigorously about action without needing a special logic of action.

---

[2] H. A. Simon, "The Logic of Rational Decision," *British Journal for the Philosophy of Science*, vol. 16 (1965), pp. 169–186.

[3] *Ibid.* For fuller discussion of the contextual conditions for a model of an action system see my "Causal Ordering and Identifiability," in *Models of Man* (New York, John Wiley & Sons, 1953), ch. 1; and J. Marschak, "Statistical Inference in Economics: An Introduction," in T. C. Koopmans (ed.) *Statistical Inference in Dynamic Economic Models*. Cowles Commission Monograph No. 10 (New York, John Wiley & Sons, 1950), ch. 1.

I. PHASES OF DECISION

The decision models of classical economics do not recognize the need either to identify the occasions of action or to devise courses of action. These models presuppose that there is a well-defined criterion for choosing among possible states of the world (a utility function), and that the actual state of the world is a function of two mutually exclusive and exhaustive sets of variables, which in the paragraph quoted above are called the command variables and the environmental variables, respectively. In the dynamic case, which is the more interesting one, each variable is a function of time; hence, the task of choice is to select a function – a time path for the command variables – for a given value of the path of the environmental variables (or a probability distribution of such paths) that corresponds to the maximum of the utility function. Virtually all of the models of classical economics are variations on this central theme.

In this picture of the world, the distinction between action and inaction is meaningless. The actor is pictured as always in action: each command variable must have some definite value at each moment in time, and there are no particular values that can be identified as "no action." Doing nothing, if it can be identified at all, is simply a particular way of doing something, not distinguished in the theory from all other forms of action.

II. THE DECISION TO ATTEND

Looking now at actual formal decision models used in industrial management, we may contrast two examples: on the one hand, a scheme for determining each week the aggregate employment level and the aggregate production level (in gallons, say) of a paint factory; on the other, a scheme for replenishing warehouse inventories of particular kinds and colors of paint. Both are dynamic programming schemes, for the optimal action during a particular period depends on future events and actions. In the first example, the decision takes the form of choosing two numbers each week – a number of workmen, and a number of gallons of product. There is no concept of "inaction" in the model. In the second example, the inventory of an item is reviewed whenever a quantity is taken from inventory for shipment. Two decisions are then made: whether to order a new supply of the item from the factory; and, if so, how much to order. Of course, if the first decision is in the negative, no quantity is calculated and no order placed – no action is taken. Action is quantized, and occurs only intermittently, when the inventory on hand falls below a specified reorder point.

Under what circumstances would we expect to use such a scheme of intermittent actions, interspersed by periods of inaction? One condition is that there be fixed costs associated with each action so that, other things being equal, it is economical to act as infrequently as possible, taking a few large actions instead of many smaller ones. A price will be paid for this economy, for it will require larger average quantities of inventory to be held (the average inventory quantity will vary reciprocally with the average frequency of ordering). In the absence of uncertainty about future sales, the classical inventory problem is to fix the reorder quantity (and consequently the reorder period) so as to minimize the sum of the reordering cost and the inventory holding cost.

A second, and more interesting, circumstance under which we would expect a system to act intermittently is one where there are many different actions to be performed, but where the system is capable of performing only one or a few at a time; where the environment makes parallel demands on the system, but the system can respond only serially. As an important special case, some of the demands may occur only infrequently but may require prompt response when they occur (e.g., a fire alarm). Here the division between action and non-action is dictated by the environment.

Under any of these circumstances, one way to design the action system is to provide inventories to meet most needs for action at the time they occur, and to permit the system to replenish inventories intermittently, thus letting it attend to its several actions serially, as its abilities require. When it is not possible to stock an inventory in anticipation of a certain kind of action, an action can be given special priority, so that the system will perform it immediately on receipt of the signal calling for it. A priority system will work satisfactorily, of course, only if the totality of occasions for high-priority action is small relative to the total action capacity of the system.[4]

In rough outline, the action systems of living organisms with central nervous systems appear to correspond to this scheme. Leaving aside actions that can be carried on in parallel with others (e.g., breathing) most behaviors requiring significant participation of the central nervous system must be performed serially. Since the environment sometimes poses real-time demands on organisms (e.g., the appearance of danger), there must be provision for priorities to interrupt ongoing actions as well as for inventorying stocks (e.g., of food and water) to permit intermittent action along each dimension.

It follows that one requirement for a comprehensive logic of decision making is that it should handle the attention-directing decisions that determine when particular kinds of actions should be initiated. In this case, as in the case of choice models, we find that there already exist formal schemes for making attention-directing decisions, phrased in terms of ordinary mathematical concepts, and making use only of the declarative logic that is

---

[4] The requirements for the design of systems of this kind are outlined in my "Rational Choice and the Structure of the Environment," ch. 15 of *Models of Man, op. cit.*

used in all mathematical reasoning.[5] No special logic of action is required.

To be more specific, the typical two-bin inventory scheme operates as follows: Associated with each item stocked are a reorder point and a reorder quantity. Whenever items are drawn from inventory, the remaining quantity is compared with the reorder point; if the latter exceeds the former an order is placed for an amount equal to the reorder quantity. The reorder point is set so as to minimize the sum of costs of holding inventory and suffering outages; while the reorder quantity is set so as to minimize the sum of costs of holding inventory and ordering (there is usually an interaction between the cost functions, so that the two minimization problems must be solved simultaneously). Once the injunction, "Minimize total expected costs!" is converted to the declarative "The order point and the reorder quantity are at the levels that minimize expected costs," the reasoning task becomes a straightforward dynamic programming problem. Its solution is then reconverted to the injunctions: "Reorder whenever the quantity in stock falls below x!" and "When you reorder, order the quantity y!"

Now if there are limits on the number of different items that may be reordered during a given period (e.g., the system may restore its inventory of food or its inventory of water, but not both simultaneously), a possibility arises that the decision rules may lead to a contradiction, that is, may call for both of two incompatible actions to be performed. In actual systems, this difficulty is handled, explicitly or implicitly, by one or more supplementary injunctions: "If several actions are to be carried out, execute first the one that has been longest on the 'want' list!"; or, "Actions of class A always take precedence over other actions!" – with or without interruption of the latter; or "Execute first the action that will replenish the smallest inventory!" – where inventories are measured in expected hours to exhaustion. Rules like these, and combinations of them, can all be found in operation in existing industrial inventory and scheduling systems, and in the programs that control the behavior of animals.

In job-shop scheduling, where each of a large number of orders is to be scheduled through a different sequence of manufacturing processes, the rules determining which order will be processed next on each machine are the heart of the scheduling system. (An especially interesting contemporary class of such systems are large computing systems with provision for simultaneous access and time sharing among many users.) The imperatives in these systems answer the question "Who's next?" The choice among alternative decision rules is made by converting the imperatives to declaratives (i.e., by assuming that the system is obeying the decision rules in question), and then estimating and comparing the costs that would be incurred under each régime.

[5] K. J. Arrow, T. Harris, and J. Marschak, "Optimal Inventory Policy," *Econometrica*, vol. 19 (1951), pp. 250–272.

The fact that, in these systems, the imperatives say "when" rather than "how much" does not in any way affect the logic involved. The standard paradigm for reasoning about decision rules is the same as it is in choice models of the kinds examined in my previous paper:[6] Convert the imperatives to declaratives – that is, consider a system that behaves in accordance with the imperatives. Evaluate the outcomes for that system; and compare them with the outcomes that could be expected with different decision rules.

To illustrate the logic of attention-directing procedures, I have mostly used examples drawn from a rather special area of industrial scheduling practice. I have done so because these decision procedures have been completely formalized, hence leave no doubt as to what logic is employed. Attention-directing imperatives play a large and important role, however, in all human behavior, for reasons that have already been suggested.

Because the central nervous system can do only a few things at a time, and because the human memory and the human environment jointly contain an enormous amount of information potentially relevant to behavior, it is essential that there exist processes to determine what tiny fraction of this totality will be evoked at any given moment, and will, during that moment, constitute the effective environment of thought and behavior. It must be possible to make decisions about what to attend to before making decisions about what to do about that which is being attended to. This factorization is reflected in the basic organization of the decision-making procedures that govern human behavior.

It is easy to construct conceptual abstractions – like those in the literature of economics and statistical decision theory – that describe decision making as a process of choosing among possible states of the world. Whatever their value for conceptualizing certain aspects of the theory of choice, these abstractions cannot be taken as descriptions of actual decision-making systems, since they ignore a central fact of the decision-making process: that it must be carried out by an information processing system whose computational powers are puny in comparison with the complexity of the environment with which they must cope. Factorization of that complexity by the device of selective attention is an indispensable adaptive mechanism.

Attention-directing and priority-fixing schemes like those described work satisfactorily only in a world that is mostly empty: that is, a world in which the demands for action, and particularly for high-priority action, are small relative to the organism's total capacity for action. In such a world, the distinction between "action" and "inaction" is meaningful. Most of the time, the organism is inactive, or is attending, at most, to "background" activities that do not impose severe real-time deadlines. Anyone who has tried to design a monitor system for a time-sharing computer, has discovered

[6] *Op. cit.*, p. 179.

that the "empty world" requirement holds not only for the human condition, but for the condition of any serial processor in a world that makes unexpected and heterogeneous demands upon it.

III. Design Decisions

The second stage in decision making is to devise or discover possible courses of action. This is the activity that in fields like engineering and architecture is called "design"; in military affairs "planning"; in chemistry, "synthesis"; in other contexts, "invention"; "composition"; or – that most approving of labels – "creation." In routine, repetitive decision making, design may play a small role, for the alternatives of action may be already at hand, to be taken off the shelf as occasion requires. In slightly less structured and repetitive situations, design may require only relatively unproblematic assembly of action alternatives from prefabricated components. In most human affairs, however, the design stage in decision making occupies a far larger part of the mind's information processing capacity than either the stages of attention directing or of choice.

Design is concerned with devising possible means for ends. In the second part of my previous paper,[7] I outlined briefly some of the characteristics of the design process: its concern with relating actions to consequences, its heavy dependence on heuristics, and the major influence exercised over it by considerations of processing capacity. I should like here to develop somewhat more fully these aspects of design, and to point up their consequences for the logic of decision making.

IV. The Space of Actions and the State Space

To introduce adequately the first problem about design that we shall consider, I must digress to the passage of the *Meno* where Meno asks:

> And how will you inquire, Socrates, into that which you know not? What will you put forth as the subject of inquiry? And if you find what you want, how will you ever know that this is what you did not know?

We are all familiar with Socrates' answer to the conundrum, his theory of recollection. No intelligent schoolboy today would accept that answer as anything but sophistic, but in our delight in Socrates' clever dialog with Meno's slave, we forgive his tricking us, and we ignore the force of Meno's still-unanswered question. In particular, Socrates completely avoids, does not even restate correctly, the last part of the question: "And if you find what you want, how will you ever know that this is what you did not know?" How do you identify the answer as the answer to *that* question?

---

[7] *Op. cit.*, pp. 179–186

If the answer to Meno's puzzle seems obvious, you have not felt the full force of the difficulty. Let me undertake a restatement. To define a problem, you must refer to the answer – that is, name it. The name may be nothing more than the noun phrase "the answer to the problem of . . . ." Now in the solution process, certain objects are discovered or created: let us call them *possible solutions*. There must be some way also of naming or referring to the possible solutions – '*A*', '*B*', and so on. Meno's question is: How do we know that the possible solution we call '*D*', say, is the same as the object called "the answer to the problem of . . ."?

The reply we give today is not Socrates' but John McCarthy's: "We call a problem well-defined if there is a test which can be applied to a proposed solution. In case the proposed solution is a solution, the test must confirm this in a finite number of steps."[8] In the problem statement, the solution is referred to as "The object that satisfies the following test: . . . ." Each possible solution can then be tested until one is found that fits the definition. Thus, if the problem is: "What is the smallest prime number greater than 10?" and if someone proposes as possible solutions the numbers 11, 12, and 13, a test can be constructed from the meanings of the terms of the problem statement that will identify 11 as the answer. The full procedure might be: (1) generate integers in order, starting with 10; (2) test each to determine if it is prime; (3) stop when a prime is found; (4) that prime is the solution, for it is the smallest greater than 10. (It is instructive that, in this example, the procedure for generating possible solutions already guarantees that one of the conditions – that it be the *smallest* – will be satisfied without an explicit test. This is a typical feature of solution processes.)

A problem will be difficult if there are no procedures for generating possible solutions that are guaranteed (or at least likely) to generate the actual solution rather early in the game. But for such a procedure to exist, there must be some kind of structural relation, at least approximate, between the possible solutions as named by the solution-generating process and these same solutions as named in the language of the problem statement. Suppose, for example, all the words in the unabridged dictionary are put on cards, which are then placed in an urn and stirred thoroughly. Finding the word "peanut" in the urn is now rather difficult; for, with the cards randomly distributed, no particular scheme of search has a better chance than any other of finding "peanut" in a short time.

On the other hand, provided one knows the English alphabet, finding the word "peanut" in the dictionary is much easier. One program runs as follows: (1) open the dictionary about in the middle; (2) if the letter encountered is earlier in the alphabet than 'p', go halfway to the end; if the

---

[8] "The Inversion of Functions Defined by Turing Machines," *in* C. E. Shannon and J. McCarthy (eds.) *Automata Studies* (Princeton, Princeton University Press, 1956), p. 177.

letter is later in the alphabet, go half way to the beginning; (3) and so on.

In sum, whenever there is a relatively simple relation mapping the names of actions on the names of solutions that can be used to guide the solution generator, finding problem solutions is simple. Where there is no such relation, finding problem solutions is difficult. There is no reason to expect the world to be constructed in such a way that simple mappings of actions on to states of the world will be common. In fact, there is reason to expect the contrary.

An adaptive organism is connected with its environment by two kinds of channels. Afferent channels give it information about the state of the environment; efferent channels cause action on the environment. Problem statements define solutions in terms of afferent information to the organism; the organism's task is to discover a set of efferent signals which, changing the state of the environment, will produce the appropriate afferent. But, *ab initio*, the mapping of efferents on afferents is entirely arbitrary; the relations can only be discovered by experiment, by acting and observing the consequences of action.[9] This, of course, is what young children begin to do in their early months – to discover the seen, heard, and felt consequences of different patterns of innervation of arms, legs, body, tongue.

When the mapping of actions on states of the world is problematic, then, and only then, are we faced with genuine problems of design. Hence, if we wish to construct a formalism for describing design processes, that formalism will need to contain at least two distinct sublanguages: a sublanguage for actions, and a sublanguage for states of the world. To the extent that these two sublanguages are related simply to each other, so that an expression in the one can be translated without difficulty into the other, the problem of design will vanish. For the problem of design *is* the problem of making that translation.

Let me give an illustration of what I consider an *un*satisfactory formalism for the design process. Consider a world with discrete time, so that points in time can be designated by integers. Denote the state of the world at time t by the vector $x(t)$.

Now, let $A(x_1, x_2)$ be the transition matrix that transforms x_1 into x_2:

$$(1) \qquad\qquad x_2 = A(x_1, x_2)x_1.$$

If we try, in this formalism, to state the problem of changing the state of the world from x_1 to x_2, we can immediately write down the answer: "Apply the action $A(x_1, x_2)$!" This is correct, but profoundly uninteresting, throwing no light on what the design problem really is.

The problem becomes interesting when we have a second way of naming

---

[9] Since the organism is a product of evolution, which may already have produced a partial matching between efferents and afferents, the "arbitrariness" of the relation may be overstated here.

transition matrices, say: $A(a_{11}, a_{12}, \ldots, a_{21}, \ldots, a_{nn})$, where a_{1j} is the element in the jth column of the ith row of the matrix. Then, the problem of finding an A such that $x_2 = Ax_1$ is nontrivial. In terms of the bilingual formalism of actions and states of the world, the problem now is to find a transition matrix, A, in the action language, whose name under translation into the language of states of the world is "$A(x_1, x_2)$." A design process is a process for finding an object that satisfies this translation requirement.

In natural language, the sublanguage of actions consists largely of verbs and their modifiers; the sublanguage for describing states of the world, of nouns and their modifiers. But natural language tends to blur the distinction wherever the translation is relatively unproblematic. Where the consequences that follow the action are well known, the noun or adjective describing those consequences may be "verbed" to name the action. Thus "to clean" is to take action that will produce a state of cleanliness. Conversely, a verb may be "nouned" to denote consequences that regularly follow from action of a certain kind. Thus "wash" is a collection of articles that is being subjected to a washing process.

Natural language blurs the distinction, because one of the main goals of learning is to discover programs of action that make the connection between actions and states of the world reliably predictable and unproblematic. Cookbook recipes, for example, are programs of action that, if followed, will produce objects having the properties of taste (and digestibility) promised by their names (assumed to be already defined in the state language). To solve the design problem of baking a pumpkin pie, use the cookbook index to find the pumpkin pie recipe, and carry out the actions prescribed there. If the cookbook is reliable, the object produced by these actions will have the properties usually associated with pumpkin pie.

To summarize the argument to this point: a problem of design exists when (1) there is a language for naming actions and a language for naming states of the world, (2) there is a need to find an action that will produce a specified state of the world or a specified change in the state of the world, and (3) there is no non-trivial process for translating changes in the state of the world into their corresponding actions.

In the decision situations treated by classical economics and statistical decision theory, the problem is considerably simplified (1) because the set of possible actions generally consists simply of the set of vectors of the known command variables; (2) the language of actions (i.e., of command variables) is essentially homogeneous with the language of states of the world; and (3) states of the world are assumed to be connected with the command variables by well-defined, and relatively simple functions. Under these simplifying conditions, algorithms often exist that are guaranteed to find, with only reasonable amounts of computation, actions corresponding to desired states of the world. Thus, the classical maximizing algorithms of the calculus, combined with the newer computational algorithms of linear programming and similar formalisms are powerful enough to handle quite large problems when the prerequisite conditions are met.

One of the earliest problems solved with the classical techniques was the following: given the cost of electricity and the cost of copper, to determine the optimal diameter of copper cable to carry a given amount of current. An early linear programming problem was the so-called diet problem: given the prices of different foods, their known content of different nutrients, and the nutritional requirements of a human being, find the lowest-cost diet that will meet these nutritional requirements. These two examples are prototypes of the wide range of practical decision problems that have yielded to the classical techniques. I have called them problems of "choice" rather than problems of "design" because the set of possible actions is given, in a very clear sense, and because the determination of the correct action involves a straightforward, if somewhat tedious, deduction – using the ordinary rules of logic – from the description of possible states of the world. In our discussion of the logic of design we shall put these kinds of problems aside.

It may be objected that our proposed meaning for "design" excludes almost everything called that in engineering and architecture. The typical solution of an engineering or architectural design problem is not a program in the action space, but a description (or picture) of an object in the state space – a blueprint or an elevation, say. But the reason why this description is regarded as a solution to the design problem is that the steps completing the translation from that description to an action program (a manufacturing or construction program) are nonproblematic. The sole action the engineer or architect has to perform (if I may indulge in a bit of heroic oversimplification) to realize the design is to turn it over to a manufacturing department or construction contractor.

In these complex, real-life situations, we may think of the design process as concerned with weaving a tight web of connections between actual physical actions (the actions of lath operators and carpenters) on one side, and realized states of the world (electric motors, office buildings) on the other. Many parts of this web can be woven using traditional patterns, without new problem-solving activity that goes beyond choice among known alternatives. At other points in the web, however, weaving together the fabric of means, coming from the left with the fabric of ends, coming from the right, requires exploration for new alternatives. It is at these interfaces (there may be more than one) that design activity takes place. Thus, a blueprint can be regarded as an encoded name for a complex action program, where a routine (in both senses of the word) exists for translating the name into the manufacturing program that corresponds to it. Given such a manufacturing algorithm, from blueprints to action, the design interface lies between the blueprint and the desired properties of the final product.

11

V. HEURISTICS

To make our discussion of the logic of design concrete, I propose to examine the structure of a particular computer program, the General Problem Solver (GPS), that embodies some of the techniques people use in solving design problems that are relatively novel to them. A number of variants of GPS have been programmed and tested on digital computers over the past eight years, with problems drawn from a dozen domains. In this way, a fair amount of experience has been acquired with the problem-solving techniques that are incorporated in GPS. In the discussion, I shall use the name "GPS" in reference to any and all of its variants.[10]

As a first example of a design problem, consider the task of discovering a proof for a mathematical theorem. The state space here may be taken as the space of syntactically well-formed sentences in the branch of mathematics under consideration, including the conjunctions of such sentences. It may be thought of as the space of "possible theorems."

A mathematical proof, as usually written down, is a sequence of expressions in the state space. But we may also think of the proof as consisting of the sequence of justifications of consecutive proof steps – i.e., the references to axioms, previously-proved theorems, and rules of inference that legitimize the writing down of the proof steps. From this point of view, the proof is a sequence of actions (applications of rules of inference) that, operating initially on the axioms, transform them into the desired theorem. The problem of discovering, or designing a proof of the expression, T, from the conjunction of axioms, A, can be phrased:

> Problem: To find a sequence of operators or
> actions that transforms A into T.

GPS attacks such a problem roughly as follows: Compare T with A, and list the differences between them (if there are none, the problem has been solved); selecting one of the differences, choose an operator that is relevant to differences of that kind; apply that operator to A, transforming it into a new object, A'. Now repeat the process, using the pair (A',T). If at any stage A'' becomes identical with T, then the desired proof is the sequence: $AA'A''A'''A''''\ldots T$. This general process is commonly called *means-end* analysis.

For GPS to operate in this way, it must be able to detect differences between pairs of expressions, and it must be able to associate with each difference one or more operators relevant to that difference. The function

---

[10] A number of descriptions of GPS have been published. For the purposes of this discussion, I recommend the one in *Contemporary Approaches to Creative Thinking*, Howard E. Gruber, Glenn Terell, Michael Wertheimer (eds.) (New York, The Atherton Press, 1962), pp. 63–119.

that maps differences onto sets of operators is usually called the *table of connections*.

In a problem space with very simple structure, the table of connections may associate with each difference an operator that precisely eliminates that difference, but makes no other change in the expression to which it is applied. In this case, each of the n differences between A and T can be detected in turn, and the corresponding operator in the table of connections applied. After n steps, the problem will have been solved.

Of course the interest of GPS lies in its attack on problems that do not have such simple structure. The operators in an interesting problem domain will not correspond simply with differences. Consider, in ordinary algebra, the distributive law, viewed as an operator for transforming expressions. Suppose A is the expression $(x + y)z$, while T is the expression $(x + z)(y + z)$. We know that the distributive law, applied to an expression like A, having three literals, will transform it into an expression having four, hence will remove that particular difference between A and T. However, when it does so, it also interchanges the multiplication and addition operations, creating a new difference. Thus, applied to A, it produces $(xz) + (yz)$, instead of $(x + z)(y + z)$.

This simple example illustrates, in a microcosm, the nature of heuristic problem solving. The available set of transformations allows only certain kinds of changes to be made in the problem expressions. These changes tend to be complex, so that in seeking to remove a particular difference between the initial expression and the desired expression, new differences are often created. Some kind of search must then be undertaken to find a successful path. Means-end analysis, the central heuristic in GPS, gives direction to the search by repeatedly comparing the state or states reached with the desired state. It does not guarantee, however, that the search will be successful, or that it will not go down a number of blind alleys before it finds a correct path.

The efficiency of means-end analysis, applied to any specific problem domain, depends in the first instance on the quality of the table of connections, as our simple example has shown. The skill of a player in ten-second chess, for example, hinges very largely on his ability to recognize the salient features of a chess position, and to evoke effective standard actions applicable to positions having those particular features. There is good empirical evidence that, even for grandmasters, actual dynamic analysis of the consequences that will follow on particular moves takes a matter of minutes, not seconds, and is therefore relatively unimportant in ten-second chess.

The problem-solving power of means-end analysis can be increased if information is available as to the best order in which to consider differences when there is more than one. The information need not be perfectly reliable – it need only be better than the scheme of taking up the differences in random order. The ordering of differences also provides information as to whether applying a particular operator has improved matters or not — whether the differences removed are more or less important than new differences that have been created. Thus, the information may be used as a *progress* test. In interesting problem domains the progress tests are not perfect; if they were, they would guide search infallibly, and the problems would be trivial. Instead, progress tests are heuristic: they usually help, but they are not guaranteed to do so.

A typical feature of the particular problems we call "puzzles" is that to solve them we must sometimes search where the progress test tells us not to. In the missionaries and cannibals puzzle, for example, the task is to move three missionaries and three cannibals from the left to the right bank of a river, under constraints aimed at preventing drowning and dining casualties. A plausible progress test is to compare numbers of persons on the right bank before and after a trip. But to solve the problem, at a certain point two persons, instead of a single one, must return with the boat to the left bank. This is the point of difficulty in the problem for most persons who try it.

With a heuristic problem solver like GPS, there is never a guarantee until the last that it is on the right path to the solution. Therefore it must try several paths and gradually generate a branching tree of possibilities. As a generalization of the progress test, we may incorporate heuristics that determine from which terminal branch of the tree already generated the next explorations should be made, and the next branches added. Two simple heuristics, or strategies, for this purpose are the rule of *depth first*, and the rule of *breadth first*.

Under the depth-first rule, the problem solver starts with the initial state, A, and generates some possible one-step paths. These are evaluated by a progress test, the best is chosen, and the process repeated. A second test terminates search along a branch if the path becomes very unpromising. In that case, the next branch above is recovered, and the next-best continuation there explored.

Under the breadth-first rule, the problem-solver generates a number of one-step paths from A. It then takes up each of the newly-generated states in turn and generates one-step paths from it.

Experience with GPS and other problem-solving programs provides fairly convincing evidence that neither the depth-first nor the breadth-first rules are efficient in state spaces of any considerable size. *Scan-and-search* rules are usually far more effective. With these rules, the problem solver generates one-step paths from A, and puts them on a *try list* in an order determined by some progress test. It repeats this, taking its starting point from the head of the try list, and putting the new paths generated back on that same list. Even if the progress test is very crude, these schemes avoid both the single-mindedness and stereotypy of the depth-first strategy, and the plodding, effort-scattering blindness of the breadth-first strategy.

Other examples could be provided of heuristics that affect the power of a problem-solving system. Some of them, like means-end analysis and the scan-and-search strategy, are general and independent of the problem domain. Others, involving improvement of the table of connections and of the progress tests, are specific to particular problem domains. Their common characteristic is that, without providing an immediate and sure-fire route to the problem solution, they generally bring about substantial reduction in the amount of search required to find a solution.

Now the output of GPS, when it is successful in solving a problem, is a recipe or program of actions – a sequence of operators, which, if applied to the initial state A, will produce the terminal state T. This interpretation is not limited to theorem proving, but is equally applicable to any of the tasks that can be attacked by means-end analysis. Thus, GPS discovers actions that are *sufficient* to realize goals. In general, there is no guarantee that the actions are necessary, unless the structure of the problem space itself guarantees the uniqueness of solutions. Uniqueness, hence necessity of the actions, will be the rare exception rather than the rule.

What do we learn from GPS about the logic of action, as it appears in the design process? First, we learn, just as in the process of choice, that the ordinary logic of declarative statements is all we need. As we have seen, that logic is adequate for describing the relation between the action programs designed by GPS and the states they are supposed to realize. The actions are sufficient conditions for transforming the initial state of the environment into the desired goal state.

Starting with the imperative: "Try to achieve the state T'," the design problem is formulated by transforming that imperative into: "Try to discover a program of action that will achieve the state T'," which is transformed, in turn, to "Apply GPS to the problem of transforming A into T'." The third imperative is not deduced from the second or the first. The logical nexus that relates them can be stated entirely in the declarative mode. Let us see how.

We consider a model of the world in which the available actions include both planning actions and performance actions. In general, if at time t_0 the world is not in state T, then it can sometimes be brought into that state at time t, by performing the planning action, $P(T)$, followed by the performance action $D(P(T))$, where $P(T)$ means the action of trying to solve the problem of realizing T, while $D(P(T))$ means the action of executing the program created by $P(T)$.

Now "Achieve T'" can be converted to "The state of the world at t_1 is T." Simplifying, in this model it is true that: "If, at t_0, action $P(x)$ is followed by $D(P(x))$, then at t_1 the state of the world will be x." If, now, the command variables are so fixed, for the time t_0, that $B(t_0) = (P(T)*D(P(T))$, where 'B' stands for "behavior" and '*' is the sign of concatenation of actions, then the sentence, "The state of the world at t_1 is T" will be true.

The phrase "try to" in the earlier statement of the problem was simply there to remind us that in the real world the actions in question usually, or sometimes, but not invariably, produce the goal state. In some cases we may incorporate these contingencies in the model itself, through probabilities or otherwise; in other cases, we may simply be satisfied to have a model that is a simplified, and idealized, representation of reality. The fallibility of the actions in producing the desired state of the world may stem from two causes: (1) the planning process may be heuristic, hence not guaranteed to produce an output in the available time (or ever); (2) the outputs produced by the planning process, the performance actions, may not be fully guaranteed to produce the desired state of the world. Many design processes can be cited suffering from either or both kinds of fallibility.

In terms of a distinction made earlier, to "try to achieve T" is a genuine action, lying clear at the efferent end of the efferent–afferent spectrum, and always capable of execution. Still more exactly, to "try to achieve T" could mean: (1) to execute the program $P(T)$; (2) if $P(T)$ has no output, stop; (3) if $P(T)$ has the output P', execute the program $D(P')$. This sequence of steps can always be executed; whether it will produce T depends on the fallibility of P and D.

VI. The Efficiency of Heuristics

The conclusion reached in the previous section might be restated thus: In those cases (and they will be the rule rather than the exception) where the achievement of a goal calls for a non-trivial planning action (discovery of alternatives) as well as a performance action (execution of alternatives) determined by the former, the model of the state space must include planning actions as well as performance actions as values of the command variables. If, further, planning actions commonly consume scarce information-processing capacity, then the theory of action will be concerned with the design of efficient planning programs as well as the design (by the planning programs) of efficient performance programs.

A considerable and growing body of applied mathematics is concerned with planning actions, or design processes, as we called them earlier. First of all, there is the subject of numerical analysis, in which some of the typical problems are:

1. Prove that, in a number of steps less than N, the algorithm A, applied to the argument x, will produce as output $f(x)$.

2. Prove that, for any epsilon however small, there exists an N sufficiently large that the difference between $f(x)$ and $A(N,x)$ – the result, after N steps,

of the operation of algorithm A on argument x – will be less than epsilon.

3. Prove that (with qualifications similar to those stated in the two previous paragraphs) the output of A is the value of x, call it x^*, that maximizes $f(x)$.

A particular topic in applied mathematics, of great importance today in management science and engineering design, is linear programming – roughly speaking, the theory of maximization of a linear form subject to constraints expressed as linear equations and inequalities. A linear programming *calculation* is a design calculation – that is, it is aimed at discovering the optimal action program in a situation that has been described in a linear programming model. But linear programming *theory* is one step removed from such calculations; it is aimed at discovering algorithms that are efficient for solving whole classes of linear programming problems. Hence, it is aimed at the design of the design processes. A typical problem in linear programming theory is to show that a particular algorithm will, in fact, find the optimum, and to provide exact or approximate estimates of the amount of computing effort that will be required for problems of various sizes.

In the past, design procedures have been formalized principally in areas where algorithms were known – that is, where it could be shown that the design procedure would always arrive at a solution to any design problem in a specified domain. Today, formal design procedures, usually taking the shape of computer programs, have been constructed for many domains where algorithmic procedures are not known to exist, or, if known, are hopelessly exorbitant in their demands upon computing effort. How are such procedures to be evaluated?

Figure 1 illustrates one way in which the *heuristic power* of a design procedure can be evaluated, independently of whether or not it possesses algorithmic guarantees. Consider a domain in which problem solution is an all-or-none matter – in which a given action program either is or is not a solution. Theorem proving is such a domain. Consider, next, some population of problems and a problem-solving program, S. We define $p(S,t)$ as the probability that a problem, drawn at random from the domain, will be solved by the program, S, in t minutes or less. The function $p(S,t)$ will then be a non-decreasing function of t.

Now, for any particular time allowance, say t_0, we can define the heuristic power of the program S as $p(S,t_0)$. Hence, we can compare the heuristic powers of different programs for some "reasonable" amount of computing effort.

We can also use Figure 1 to define various algorithmic guarantees. For example, we might call a program algorithmic if, for some t_1, $p(S,t_1) = 1$. Or, we might call a program asymptotically algorithmic if we can make $p(S,t)$ as close to 1 as we please by making t sufficiently large. The important point is that whether a particular program does or does not possess such

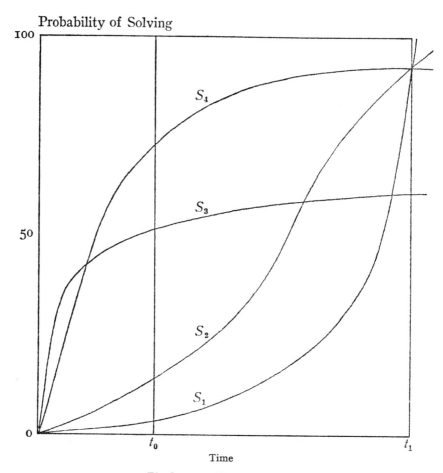

The Concept of Heuristic Power

The function $p(S,t)$ is graphed for four hypothetical problem-solving programs. S_1 is an algorithm, guaranteed to solve any problem in time t_1. S_2 is asymptotically algorithmic. S_3 is the most powerful of the programs for very small t, but S_4 has the greatest heuristic power for t_0.

FIGURE 1

algorithmic properties is quite independent of its heuristic power for moderate t. For example, the only algorithm for chess (which consists of considering all possible games and minimaxing backward from the end) would almost never find a move during the lifetime of the universe, much less in a reasonable computing time.

If problem-solving in a particular domain is not an all-or-none matter, but solutions of different quality can be distinguished, the measure of heuristic power has to be modified somehow. If there is some way of measuring the

18

value of the improvement in the solution that would be attained by increasing the computing time, and measuring this value in units comparable to the measure of computing cost, then the problem can be formulated of determining the optimal computing time. So-called sequential sampling problems in statistics, and search problems in operations research take this general form.

In many cases of practical importance programs having considerable heuristic power can be obtained by taking care to define the notion of "problem solution" with an eye to the effect that this definition will have on the computing requirements. An illustration that I find instructive on this point is the problem of finding a needle in a haystack.

Suppose we have a haystack in which needles are distributed at random with a specified density. What procedure can we devise to find the sharpest needle in the stack? The only algorithm that suggests itself is finding all the needles and measuring or comparing their sharpness to determine which is sharpest. If the stack is very large, we shall content ourselves with searching some portion of it, and selecting the sharpest needle of those in that portion. If we search one n^{th} of the stack, our chance of finding the sharpest is $1/n$.

How can we tell when to stop searching? One rule is to stop when we have used a specified amount of effort. Another quite different rule is to stop when we have a needle sharp enough to sew with. A good feature of this rule is that it calls for a search time inversely proportional to the density of sharp needles in the stack, and independent of the size of the entire stack. In a world full of haystacks that for all practical purposes are infinite, this is a highly desirable property for a problem-solving procedure.

Now an economist would say that the proper rule is to search until the expected improvement in sharpness per minute of additional search is worth less than the cost of the search. This is true, but not always helpful, because it is often far easier, in practice, to define what is meant by a "sharp enough" needle than to measure the marginal value of additional sharpness, or to estimate the amount of search that would be required to produce it.

The process of searching for "good enough" solutions is called *satisficing*. It is one of the most general and effective means for attaining heuristic power with modest amounts of computation. The fundamental reason for its effectiveness is that it does not require the comparison of all possible solutions with each other, but only the comparison of each possible solution, as it is generated, with a standard.[11] It is easy to see how GPS can be made into a satisficer. If differences are signed, so that the directions of better and worse can be distinguished, then GPS can simply be given the task of transforming the initial state into a state that is, along certain dimensions, as good as, or better than, a standard state.

[11] For a more thorough discussion of satisficing see "A Behavioral Model of Rational Choice," in *Models of Man, op. cit.*

19

VII. Conclusion

Human beings are information-processing systems operating largely in serial fashion, and possessing very modest computational powers in comparison with the complexity of the problems with which their environment confronts them. Their survival depends on attending selectively to that environment, and on finding satisfactory behavioral alternatives for handling those problems to which they attend.

Hence a theory of decision making is concerned with processes for selecting aspects of the environment for attention, processes for generating alternatives and processes for choosing among alternatives. In the design of these processes, the conservation of attention and of computing effort is a vital consideration. To reason about these matters, models must be constructed that contain command or action variables and environmental variables. With these models, the reasoning used to make decisions, or to design decision-making processes embodies no special logic, but employs declarative logic of the ordinary kind.

Design problems – generating or discovering alternatives – are complex largely because they involve two spaces, an action space and a state space, that generally have completely different structures. To find a design requires mapping the former of these on the latter. For many, if not most, design problems in the real world systematic algorithms are not known that guarantee solutions with reasonable amounts of computing effort. Design uses a wide range of heuristic devices – like means-end analysis, satisficing, and the other procedures that have been outlined – that have been found by experience to enhance the efficiency of search. Much remains to be learned about the nature and effectiveness of these devices.

Our brief survey of the kinds of reasoning that can be applied to the design of planning programs demonstrates again the central thesis of this paper: ordinary mathematical reasoning, hence the ordinary logic of declarative statements, is all that is required for a theory of design processes. The actions in question in a planning theory are the actions of using particular processes as planning programs. The relevant imperatives are of the form: "Prove this theorem!" and "Apply GPS to the problem!" The route from the first to the second of these imperatives lies through an empirical or theoretical analysis (requiring no imperatives) of the heuristic power of GPS for theorems of the kind in question.

A. COMMENTS ON H. SIMON'S
"THE LOGIC OF HEURISTIC DECISION MAKING"

ROBERT BINKLEY

PROFESSOR SIMON'S main thesis, both in this paper and in the earlier paper to which he makes reference, is that we do not need a special imperative logic. A subordinate thesis, which appears mainly in the second paper, is that decision theory needs to consider not only the choice of an action from among a given set of action alternatives, but also the discovering of these alternatives as well as the selection of the occasion for action.

My comments will mainly concern these two themes. With respect to the first I shall say that there is a sense in which the philosopher at any rate can be said to need a special logic of imperatives, however things may stand with the decision theorist. And with respect to the second I shall suggest that all of decision theory, or at least all the parts of it that Simon discusses in his paper, can be reduced to the theory of choice of action from among a set of given alternatives. But let me mention at once that I do not think that in saying these things I shall be expressing any disagreement with Simon's views, except perhaps on some merely verbal points. I am trying instead to give a special emphasis to certain of his results, and also to view them from a perspective somewhat different from the one that Simon had in mind.

It might be possible to be puzzled about what Simon means by saying that no special imperative logic is needed in decision theory. After all, he does include imperatives in the reasonings he describes, and gives rules for converting certain imperatives into declaratives, and certain declaratives into imperatives. These imperatives were not already there in declarative logic, and so this must be described as an enrichment of declarative logic with imperatives. What more, it might be asked, do we have to do to have a special logic of imperatives? But to press this point, I think, would be to misunderstand Simon's intention. What he means can be set out as the following two claims. First, Simon is holding that declarative logic suffices for formulating and establishing means-end statements. Second, he is holding that the sole function of distinctively practical reason is the application of means-end statements in actual decision.

This is, of course, my way of putting it, not his. Simon is not at all given to general remarks about the function of practical reason, and he on the whole very carefully avoids the vocabulary of means and ends. Let me explain these divergences.

I feel justified in bringing practical reason into it because I suspect that that is what those who talk about imperatives in the context of decision theory really have in mind. There is no reason why imperatives as a *grammatical* category should figure at all in decision theory. "Get a little drunk and you land in jail" is or contains an imperative, at least according to some grammarians,[1] but has no special interest for decision theory. Nor do imperatives conceived as the linguistic vehicles of commands. A command is, or involves, a complex relation between two persons, the commander and the one commanded. It is true that the relation between commander and commanded is sometimes relevant in decision making, but it is not of the essence. Whether a certain command is to be issued, and whether a certain command is to be obeyed are sometimes things that decisions have to be made about. But a decision what to do is made by a single decision maker who then does what he has decided to do, without necessarily either issuing or obeying a command.

What has happened is that, for various reasons, philosophers have come to connect the distinction between practical and theoretical thinking – thinking what to do and thinking what is the case – with the distinction between prescriptive and descriptive discourse – *telling* someone what to do and *telling* someone what is the case. The latter distinction is expressible in the syntactic mode of speech as a distinction between imperative and declarative sentences, and so the imperative-declarative distinction has come to stand in the minds of philosophers for the practical-theoretical distinction. I believe this to be a philosophical mistake, but, for the purpose of understanding Simon's paper, and lots of other papers, I think we can accept it as a harmless convention that philosophers use to provide themselves with a grammatical category for representing practical thinking in language. Viewed in this way, Simon's claims about the role of imperatives in decision making become claims about the function of practical reason.

By "means-end statement" I mean statements to the effect that in a set of circumstances C, some course of action M is the best means to some final state of affairs E. Were it not for the risk of adding still further to the confusions just discussed, I would call them hypothetical imperatives. But I do not mean to suggest that this formula, "In C, M is the best means to E," has in itself any very clear or definite meaning. Quite the contrary. In fact it seems to me that one of the most valuable contributions of decision theory in general, and of Simon's paper in particular, as far as philosophy is concerned, is the light it sheds on what we mean, or ought to mean, by such formulae. Nevertheless, the import of the formula in the present context is straightforward.

Simon says, roughly, that decisions are made in the following way. (Or perhaps that they are *to be* made in the following way. Recall that egregiously casual disjunction with which he defined the task of theory of action as that of describing *or* prescribing certain features of action.) We

---

[1] R. W. Pence and D. W. Emery, *A Grammar of Present-day English* (2nd ed., New York, 1963), p. 25.

begin with an imperative which specifies the end. We convert this to a declarative; that is, we assume that the end is achieved. Combining this with other declaratives which define the circumstances, we draw an inference about what actions must have been done. These action declaratives are finally converted to imperatives which tell us to perform the means to our end. It is a logical process with imperatives at the top and imperatives at the bottom, but with a lot of purely declarative reasoning in between.

A theory of decision is mainly interested in the intervening declarative reasoning. As Simon points out, an applied science tends to drop off the imperatives altogether, and to give us just the central core of declaratives, which can then be used in either a positive or a normative way. Thus the economist not only predicts that firms will operate at the point where marginal revenue equals marginal cost, a great many other things being equal; he will also advise firms so to operate.

However, from the point of view of the philosopher concerned with the problem of practical reason, it is the links with imperatives at top and bottom that hold all the interest. In his thinking, therefore, the philosopher will naturally tend to compress the middle part as much as possible, and in fact to sum it all up in a single statement. This is the means-end statement I have been talking about. And, given this interest, the philosopher will focus his attention on the rules connecting imperatives to the means-end statement, Simon's "conversion" rules. These rules will have so great an importance for the philosopher that he will be bound to refer to them as a special logic of imperatives. So, without disagreeing with Simon, the philosopher can hold that he *does* need a special logic of imperatives; it all depends on what you mean by "special".

Perhaps I should say a word about just what this philosopher's problem of practical reason is. It is, as I see it, the problem of understanding how action, or decision to act, can be said to be rational. In general, if there is a problem understanding how X can be said to be Y, it is because there is some reason to suppose that X cannot be said to be Y. And there *is* some reason to suppose that action, or decision to act, cannot be said to be rational. For throughout the history of philosophy the idea of rationality has, if we leave pragmatism out of it, always been explicated primarily with reference to theoretical reason, the rationality of belief, and has been connected with ideas about valid argument and inference. The pattern has been roughly this. Certain beliefs have grounds, the ground of a belief being some other belief. A belief is said to be rational relative to its ground when the declarative affirming the belief follows from the declarative affirming the ground – follows from it in some declarative logic.

Something similar must be found on the practical side if action is to be said to be rational. This is where imperative logic comes in. For we might say that actions, or decisions to act, also have grounds. The ground of a decision would either be some other decision or some belief or some combination of beliefs and decisions. And a decision would be rational relative to its ground when the imperative prescribing it follows from imperatives prescribing the decisions in its ground taken together with declaratives affirming the beliefs in its ground – follows from these in some imperative logic.

It is considerations of this sort that lead me to attribute to Simon a view about the sole function of practical reason. For he says that these conditions for rationality of decision are met in the case of deciding to adopt means to an end, provided only that the appropriate means-end statement can be established. So he admits this much of a function to practical reason. And since he holds that imperatives play no other role in decision, he must hold that this is the sole function of practical reason.

It might be thought that there is at least one other function of practical reason, the reasoning involved in obeying a law or command. But I think that we are here construing the idea of means and end so broadly that even this would come under it.

Means-end statements, I have said, are statements summing up the declarative reasoning that links end-imperatives with means-imperatives in Simon's theory of decision. I now want to explain more exactly what I meant by saying that Simon's theory contributes to the clarification of the meaning of the means-end formula, "In circumstances C, action M is the best means to end E."

We have two main questions about this formula. By what criteria is M judged to be best? From what class of alternatives is M selected? Simon helps us to answer both these questions.

The end E, he says, is specified by laying down certain conditions on the environment variables, which are described in the language of states. The means M, on the other hand will be given by a program described in the language of action which fixes the values of the command variables. To say that M thus specified is the *best* means to E seems to me to involve two factors; the degree to which the expected results of M fulfill the conditions defining E, and the likelihood that M will have these results. (Other possible grounds for preferring one means to another, such as cost, are already included in the specification of the end.) Probability and degree of fulfillment, of course, do not always go hand in hand, and one must frequently choose between the bird in hand and the two in the bush. Theories can be worked out for this, but that is not a main point in Simon's paper.

Simon's views about heuristics become relevant when we try to answer the question about the class of alternatives from which M is selected as best. It might be thought that the class is that of all actions which the agent could do if he tried. But I think that Simon holds, rightly, that that class is too large, since it may include actions which the agent does not know about, and which it would not be wise for him to try to discover. On the other hand, the class of actions known to the agent is too small, since perhaps he should come to know more. I think instead that Simon is saying that the class of alternatives should be the class of available actions that emerge from some heuristically sound planning action.

A planning action is an action that is supposed to discover means to an end, programs of action having some likelihood of realizing the requirements of the end to some degree. Sometimes, as Simon points out, the planning action is trivial, since the alternatives open to the agent, and their results, are well known. Let me remark, however, that even here there is always at least potentially a non-trivial design problem requiring a planning action, since there is always the option of searching for and considering some radical restructuring of the situation. It just might turn out, for example, that the best solution to a two-bin inventory problem will be not to stock the item at all, but to get out of that line of business altogether. Such restructuring, of course, would involve changing the end.

In other cases, while the alternative actions and their results are not known, some definite planning action is known, and one has merely to sit down to work. In still other cases, the planning action itself may be unknown, except under such unhelpful descriptions as "mulling it over".

A planning action of this last indefinite kind will always be included among the alternatives for any decision, since there is always the possibility of thinking further about the problem. There may be planning actions of the second, definite type. There may be performance actions, or it may be that all we can do is decide how to plan. Simon has pointed out that the decision whether to adopt one of the definite planning actions, and if so, which, can be based on the heuristic efficiency of the planning action, where this is based both on how likely the action is to produce a plan and how good the plan is likely to be. That is, the same criteria of probability and degree of fulfillment apply here as in the case of performance actions. But how are we to evaluate the indefinite, "Try to think of something else" planning action? I don't think we can simply apply the same considerations of heuristic efficiency, because this planning action, by holding out among other things the possibility of radical restructuring of the problem, transcends the definition of the problem in terms of which heuristic efficiency would be defined.

I think instead that we must realize that we *have* a set of alternatives to choose between only as the result of a prior planning action. This prior planning action, however, need not itself have been decided upon as the best means to the end; that would lead to the regress of needing to plan before we act, yet needing to plan to plan before we plan, yet . . . and so on. The "first" planning act is simply *done*. The question we face at the time of decision is whether it has been done well. To say that it has been done well is to say that we may rest satisfied with its results, that it is not worthwhile searching for still further alternatives, but that our decision can be made on the basis of those we have. This is what I mean by saying that a planning action is heuristically sound.

I am holding that the statement that M is the best means has as part of its force the claim that the planning action generating the alternatives from which M is selected as best is a heuristically sound one. We are not obliged to select the best member of a class unless there is a reason why we should select from that class, and not a larger one.

But, if all this is so, then the choosing of a planning action is no different in principle from the choosing of a performance action, and so far, all decision can be reduced to choosing from a set of given alternatives. And I do not think that the selecting of occasion for action is an exception to this, as Simon perhaps suggests. For I think it is fairly clear that the decisions about occasions that he discusses are really second order decisions about rules or policies governing the selection of occasions. The manager, by fixing the reorder point and quantity, lays down a general rule. As a result of this, the stock boy finds himself on occasions where he must decide whether or not to obey.

In this broad sense, then, all decision can be reduced to choosing from given alternatives. However, I don't think that this is inconsistent with what Simon has said.

B. COMMENTS ON H. SIMON'S
"THE LOGIC OF HEURISTIC DECISION MAKING"

Nuel D. Belnap, Jr.

Professor Simon's "central proposition" is that "ordinary mathematical reasoning, hence the ordinary logic of declarative statements, is all that is required for a theory of design processes" (p. 20).[1] Hence, he says, "there is no need for a special 'logic of imperatives' or 'logic of action'," (p. 2), since practitioners among engineers and management scientists (p. 1) are able to do everything they need to do and say everything they need to say without one.

It seems to me that Simon has not given an altogether satisfactory reason for abandoning the attempt to articulate logical systems having to do with action, if indeed this is what he takes to be the cash value of his remarks. Engineers and their cousins are, or so at least the tradition holds, unreliable judges of which abstract systems need development or of which levels of abstraction are likely to be theoretically the most fruitful. The engineer, by his very definition as an *applied* scientist, wants something that *works* for his purposes and in his context, not caring whether or not it is logical or rigorous. For example, Professor Simon remarked in an earlier paper that economists often do not distinguish in their writing between descriptive and normative economics (p. 4 of LRD), and he used this as part of an argument for identifying the logic of descriptive statements with the logic of imperatives. I can only compare the practicing economists' ignoring of the distinction between "ought" and "is" with the position of the Plumber in J. M. Synge's delightful tale, "Kandleman's Krim." Synge has his Plumber argue against the Orc that he in his plumbing has no need to distinguish between *pi* conceived on the one hand abstractly as the ratio of the circumference to the diameter of a circle, and on the other hand taken concretely as the fraction *three and one seventh*. For the Plumber, as one of Simon's "practitioners in a field of action," (p. 1), to distinguish abstract *pi* from *three and one seventh* would be to make a distinction without a difference. And just as Simon says that "ordinary mathematical reasoning" (p. 20) suffices for the logic of design planning in the spirit of his General Problem Solver computer program, so the Plumber might well go on to say that good old rational arithmetic suffices for the Logic of Plumbing. But although this is true of *routinized* plumbing, it seems to me incredible to suppose that there could have been a Logic of Plumbing at all without a conceptualization of the abstract *pi* layed up in Plato's heaven.

The moral I wish to draw is that when it comes to foundational questions,

---

[1] Page references are to the indicated paper, except that "LRD" refers to Professor Simon's "Logic of Rational Decision."

there is no point asking the applied scientist *which* foundational questions are not worth the asking, for from his point of view there are *no* foundational questions worth asking. But the summary dismissal of higher levels of abstraction is not restricted to engineers. Even the most theoretical of physicists is ordinarily satisfied to take the calculus much as he finds it, not really caring very much whether or not one expresses it self-contradictorily in terms of infinitely small quantities. The mathematical revolution of the nineteenth century through which the calculus was provided with something like a firm foundation is simply irrelevant to such a physicist. Indeed, we need not stop with the physicists: mathematicians themselves are more often than not impatient with problems in the foundations of mathematics. I am reminded of a luncheon conversation between Professor Alan Ross Anderson and an eminent mathematician, in the course of which Anderson laid out on the table cloth in some detail the Gödel-Herbrand theory of primitive recursive functions. In this theory, one begins with a few very elementary functions, and then proceeds to construct the rest bit by bit in little tiny tippy-toe steps. At the conclusion of Anderson's account of how these functions are so carefully and rigorously constructed, the eminent mathematician agreed that it was very interesting, but replied he *already* had all *his* functions!

And I think Simon feels like that, too. He *already* has all *his* logic. Which is to say that he finds foundational questions concerning action logic irrelevant for his practical and theoretical needs, concerning which he is doubtless to be taken as final authority. But it seems to me to be extremely dangerous to take Simon's reflections as prescriptive for the worth of the logician's highly abstract approach to normative logic. To do so would be like asking the arithmetician whether or not there is any point in the Frege-Russell analysis of the concept of number in set-theoretical terms. Or, to be a trifle *ad hominem*, it would be like asking the chess player whether or not he finds any point in Professor Simon's well-known, rigorous, and highly complex analysis of chess strategy. For, of course, a non-electronic, human-type chess player cannot consciously put to use Professor Simon's masterful analysis, just because it is so rigorous and complex. But it would be absurd to conclude that the analysis is irrelevant to chess playing.

Let me make it clear that my sword has only one edge: though I have profound reservations concerning the wisdom of listening to practitioners or scientists or even mathematicians when they try to tell me which foundational questions are *not* interesting, I am full of attention when instead they come forward with grist for the foundational mill. And there is no question but what Simon has himself both contributed to and located areas for possible contributions by others in the region which he sometimes seems to claim does not or should not exist; that is, in the region of action logic. For example, Simon has found that the theory of design requires positing two different domains of discourse, one concerned with actions and one concerned with states of the world. In much the same way, he finds that in choice theory one must distinguish between what he calls "command" or sometimes "action" variables and what he calls "environmental" variables; the former are those over which alone we have control. Now it seems perfectly plain to me that what Simon calls "declarative logic of the ordinary kind" makes no such distinctions as these. In articulating the difference and in pointing out that the theories of choice and design make the distinction mandatory, and even in explaining those circumstances in which it is not to much practical effect to make the distinction, Simon is, in spite of himself, making a contribution to the logic of action.

Even though, as it seems to me, one must reject the entire scheme of Simon's negative argument as a kind of appeal to authority – which in this instance might be called "The Plumber's Fallacy" – nevertheless, I want in the second part of my remarks to suggest very briefly some reasons of detail why Simon's dismissal of the work of the philosophers seems more plausible than it should. I have selected three points for comment.

In the first place, the claim that action logic is already manageable by "ordinary" declarative logic has a spectrum of senses varying with the standards set for counting a task as manageable with the logic at hand. To reduce to absurdity one end of this spectrum of senses, consider for a moment Gödel's celebrated observation that every formalizable theory can be treated as a set of natural numbers – Gödel numbers, of course. Does it follow from this observation that all science, be it mathematical, natural, or social, is, insofar as it is formalizable, a branch of the elementary arithmetic of natural numbers? Yes, I suppose in some sense it does. But it is obviously not the sense required to justify an assertion that all the practicing scientist needs is elementary arithmetic. To justify this latter claim, one would have to show that Gödel-numbering is the only useful and illuminating way of looking at theories, or at least that it is just as illuminating and helpful as any alternative. Just so, for Simon's thesis to stand, he needs to argue in detail that the ordinary declarative logic is in every case just as illuminating as any alternative such as an imperative logic or a logic of action. It will not suffice to show that imperatives and the like can be so tortured as to fit the Procrustean bed of standard logic.

Secondly, Simon argues that we should look at the logic actually employed by sophisticated practitioners to elicit an appropriate logic of decision. Though I agree with the general spirit of this suggestion, its dangers need emphasizing. Simon, above all others, must be sensitive to how recently sophisticated decision makers have come to employ the differential calculus, probability theory, linear programming, or the General Problem Solver, a thought which leads one immediately to the conjecture that a survey of which conceptual tools are of use to practitioners today is likely to tell us very little about which ones will be in the van some fifty years hence. Surely a survey of "sophisticated" management experts of fifty years ago, say around the turn of the century, would have had to conclude that the logic of heuristic decision making is not even the ordinary declarative logic of the logicians, much less linear programming, but just good old common sense – with possibly an occasional *soupçon* of a syllogism. And if such a survey had been taken as prescriptive. Simon would never have had the opportunity of developing the really powerful conceptual tools which he himself has provided for the theory of decisions.

Thirdly, the keystone of Simon's claim that a logic of imperatives is unnecessary lies in his view that an imperative can be completely disposed of by translating it into what Professor Nicholas Rescher calls a "termination statement,"[2] that is, a statement expressing declaratively a set of conditions under which the imperative can in some sense be counted as being satisfied. Of course this is irrelevant to a logic of action in the sense of Professors Davidson and von Wright, since they already confine themselves to declaratives. But putting that aside, what I wish to point out is that Simon's "quick-translation" thesis is only plausible to the extent that one sweeps all the hard cases under the rug. For example, conditional imperatives, although indeed and of course connected intimately with declarative sentences, as Rescher has indicated in his book on imperatives, resist the quick translation Simon proposes. Furthermore, by considering only utilitarian kinds of cases, Simon ignores certain problems arising in deontic logic, where the background is a set of rules rather than a set of utility variables to be maximized. In certain such situations, which may well be quite other than those faced by the management scientist, the technique of quick translation is wholly inapplicable. The reason is that in these contexts it is essential to consider sentences in which the deontic modalities are nested one within another. For example, in making a contractual offer, I bring about the deontic state in which the recipient of the offer is permitted to bring about by his acceptance of the offer the deontic state in which I am obligated (in the best deontic sense) to fulfill the terms of the contract. And since making offers is permitted by law, the nesting can be at least three deep. In such circumstances, no facile translation into the declarative mode is likely.

In conclusion, I should like to make some programmatic observations about the possibilities for action logics, and especially imperative logic, based on a consideration of its cousin, erotetic logic – that is, the logic of questions and answers. Some early attempts to construct an erotetic logic took the point of view that logic is inferential if it is anything, and so attempted to make sense out of inferences involving questions as either premisses

---

[2] N. Rescher, *The Logic of Commands* (London, 1966), ch. 5.

or conclusions. The results were not, in my judgment, happy. Erotetic logic found a suitable starting point only when the nature of the task was re-described, still in analogy with inferential logic, but with a better analogy. What, after all, *is* inferential logic? I should characterize it as having two more or less distinguishable parts. It is, in the first place, a linguistic apparatus added to a grammar – I am thinking of a formal language with a formal grammar – which is normative for inferential behavior. But secondly, logic provides us with a set of semantic and syntactic concepts for *talking about* inference, concepts such as truth, validity, consistency, provability, and the like. If you will let me hang the difference on some ugly and misleading but very temporary pegs, I shall call the former "object-logic", as being part of the object-language, and the latter "meta-logic". It was this description which provided the analogy which led to a viable logic of questions, for then the task of erotetic logic could be construed as the provision *first* of a suitable apparatus, to be thought of as added to a formal language, for asking and answering questions, and *second*, of a set of metalinguistic concepts adequate for talking about the various syntactic and semantic aspects of the interrogative situation. And so we have both an erotetic object-logic and an erotetic meta-logic, in exact analogy to the inferential situation, but without having to think of a good thing to mean by drawing inferences involving questions. I might add that the thinking of those involved in information retrieval – even the most sophisticated – was in the early stages of no use whatsoever in this enterprise. It was necessary to become very general, very abstract, and very impatient with requests for applications in order to make any headway. Only *after* the foundations of the abstract theory were laid did it become fruitful to consider the requirements of those charged with the world's work.

The lesson for imperative logic is straightforward: what is wanted is first an imperative object-logic – which is to say, an apparatus added to a formal language suitable for constructing imperatives – and second, a set of concepts useful for talking about the various syntactic and semantic aspects of the imperative situation. Of course those participating in the construction of imperative logic have been involved in just such an enterprise, and my remarks are directed at them only to the extent of suggesting that one ought not be preoccupied to the exclusion of all else with inferences or putative inferences involving imperatives. And I also wish to insist that Simon's reflections on the decisional and design situations provide a rich source of guidelines for those engaged in the enterprise of formalization. But I do wish to urge that the comparison with erotetic logic suggests that arguments purporting to show that imperatives do not or cannot figure in inferences, or as Simon suggests, figure only as almost unnecessary ultimate premises and ultimate conclusions, are simply not arguments against the possibility of a viable imperative logic.

C. REPLY TO COMMENTS

HERBERT A. SIMON

A. *Reply to Professor Binkley's Comments*

I agree in general with most of Professor Binkley's emphases, and his elucidations of what I have said; the points on which we differ are mainly points on which I disagree with Professor Belnap also, and hence I shall deal with them in one place.

1. I would omit the word "best" in speaking about the relations of means to ends – for most schemes of practical action are workable only because they seek the *satisfactory* instead of the *best*. This is an important point, for the greatest limitation of classical decision theory is its preoccupation with optimizing, to the neglect of satisficing.

2. Philosophers, says Binkley, will focus their attention on the rules connecting imperatives to the means-end statements, and will be relatively uninterested in the reasoning that leads from the ends to the means. Of course, if philosophers *had* thus concerned themselves only with the bread and had ignored the sandwich filling in between, there would have been no reason for my paper. In point of fact, that isn't what they have done. The literature on the logic of imperatives gives primary, if not quite exclusive, attention to formal procedures for *inferring* an imperative from one or more others. I (partially) except Professor Rescher in his recent book, *The Logic of Commands*, as well as Jörgensen and perhaps a few others, but it is a fair characterization of the vast bulk of work on normative logics.

My thesis, to which Binkley appears not to object, is that the construction of special rules of inference for normative logics, and the demonstration (often unsuccessful and never complete) that these rules will not produce paradoxical or counter-intuitive results is work of supererogation. By introducing appropriate conversion rules, of the kind I have proposed, we can take over the whole apparatus of declarative logic, whose strengths and difficulties are already well understood, and do not need to puzzle about the properties of new rules of inference. The former course has been followed in the applied literature I have discussed, and I recommend it to philosophers. If they will accept the recommendation, they can then move on to other, unsolved, problems that require attention.

3. Binkley observes that choosing a planning action is no different *in principle* from choosing a performance action, hence that all decision can be reduced to choosing from a set of given alternatives. If he will allow me always to put the "in principle" in italics, I will accept his formulation. But it is worth keeping in mind that one chooses a *planning* action in order to obtain some *performance*, or *design* alternatives, which were not given in advance. Hence, Professor Binkley and I appear not to disagree that in

interesting design problems the design alternatives are not given in advance – that what is unique and interesting about this class of problems is their two-level structure.

4. The last-resort planning action that Binkley calls "mulling it over" is perhaps not as vague as its name would imply. Suppose that we did not permit the planner to carry his memory around inside his head, but required him, instead, to externalize it in a big, indexed encyclopedia. I expect that if we then observed him while he was "mulling things over," we would find him searching through the encyclopedia for planning actions already stored there, perhaps adapting one of them to the task at hand. We do not know enough yet, about human problem solving in ill-structured situations to describe more specifically than this what might be going on, but we should not be surprised if, on closer acquaintance, it turns out to be simply "more of the same".

This does not explain how the primordial planning actions were stored in the encyclopedia in the first place. I would agree entirely with Professor Binkley's proposal for avoiding an infinite regress of planning actions. As he says, "The 'first' planning act is simply *done*."

B. *Reply to Professor Belnap's Comments*

My quarrels with Professor Belnap are more fundamental. To put it simply, he misunderstands my whole paper. That of course is my fault, not his. Evidently the paper does not express what I intended it to express, and I should clarify my meaning.

1. I gladly admit to being a Plumber, but I am a Plumber with philosophical purposes. A study of the literature of modern decision theory (I have in mind the work of Ramsey, de Finetti, Arrow, Savage, von Neumann, Luce, Wald, Suppes, to mention a few) should convince Professor Belnap that this field has been favored with some Plumbers who were highly sensitive (sometimes almost impractically sensitive) to logical issues. I think it safe to assume that they were quite as concerned with the rigor of their logic as with the nonleakiness of the pipes, and perhaps as competent in logic as in plumbing. Hence, in suggesting that this body of analysis may be insufficiently rigorous for the purposes of philosophy, Belnap is picking an unlikely target.

My claim is not that declarative logic *cum* conversion rules is adequate for economists and engineers, but that it is adequate for logicians. In the philosophical literature, the adequacy of proposed formalisms has too often been tested only against simple hypothetical cases, often contrived to be paradoxical, but none the less contrived. My purpose in pointing to actual applications was to have examples formidable enough to demonstrate adequacy to handle real-world complexity, and not simply adequacy to handle toy situations. This kind of slumming in the real world can have genuine value for philosophy, and I urge Professor Belnap not to allow snobbishness about plumbers to deprive him of interesting experiences.

2. One of Belnap's comments shows a misunderstanding of the goals and practices of cognitive simulation. He says: "For of course a non-electronic human-type chess player cannot consciously put to use Professor Simon's masterful analysis, just because it is so rigorous and complex." On the contrary, the computer chess-playing program to which he refers was intentionally designed to use only processes of which human chess masters are capable. In fact, any chess master or expert (partly consciously) uses a more "rigorous and complex" analysis program than the best we have yet devised for a computer. Our mating combinations program does not substitute speed or complexity for the sly cleverness of human players, but imitates the latter. The purpose of this particular line of research was to understand human problem solving, and the program has been shown empirically to match human data in a number of important respects.

3. Belnap observes that "declarative logic of the ordinary kind" distinguishes no such categories as "command," "action variables," and so on. Agreed. Formal logic also distinguishes no such categories as "complex number," "fiber bundle," "electron." This does not imply that whenever, either in mathematics or empirical science, we wish to introduce terms like these we must introduce them into the structure of our logic, and then devise new rules of inference so that we can reason about sentences containing these terms. Mathematics and science have followed the alternative path of keeping their special terms outside the central core of logic so that the ordinary rules of inference of declarative logic would suffice. Modern decision theory, following the same route, has succeeded in handling with complete rigor the problems to which normative logics address themselves. This seems to me the parsimonious route to take – especially since explorers have already gone this way and marked the road for us.

4. Belnap paints for us a poignant picture of "imperatives tortured to fit the Procrustean bed of standard logic." But since this "torture" has been carried out successfully for quite complex situations, he must be mistaken about the shape either of the imperatives or of the bed of standard logic. As matters have turned out, the imperatives slid into bed without bending or twisting, and rest there quite comfortably. It is a little futile to oppose demonstrated feasibility with hypothesized impossibility.

5. Belnap suggests that, while the direct method I propose has worked for practitioners up to the present time, they should look toward the future. Of course, I cannot guarantee that declarative logic *cum* conversion will suffice for all the future needs of normative logic. However, since alternative proposals have not even been shown adequate for *present* needs, and have been applied only to toy examples, I would strive for further development of the successful approach before spending much effort trying to bring other

approaches up to the level of contemporary practice. If someone wants to place his bets elsewhere, I can only agree that gambling on the future is of the essence of the scientific or philosophic life. I myself believe, for the reasons stated in my paper, that constructing independent normative logics is a bad bet.

6. Belnap accuses me of sweeping all the hard cases under the rug. His first example of a "hard case" is the conditional imperative. Since conditional imperatives are simply strategies – functions with command variables as the dependent variables, environmental variables as the independent variables, they have certainly not been swept under the rug by modern decision theory. The theory of games and dynamic programming theory, to mention just two examples, are full of them.

The theory of games also offers a counterexample to Belnap's claim that declarative logic cannot handle contractual offers. The game of contract bridge contains all of the complexities that he attributes to contracting, but contract bridge is readily formulated as a game in the von Neuman-Morgenstern sense.

The diet problem, used as an example in my paper in *The British Journal for the Philosophy of Science* (*op. cit.*), refutes the claim that I "ignore certain problems arising in deontic logic, where the background is a set of rules rather than a set of utility variables to be maximized." The diet problem requires the cost of the diet to be minimized, say, subject to all sorts of rules as to how much of which kinds of foods may be eaten. There is no difficulty in adding to the problem, for example, constraints corresponding to the Jewish dietary laws or the Catholic rules on fasting during Lent.

7. Since my paper is not concerned with erotetic logic, I shall not comment at length on the analogy Professor Belnap draws between this and imperative logic. He claims that erotetic logic has made essential contributions to information retrieval. No special erotetic logic is involved in the particular information retrieval programs I have studied (e.g., BASEBALL, SYN-THEX, SKETCHPAD), but I cannot claim to be familiar with all such programs, or the particular one to which he alludes. I observe only that he does not claim that new rules of erotetic *inference* were essential, and hence the analogy appears not to apply to the case at issue.

8. This last example and Belnap's concluding remarks reveal our mutual failure in communication. He appears to attribute to me the view that practical men have nothing to learn from theorists, while I thought I was arguing that, in a particular instance, some sophisticated theorists had done a good job by looking at practical situations for inspiration. He interprets my paper as an argument against the possibility of an imperative logic, while I thought I was arguing only that such a logic has been proved unnecessary.

II

SEMANTIC FOUNDATIONS FOR THE
LOGIC OF PREFERENCE

Nicholas Rescher[1]

CONTENTS

	Page
I. Historical Introduction	38
II. Modes of Preference	39
1. Two Modes of Goodness	39
2. The Two Corresponding Modes of Preference	41
III. Semantical Machinery	42
1. The Line of Approach	42
2. Formal Machinery of Analysis: Semantical Considerations	43
3. A Purely Qualitative Alternative Approach	46
4. Relations Between the Two Modes of Preference	47
5. The von Wrightean Semantics	47
6. Preference-Tautologies	49
7. Restricted and Unrestricted Quantification	51
IV. An Examination of Some Preference Principles	52
V. A Measure-Theoretic Perspective upon the Logic of Preference	57
VI. Conclusion	59
VII. Appendix: Restricted vs. Unrestricted Quantification	59
VIII. Bibliography	62

[1] Certain basic ideas of the present paper were developed in discussion with my colleague John Robison. In working these ideas out in the form in which they are presented here, I benefited substantially by the able assistance of Anne (Mrs. Michael) Pelon.

I. Historical Introduction

THE FOUNDER of the "logic of preference" is the founding father of logic itself, Aristotle. Book III of the *Topics* – where Aristotle is concerned to spell out principles governing the concept of preferability ($\grave{\alpha}\iota\rho\varepsilon\tau\widehat{\omega}\varepsilon\rho o\nu$ = the worthier of choice) – must be regarded as the inaugural treatment of the subject. The treatment there, however, is such that no adequate distinction is drawn between material and formal considerations. The bulk of the principles listed are of a strictly substantive, non-formal sort. For example:

> That which is more permanent or durable is preferable to that which is less so. (116a13-14)
> That which is to be chosen for its own sake is preferable to that which is to be chosen for the sake of another. (116a29-30)

Other principles given are of a more formal and logically more tractable sort. For example:

> The possible (practicable) is preferable to the impossible (impracticable). (316b27)
> That is preferable which is the more applicable on every occasion or on most occasions (for example, justice and self-control are preferable to courage, for the first two are always applicable, but courage only sometimes). (117a35-37)
> If A be absolutely better than (preferable to) B, then also the best specimen of A is better than (preferable to) B; e.g., if man is better than horse, then also the best man is better than the best horse. (117b33-35)

The study of preference-principles acceptable upon abstract, formal, systematic grounds rather than upon any particular substantive theory of preferability-determination is the task which the philosophically oriented "logic of preference," as we envisage it, is to set for itself.

In recent philosophy, this enterprise was revived in the orbit of influence of the school of Brentano – particularly by Hermann Schwarz and Max Scheler.[2] The relevant work of this school has been carried forward by several continental investigators before World War II,[3] and since that time this line of inquiry has flourished especially in Scandinavia.[4] Only recently has the subject begun to arouse interest in the U.S.A. – a phenomenon for which R. M. Martin and R. M. Chisholm have been largely responsible.[5]

Interest on the part of economists in the theory of preference as a special application of the concept of utility antedates this philosophical tradition. For the traditional theory, the reader should consult ch. VI, "Value and

[2] See *Schwarz* (1900) and *Scheler* (1913–14). For all citations of this sort see the Bibliography at the end of this paper.
[3] See *Katkov* (1937) and *Kraus* (1937).
[4] See *Halldén* (1957), *von Wright* (1963), and *Aqvist* (1963).
[5] See *Martin* (1963), *Chisholm* (1964), and *Chisholm and Sosa* (1966).

Utility," of Alfred Marshall's classic *Principles of Economics*.[6] The recent formal development of this utility concept has primarily been in the direction of the mathematical theory of games.[7] The concept of valuation (and thus of preference) also plays a prominent and illuminating role in modern decision-theory.[8]

It is a central part of the motivation of this paper to try to develop the logic of preference in such a way as to build a bridge connecting these traditions: the logico-philosophical on the one hand, and the mathematico-economic on the other.

II. Modes of Preference

1. *Two Modes of Goodness*

The locutions "it is a good thing that p" or "p's being the case is a good thing" – involve a serious ambiguity in the notion of "good" at issue. Certain essential distinctions must be drawn if confusion is to be avoided. The need for these distinctions becomes manifest if we examine some specific illustrative situations. Consider, for example, the following case:

If it is the case that	then one is to get
p	+ \$1
not-p	(unspecified)

Here p's being the case is a "good thing" in the precise sense that, supposing p to be so, a positive result ensues. (Locutions of the type "there is something in it for me" and "I am better off than I was before" come to be applicable.) The basis of comparison here is that between:

(1) my situation *before* it eventuated that p was the case, and
(2) my situation *after* the eventuation of p.

Correspondingly, by this standard of comparison, the p of the following situation

If it is the case that	then one is to get
p	—\$1
not-p	(unspecified)

is a bad thing, again in the precise sense that when p comes about "I stand to lose something" and "I am worse off than I was before."

---

[6] London, Macmillan and Co., 1890; 8th ed., 1920. For a helpful history of the recent history of economic utility theory see D. Braybrooke, "Farewell to the New Welfare Economics," *Review of Economic Studies*, vol. 23 (1955), pp. 180–193.

[7] See R. D. Luce and H. Raiffa, *Games and Decisions* (New York, Wiley, 1957), where a comprehensive bibliography is also given.

[8] See R. Jeffreys, *The Logic of Decision* (New York, McGraw-Hill, 1965).

Let us call this mode of goodness and badness – as based on a straight-forward comparison of (1) and (2) – *first-order* goodness and badness, choosing this qualification because the mode of "goodness" at issue turns on the value of the result of only one possible alternative in the situation in question (viz., *p*'s being the case) to the exclusion of any concern with the result of the other alternative (viz., *p*'s not being the case).[9]

That considerations over and above those involved in first-order goodness (or badness) must be introduced is readily established by the example of situations such as the following:

If it is the case that	then one is to get
p	+ $1
not-*p*	+ $10

By the standards of comparison (1) and (2) laid down above, it is clear that *both* *p*'s and not-*p*'s coming to be the case are first-order "good things." Nevertheless, it is also plain that one is entitled to regard *p*'s happening as in some (different) sense a "bad thing" because *p*'s happening of course precludes not-*p*'s happening, and not-*p*'s happening is – under the circumstances – a good thing of such a magnitude that one cannot but regard its preclusion as a "bad thing."

The contrast at issue here is brought out even more explicitly in the following situation:

If it is the case that	then one is to get
p	—$1
not-*p*	—$100

Neither *p* nor not-*p* are first-order "good things." Yet one cannot, under the circumstances, regard *p*'s happening as other than a very "good thing" indeed, since it averts the minor catastrophe that ensues when not-*p*.

The contrast at issue in such cases, then, is not that between (1) and (2) as above, but that between

(2) my situation after the (assumed) eventuation of *p*, and

(3) my situation after the (assumed) eventuation of not-*p*.

We shall call the type of goodness at issue here *differential goodness*. It is assessed by taking into *comparative* account – not just the situation under consideration, but – the possible *alternatives* to the situation under consideration. As our examples have shown, it is clear that there is no inevitable correlation between first-order goodness (and badness) and differential goodness (and badness). First-order goods can be differential evils, and conversely.

---

[9] This conception would, I suppose, come reasonably close to capturing some aspects of the intent of the traditional notion of *intrinsic* goodness, but this idea has been used in such a variegated (and sometimes loose) way that it is pointless to employ it for our purposes.

2. *The Two Corresponding Modes of Preference*

As one would suspect, the distinction between *first-order* and *differential* goodness carries over into a parallel distinction between two corresponding modes of preference. This is again brought out most sharply by an examination of examples. Consider the following situation where its coming-about-that-p and its coming-about-that-q are assumed to be independent events:

If it is the case that	then one is to get
p	+ $10
not-p	(unspecified)
q	+ $1
not-q	(unspecified)

Here one obviously prefers p's being the case to q's being the case, in the precise sense that the former conduces more to my benefit (i.e., is such that one "stands to gain more by it"). This point can be made in the following terms: that the *extent* of p's first-order goodness (viz., a "gain" of $10) is greater than the extent of q's first-order goodness (viz., a "gain" of $1). We shall designate the mode of preferability at issue here as *first-order preference*. This mode of preference then is based upon a contrast of *the comparative extent of the first-order goodness* of the two items being compared.

Consider now the contrasting situation:

If it is the case that	then one is to get
p	+ $2
not-p	+ $2
q	+ $1
not-q	−$100

The significant features to be noted with respect to this situation are: (i) There is no question that p is first-order preferable to q (the first-order goodness of p stands to that of q in a ratio of 2 : 1). Nevertheless (ii) it is a matter of genuine indifference to oneself whether p is or is not the case – exactly the same result accrues either way. Moreover, (iii) it is highly important to one that q rather than not-q be the case (more than $100 being at stake with respect to these alternatives). In view of this – and despite the first-order preferability of p to q – there is a definite and important sense in which we prefer q's being the case to that of p. This point can perhaps be sharpened by retabulating the alternatives as follows:

If it is the case that	then one is to get
$p \mathbin{\&} q$	+ $3
$p \mathbin{\&} \sim q$	−$98
$\sim p \mathbin{\&} q$	+ $3
$\sim p \mathbin{\&} \sim q$	−$98

Our intuitive preference for q's being the case in contrast to p's being the case is based on the impressive contrast between the facts that, as this tabulation renders palpable:

1. When q is the case, one cannot fail to gain \$3 regardless of whether p is or is not the case.
2. When p is the case, then one either gains \$3 or *loses* \$98 depending upon whether q is or is not the case.

The sort of preference at issue here is clearly based upon a contrast of *the comparative extent of the differential goodness* of the two items being compared. Correspondingly, this type of preference will be designated as *differential preference*.

Our aim in this paper will be to lay the groundwork for a detailed study of the logical theory of preference relationships of this general sort: to elucidate what is involved in preference-commitments of various types. The question of special interest to the economists – viz., how to *combine* the preference-commitments of diverse individuals into one coherent inter-personal preferential scheme – lies outside the purview of our discussion.

III. Semantical Machinery

1. *The Line of Approach*

The basis for the semantical considerations we are attempting to develop is the concept of a propositional preference ordering. Presupposing a propositional logic of the familiar sort – and representing propositions by the meta-variables 'α', 'β', 'γ', etc. – we introduce the propositional relationship P (for preferability) with the understanding that

$$\alpha P \beta$$

is to be understood as "α's being the case is preferred (preferable) to β's being the case." The only indispensable requirements we shall impose on the relationship P are:

1. That P be an ordering relation, i.e., that it be transitive, asymmetric, and irreflexive.
2. That P be an extensional relation among propositions, i.e., that it admit the substitution of provable equivalents.

The exact interpretation of the sort of preference at issue in P is to be left open. Specifically we shall not try to settle whether this is to be

(1) A matter of being *preferred* by a given individual (or group),

or

(2) A matter of being *preferable* by some impersonal criterion.

Nor shall we make any specification as to whether the preference at issue is a *synoptic* preference ("preferable when everything is taken into account") or an *aspectival* preference ("preferable in point of cost, or convenience, or the like"). However important these distinctions may be of themselves, they should be indifferent to the sort of abstract and "structural" considerations to which a *logic of preference* devotes itself.

*   *   *

There are two alternative approaches to the development of a logic of preference: the *axiomatic* and the *semantic*. On the axiomatic approach, one lays down certain *basic formalized rules* – presumably underwritten by intuitive considerations – as guiding basis for the formal development of a theory. From these basic rules the theory itself is then derived as a logical consequence. On the semantic approach one sets up a *criterion of acceptability* for such rules and includes in one's system all those rules classed as acceptable by the criterion. The former, axiomatic approach has to date been the standard for the logic of preference. The systematizations of von Wright, Halldén, Chisholm-Sosa, and Martin have all proceeded in its purview. The approach is, however, unsatisfactory because of the wide divergence among these pioneers as to just what the "obviously acceptable" principles of a logic of preference are. (Only the irreflexivity, asymmetry, and transitivity of preference lie in the range of the clearly unproblematic.) We ourselves shall pursue various *alternative but in principle reasonable* possibilities along the line of the semantical approach. Here divergences are less harmful and issue not in outright inconsistencies of a system but in alternative plausible specifications of one intrinsically ambiguous idea. The approach is an experimental one: we do not seek to find "the correct" logic of preference but to explore some of the more promising systems that can be built up by way of tracing out various, of themselves plausible, conceptions of the nature of the preference relation. We hope in this way to be able to provide a *rationale* capable of explaining the divergencies between the several mutually incompatible axiomatizations that have been proposed for preference-logic by various recent writers on the subject.

2. *Formal Machinery of Analysis: Semantical Considerations*

To develop the semantical groundwork of a theory that deserves the name of a "logic of preference", the sorts of considerations with which we have been dealing must be provided with a somewhat more systematic grounding.

Assume that we have a list

$$w_1, w_2, \ldots, w_n$$

of "possible worlds" (state descriptions in the sense of Carnap). Our starting-point is provided by an *index of merit* measure $\#$ which assigns to each possible world w_1 a real-number value $\#(w_1)$. We shall not now enter upon a discussion of the specific substantive character of this measure, i.e., the specific respects in which it assesses the characteristics of the possible worlds, the sorts of considerations of which it takes account, and the relative importance with which it endows them. Considerations of this sort relate to the material side of the concrete application of the machinery and not to the formal side of the abstract logic of the matter, which alone concerns us at present.

Given this measure-of-merit or desirability for the possible worlds, we then assign to any proposition α that can be generated as a truth-functional compound of the w_i the real number value $\#(\alpha)$ to be *the average (arithmetical mean) of the $\#$-values of all the possible worlds w_i within which α is true.*[10] (This leaves $\#(\alpha)$ undefined when α is a contradiction; a difficulty which we shall simply lay aside for the time being.)[11]

We may construe $\#(\alpha)$ as measuring the extent of the first-order goodness of α (i.e., of the circumstance of α's being the case). And in this case the corresponding mode of preference will obviously be represented by the definition:[12]

$$\alpha P^\# \beta \text{ for } \#(\alpha) > \#(\beta)$$

Our $\#$-measure for first-order goodness is readily applied to a derivative measure for differential goodness – let it be represented by $\star$:

$$\star(\alpha) = \#(\alpha) - \#(\sim\alpha)$$

This measure has the interesting feature, which is of far-reaching significance – and whose counterpart emphatically does not hold for $\#$ – that

$$\star(\sim\alpha) = -\star(\alpha)$$

The corresponding mode of preference will obviously be represented by the definition

$$\alpha P^\star \beta \text{ for } \star(\alpha) > \star(\beta)$$

For the sake of an illustration of this group of ideas, consider the following:

Possible worlds	$\#$-values
w_1: $p \,\&\, q$	a
w_2: $p \,\&\, \sim q$	b
w_3: $\sim p \,\&\, q$	c
w_4: $\sim p \,\&\, \sim q$	d

[10] An interesting variant of this approach would be to consider a distribution of probabilities across the possible worlds w_i and then consider the correspondingly weighted average of the w_i, rather than their arithmetical mean. This approach is adopted as standard in Jeffrey's monograph [see *Jeffrey* (1965), ch. 5], where, however, the propositional logic of the situation is not worked out. We shall return to the matter in footnote 17 below.

[11] The reader, can, if he likes, remove this gap by thinking of $\#(a)$ as fixed at 0 in this case.

[12] Note that we must throughout *exclude substitutions* that make a or β into *contradictions*, once we have left $\#$ undefined in this case.

On this basis we may calculate, by way of illustration:

$$\#(p) = \frac{a+b}{2} \qquad\qquad \star(p) = \frac{a+b}{2} - \frac{c+d}{2}$$

$$\#(\sim p) = \frac{c+d}{2} \qquad\qquad \star(\sim p) = \frac{c+d}{2} - \frac{a+b}{2}$$

$$\#(q) = \frac{a+c}{2} \qquad\qquad \star(q) = \frac{a+c}{2} - \frac{b+d}{2}$$

$$\#(\sim q) = \frac{b+d}{2} \qquad\qquad \star(\sim q) = \frac{b+d}{2} - \frac{a+c}{2}$$

$$\#(p \vee q) = \frac{a+b+c}{3} \qquad\qquad \star(p \vee q) = \frac{a+b+c}{3} - d$$

$$\#(p \,\&\, q) = a \qquad\qquad \star(p \,\&\, q) = a - \frac{b+c+d}{3}$$

Thus, to say that $pP\#q$ would be to have it that

$$\frac{a+b}{2} > \frac{a+c}{2} \text{ or } b > c$$

Or again, to say that $(p \vee q)P\star p$ would be to have it that:

$$\frac{a+b+c}{3} - d > \frac{a+b}{2} - \frac{c+d}{2} \text{ or } 5c > a+b+3d$$

However, the salient difference between these two modes of preference is brought out by the fact that the principle

$$pPq \rightarrow \sim qP \sim p$$

which fails in general for $P\#$ does hold for $P\star$. (See the discussion of the principle (R1) in Sect. IV below.)

(A mode of preference with which it would also be interesting to deal is *preferability-other-things-being-equal*, that is, a relation P' such that (say):

$pP'q$ iff $\#(p \,\&\, r) > \#(q \,\&\, r)$ whenever r is independent of p and of q.

Although this sort of conception can be handled with the machinery here introduced, its treatment involves additional complications which militate against our dealing with it here. Compare, however, the treatment of the principle (W5) in Sect. IV below.)

Viewed in somewhat general terms, our approach to the logic of preference thus proceeds in terms of a numerical criterion of merit. Given a proposition α, we determine in some suitable way a numerical *measure of merit* $\mu(\alpha)$. And then we introduce a corresponding preference relation P^μ with the convention that

$$\alpha P^\mu \beta \text{ for } \mu(\alpha) > \mu(\beta)$$

45

3. *A Purely Qualitative Alternative Approach*

To the mind of some readers, the preceding quantitative line of approach might seem to have an air of unrealistic oversophistication. To assign to each possible world a specific real-number as its "measure of merit" might appear a procedure that presupposes an unattainable differentiation in degrees of value. This line of criticism could, however, be accepted without vitiating the strategy of approach. We reply to the critic: "Have it your way – don't even try for precise distinctions! Grade possible worlds into (say) just three classes: desirable, undesirable, and neutral. You can still apply – and benefit from – the application of the machinery here constructed."

The fact is clear that our entire procedure could be carried on in the setting of just three rough, individually undifferentiated entries of an index of merit measure. Merely let the w_i assume just one of three #-values, as follows:

$$+ 1 \quad \text{favorable (desirable)}$$
$$0 \quad \text{neutral}$$
$$- 1 \quad \text{unfavorable (undesirable)}$$

The whole of the semantical machinery we shall construct now can be applied on the basis of such very rough and unsophisticated purely qualitative merit-assessments – assessments so crude and rough-cut[13] that even the reader favorably inclined to the sentiments of our hypothetical critic, could hardly demur from following the direction of our quantitative method for so slight a distance.

* * *

It must, however, be made clear that our semantical approach to the logic of preference is not a *purely comparative* or *strictly ordinal* one based solely upon the conception of preferability as such, but an *evaluative* one in which preference relations are based derivatively upon an essentially *quantitative* approach, the assessment (measure) of the intrinsic merit (goodness) of the objects involved. We treat preference as being *derivative* from merit assessments and not as an ultimately self contained comparisory. To illustrate the distinction at issue, suppose that we are to deal with four possible worlds w_1–w_4, and suppose that we knew them to be so listed in *order of preference*. If this purely comparative preference-information were all that we knew, we would be wholly unable to say (1) by *how much* w_1 (say) is preferred to w_2, let alone (2) what *the intrinsic merit* (goodness/badness) of w_1 (say) might be. This purely comparative basis would prove insufficient

---

[13] Our simplified approach, for examp le, fails entirely to distinguish different degrees of favorableness and unfavorableness. But, of course, to the extent that such distinctions are drawn we move away from the aspirations of our simplicistic critic back toward our initial starting point.

for the quality-assessment (and thus essentially quantitative) processes that underlie the preferability-comparison of our semantics.

4. *Relations Between the Two Modes of Preference*

There is an interesting kinship between the two types of preference we have distinguished. Consider again the four possible worlds w_1–w_4 of the preceding section. Notice that

$$pP^{\#}q \text{ becomes } \frac{a+b}{2} > \frac{a+c}{2} \text{ or } b > c$$

and that

$$pP^{\star}q \text{ becomes } \frac{a+b}{2} - \frac{c+d}{2} > \frac{a+c}{2} - \frac{b+d}{2} \text{ or } b > c$$

This suggests that $\#$-preference and $\star$-preference are equivalent. But it is readily seen that this is not the case. For our procedure and our tabulations have to this point been based on the supposition that the variables involved – 'p', 'q', etc. – represent *independent* propositions: propositions devoid of logical interconnections of such a kind that the $\#$-value assigned to one must have a bearing upon that assigned to the other(s). *Only under this independence presupposition that 'p', 'q', etc. represent independent propositions do $\#$-preference and $\star$-preference come to coincide.* When this presupposition is not satisfied, the equivalence no longer obtains, as is shown by the following example. Consider:

$$pP(p \vee q)$$

First, let P represent $\#$-preference, and let us go again to the four w_i of the preceding section. Then

$$pP^{\#}(p \vee q)$$

will represent

$$\frac{a+b}{2} > \frac{a+b+c}{3} \text{ or } a+b > c$$

If, on the other hand, P represents $\star$-preference, then

$$pP^{\star}(p \vee q)$$

will represent

$$\frac{a+b}{2} - \frac{c+d}{2} > \frac{a+b+c}{3} - d \text{ or } a+b+3d > 5c$$

and it is perfectly clear that these two inequalities are not equivalent. Thus it will only be in the special case of independent relata (essentially, those which do not share a common variable) that the two modes of preference will coincide.

5. *The von Wrightean Semantics*

We turn now to a variant approach to the semantics of preference-logic which is designed to codify the approach of G. H. von Wright's recent monograph. We again suppose as starting point a series of possible worlds (state descriptions):

$$w_1, w_2, \ldots, w_n$$

We suppose that the propositions at issue are generated by truth-functional compoundings of the w_i. We suppose further a "ground floor" preference ordering of the w_i, allowing the possibility of indifference, say, for example

$$w_4 > w_3 \simeq w_5 > w_1 > w_2$$

(In such a list every possible world can occur just once, and a well ordering must result when $\simeq$-connected entries are identified.)

Let us now construe

$$\alpha P^w \beta$$

to mean:

For every γ (independent of α and β[14]) we have it that every possible world w_i in which $\begin{Bmatrix} \alpha \text{ true} \\ \beta \text{ false} \\ \gamma \text{ true} \end{Bmatrix}$ is $>$-preferable to all the corresponding possible world(s) w_j in which $\begin{Bmatrix} \alpha \text{ false} \\ \beta \text{ true} \\ \gamma \text{ true} \end{Bmatrix}$

Note that the condition on γ here plays the role of a requirement of "other things being equal".

This specification of a semantical interpretation of the P^w-relationship corresponds exactly to the system of von Wright's theory. It accords entirely with the motivations and explanations of his discussion, and is such that all of his "basic principles" prove acceptable.

Let us illustrate the workings of this von Wrightean semantics in a numerical rather than merely comparative setting. Consider the following eight possible worlds:

World	p	q	r	$\#(w_i)$
w_1	$+$	$+$	$+$	x_1
w_2	$+$	$+$	$-$	x_2
w_3	$+$	$-$	$+$	x_3
w_4	$+$	$-$	$-$	x_4
w_5	$-$	$+$	$+$	x_5
w_6	$-$	$+$	$-$	x_6
w_7	$-$	$-$	$+$	x_7
w_8	$-$	$-$	$-$	x_8

Note now that on the von Wrightean semantics we have:

$$p P^w q \text{ iff } x_3 > x_5 \text{ and } x_4 > x_6$$

On the $P\star$-semantics, on the other hand, we have

$$p P^w q \text{ iff } x_3 + x_4 > x_5 + x_6$$

---

[14] Actually, in realistic applications of this machinery, one would want to require here not merely logical independence alone, but causal independence as well.

It is thus obvious that P^w preferability entails $P\star$ preferability, but not conversely, so that the former is significantly more restrictive than the latter. (Indeed we shall shortly argue that there is good reason to think it to be actually too restrictive.) Again, by way of application of this machinery, note that "$(p \supset q)P^w p$" is a perfectly possible preference-situation, which would prevail under the circumstance that both $[x_1, x_5, x_7] > x_3$ and $[x_2, x_6, x_8] > x_4$.

Let us now develop the argument as to the restrictiveness of P^w. Let the case with the possible worlds be as above, and let it be supposed that:

$$x_3 = +1000$$
$$x_4 = \quad 0$$
$$x_5 = -1000$$
$$x_6 = +.0001$$

Surely, in any intuitively plausible sense of the term, p is now "preferable" to q (for when p is true we may gain as much as 1,000 but can lose no more than 0, whereas when q is true we may lose as much as 1,000, but can gain no more than .0001). But on the (overly safe) construction of the von Wrightean semantics we cannot say that p is preferable to q because in one case (among potentially countless ones) we may lose a bit more by p than by q.

Despite the interpretative shortcoming brought out in such examples, the von Wrightean semantic does, however, enjoy one important systematic advantage. It proceeds simply and solely on the basis of an ordinal preference ordering of the possible worlds, and does not call – as do the $P\star$ and $P\sharp$ relations, for an actual cardinal valuation of them. But actually this advantage is more seeming than real, since an ordering can always be transformed into a valuation by such devices as letting every possible world score 1 point for every other one that it excels in the rank ordering.

6. *Preference-Tautologies*

On the basis of the semantical machinery developed in Sect. III above, we are able to introduce the concept of a *preference-tautology*. Consider a preference-principle of the type:

$$pPq \rightarrow \sim(qPp)$$
$$pPq \rightarrow \sim qP \sim p$$
$$(pPq \;\&\; qPr) \rightarrow pPr$$

Such a principle will be a $P\sharp$-tautology (or a $P\star$-tautology, respectively) if, when P is interpreted throughout as $P\sharp$ (or $P\star$, respectively), the principle goes over into a truth – *i.e.*, an arithmetical truth – with respect to every possible assignment of $\sharp$-values to the possible worlds generated out of truth-combinations of the variables that are involved.

For example, to see that the second principle of the preceding list is a $\#$-tautology, we consider the $\#$-value assignment

Possible world	$\#$-value
w_1: p & q	a
w_2: p & $\sim q$	b
w_3: $\sim p$ & q	c
w_4: $\sim p$ & $\sim q$	d

Now "$pP^\#q \rightarrow \sim qP^\# \sim p$" amounts to:

$$\frac{a+b}{2} > \frac{a+c}{2} \rightarrow \frac{b+d}{2} > \frac{c+d}{2}$$

that is, to

$$b > c \rightarrow b > c$$

which is an arithmetical truth.

On the other hand, it can be seen that the principle

$$pP^\#q \rightarrow \sim qP^\# \sim p$$

breaks down under substitution for the variables involved. For if we substitute "$p \vee q$" for "q" we obtain

$$pP^\#(p \vee q) \rightarrow \sim(p \vee q)P \sim p$$

which amounts to:

$$\frac{a+b}{2} > \frac{a+b+c}{3} \rightarrow d > \frac{c+d}{2}$$

that is, to

$$a + b > 2c \rightarrow d > 2c$$

which is obviously falsifiable.

It is thus crucially important to distinguish between *unrestricted* preference-tautologies such as

$$pP^\#q \rightarrow \sim(qP^\#p)$$

which – as the reader can check – proves acceptable under *any and every* substitution of the variables involved, and *restricted* preference-tautologies like

$$pP^\#q \rightarrow \sim qP^\# \sim p$$

which has unacceptable substitution instances. On the other hand it is readily shown that

$$pP^\star q \rightarrow \sim qP^\star \sim p$$

is unrestrictedly acceptable.

It is an interesting fact, inherent in their "restricted equivalence," that despite their very great *conceptual* difference (*i.e.*, the very different meanings that attach to them), essentially the same preference theses obtain for $P^\#$ and $P^\star$: the only differences that can arise between them are that growing out of substitution restrictions. The sorts of preference theses that can bring out on the side of formal acceptability the conceptual difference between the two concepts will be those that turn on substitution-restrictions, such as:

$$pP(p \lor q) \to \sim(p \lor q)Pp$$

which is acceptable for $P^\star$ but not for $P^\sharp$.

The possession of a semantically viable concept of a *preference tautology* is of the utmost importance from the logical point of view. For with its guidance, the question of the axiomatization of preference logic can meaningfully be raised and fruitfully dealt with. Our interests here falling on the semantical rather than the formal/axiomatic side, we shall not pursue this prospect further on the present occasion.

7. Restricted and Unrestricted Quantification

To provide ourselves with a systematic formal mechanism for recording the (for our purposes) pivotal distinction between two different modes of quantifications, we shall introduce the unrestricted propositional quantifier $\forall$ with

$$(\forall p)(- - - p - - -)$$

to be construed as asserting that "$- - - p - - -$" holds with respect to *any and every* substitution for 'p', and the restricted propositional quantifier A with

$$(\mathsf{A}p)(- - - p - - -)$$

to be construed as asserting (only) that "$- - - p - - -$" holds for all those substitutions for 'p' which do not involve other variables that occur in "$- - - p - - -$".

Thus, for example, we would be in a position to assert the principle

$$(\forall p)(\forall q)(pP^\sharp q \to \sim[qP^\sharp p])$$

On the other hand it would not be correct to assert the principle,

$$(\forall p)(\forall q)(pP^\sharp q \to \sim qP^\sharp \sim p)$$

although it would, by contrast, be correct to assert the principle,

$$(\mathsf{A}p)(\mathsf{A}q)(pP^\sharp q \to \sim qP^\sharp \sim p)$$

The possibility is (of course) not to be excluded that in certain cases a mixture of these quantifiers is appropriate, so that one could assert a principle of the form

$$(\mathsf{A}p)(\forall q)(- - - p,q - - -)$$

claiming, in effect, that 'p'-substitutions must be restricted, although 'q'-substitutions can be made unrestrictedly.

The ideas and procedures at issue here are applied and illustrated in the Appendix.

IV. An Examination of Some Preference Principles

The most extensive, and doubtless the best-known treatment of preference logic is that of G. H. von Wright's book on *The Logic of Preference* (Edinburgh, 1963). Some brief suggestions are offered in ch. II of R. M. Martin's book *Intension and Decision* (Englewood Cliffs, N.J., 1963). A suggestive discussion can also be found in an article by R. M. Chisholm and E. Sosa, "On the Logic of 'Intrinsically Better'" (*American Philosophical Quarterly*, vol. 3, 1966). On the semantical side, these writers all proceed on the basis of intuitive, unformalized considerations. It is thus of interest to examine their preference-principles from the angle of their $P^\sharp$ and $P^\star$-tautologousness. The results of such an examination are tabulated below:

Von Wright	$P^\sharp$	$P^\star$
(W1) $pPq \to \sim(qPp)$	+	+
(W2) $(pPq \ \& \ qPr) \to pPr^{15}$	+	+
(W3) $pPq \to (p \ \& \sim q)P(\sim p \ \& \ q)$	+	+
$\quad\ \ (p \ \& \sim q)P(\sim p \ \& \ q) \to pPq$	+	+
(W4) $[\sim(\sim p \ \& \sim q)P\sim(\sim r \ \& \sim s)] \to [(p \ \& \sim r \ \& \sim s)P$ $\quad (\sim p \ \& \sim q \ \& \ r) \ \& \ (p \ \& \sim r \ \& \sim s)P(\sim p \ \& \sim q \ \& \ s)$ $\quad \& \ (q \ \& \ r \sim \ \& \sim s)P(\sim p \ \& \ q \ \& \ r) \ \& \ (q \ \& \sim r \ \& \sim s)$ $\quad P(\sim p \ \& \sim q \ \& \ s)]$	—	—
$\quad\ \ [(p \ \& \sim r \ \& \sim s)P(\sim p \ \& \sim q \ \& \ r) \ \& \ (p \ \& \sim r \ \& \sim s)P$ $\quad (\sim p \ \& \sim q \ \& \ s) \ \& \ (q \ \& \sim r \ \& \sim s)P(\sim p \ \& \sim q \ \& \ r) \ \&$ $\quad (q \ \& \sim r \ \& \sim s)P(\sim p \ \& \sim q \ \& \ s)] \to [\sim(\sim p \ \& \sim q)$ $\quad P\sim(\sim r \ \& \sim s)]$	—	—
(W5) $pPq \to [(p \ \& \ r)P(q \ \& \ r) \ \& \ (p \ \& \sim r)P(q \ \& \sim r)]$	—	—
$\quad\ \ [(p \ \& \ r)P(q \ \& \ r) \ \& \ (p \ \& \sim r)P(q \ \& \sim r)] \to pPq$	$(+)^1$	$(+)^2$

Chisholm-Sosa	$P^\sharp$	$P^\star$
(A1) $= $ (W1)	+	+
(A2) $[\sim pPq \ \& \sim(qPr)] \to \sim(pPr)$	+	+
(A3) $[\sim(pP\sim p) \ \& \sim(\sim pPp) \ \& \sim(qP\sim q) \ \& \sim(\sim qPq)] \to$ $\quad [\sim(pPq) \ \& \sim(qPp)]$	+	+
(A4) $[\sim(qP\sim q) \ \& \sim(\sim qPq) \ \& \ pPq] \to pP\sim p$	+	+
(A5) $[\sim(qP\sim q) \ \& \sim(\sim qPq) \ \& \ qP\sim p] \to pP\sim p$	+	+

KEY

— unacceptable
+ unrestrictedly acceptable
(+) restrictedly acceptable

ANNOTATIONS

1. The appropriate quantifier-prefix is:
$(\forall p)(\forall q)(Ar)$
2. The appropriate quantifier-prefix is:
$(Ap)(Aq)(Ar)$

---

[15] (W1) and (W2) represent the *antisymmetry* and the *transitivity* of the preference relation. (Between them they entail irreflexivity, viz.: $\sim(pPp)$.) These are the minimal rules for "preference" classically insisted upon in *all* treatments of the subject by logicians, economists, etc.

R. M. Martin (*op. cit.*) accepts inter alia two principles whose status is as follows:

	$P\sharp$	$P\star$
(M1) $(pPr \lor qPr) \to (p \lor q)Pr$	—	—
(M2) $pP(q \lor r) \to [pPq \,\&\, pPr]$	—	—

Moreover, the converses of these two principles also fail to obtain for both of our modes of preference:[16]

	$P\sharp$	$P\star$
(M3) $(p \lor q)Pr \to (pPr \lor qPr)$	—	—
(M4) $(pPq \,\&\, pPr) \to pP(q \lor r)$	—	—

The same goes for various cognate rules, as may be seen from the tabulation:

THE STATUS OF VARIOUS PREFERENCE PRINCIPLES

Preference Principle	Von Wright	Chisholm Sosa	Martin	$P\sharp$	$P\star$	P^w
1. $pPq \to \sim(qPp)$	√	√	√	+	+	+
2. $(pPq \,\&\, qPr) \to pPr$	√	√	√	+	+	+
3. $pPq \to \sim qP\sim p$		x	√	$(+)^1$	+	+
4. $\sim qP\sim p \to pPq$		x	√	$(+)^1$	+	+
5. $pPq \to (p \,\&\, \sim q) P(\sim p \,\&\, q)$	√	x		+	+	+
6. $(p \,\&\, \sim q) P(\sim p \,\&\, q) \to pPq$	√	x		+	+	+
7. $[\sim(pP\sim p) \,\&\, \sim(\sim pPp) \,\&\, \sim(qP\sim q) \,\&\, \sim(\sim qPq)] \to [\sim(pPq) \,\&\, \sim(qPp)]$	√	√		+	+	+
8. $[\sim(qP\sim q) \,\&\, \sim(\sim qPq) \,\&\, pPq] \to pP\sim p$	√	√		+	+	—
9. $[\sim(qP\sim q) \,\&\, \sim(\sim qPq) \,\&\, qP\sim p] \to pP\sim p$	√	√		+	+	—
10. $pPq \to [(p \,\&\, r) P(q \,\&\, r) \,\&\, (p \,\&\, \sim r) P(q \,\&\, \sim r)]$	√			—	—	+
11. $[(p \,\&\, r) P(q \,\&\, r) \,\&\, (p \,\&\, \sim r) P(q \,\&\, \sim r)] \to pPq$	√			$(+)^2$	$(+)^3$	+
12. $[\sim(pPq) \,\&\, \sim(qPr)] \to \sim(pPr)$		√		+	+	
13. $(pPr \lor qPr) \to (p \lor q) Pr$			√	—	—	—
14. $(p \lor q) Pr \to [pPr \,\&\, qPr]$	√			—	—	—
15. $[pPr \,\&\, qPr] \to (p \lor q) Pr$	√			—	—	—
16. $(p \lor q) Pr \to (pPr \lor qPr)$				—	—	—
17. $pP(q \lor r) \to (pPq \,\&\, pPr)$			√	—	—	—
18. $(pPq \,\&\, pPr) \to pP(q \lor r)$				—	—	—
19. $(pPr \,\&\, qPr) \to (p \,\&\, q) Pr$				—	—	—
20. $(p \,\&\, q) Pr \to (pPr \,\&\, qPr)$				—	—	—
21. $pP(q \,\&\, r) \to (pPq \,\&\, pPr)$				—	—	—
22. $(pPq \,\&\, pPr) \to pP(q \,\&\, r)$				—	—	—
23. $[\sim(\sim p \,\&\, \sim q) P\sim(\sim r \,\&\, \sim s)] \to [(p \,\&\, \sim r \,\&\, \sim s) P(\sim p \,\&\, \sim q \,\&\, r) \,\&\, (p \,\&\, \sim r \,\&\, \sim s) P(\sim p \,\&\, \sim q \,\&\, s) \,\&\, (q \,\&\, \sim r \,\&\, \sim s) P(\sim p \,\&\, \sim q \,\&\, r) \,\&\, (q \,\&\, \sim r \,\&\, \sim s) P(\sim p \,\&\, \sim q \,\&\, s)]$				—	—	+
24. $[(p \,\&\, \sim r \,\&\, \sim s) P(\sim p \,\&\, \sim q \,\&\, r) \,\&\, (p \,\&\, \sim r \,\&\, \sim s) P(\sim p \,\&\, \sim q \,\&\, s) \,\&\, (q \,\&\, \sim r \,\&\, \sim s) P(\sim p \,\&\, \sim q \,\&\, r) \,\&\, (q \,\&\, \sim r \,\&\, \sim s) P(\sim p \,\&\, \sim q \,\&\, s)] \to [\sim(\sim p \,\&\, \sim q) P\sim(\sim r \,\&\, \sim s)]$	√			—	—	+

KEY:
— unacceptable
+ unrestricted acceptable   [1] The appropriate quantifier-prefix is: $(Ap)(Aq)$.
(+) restrictedly acceptable   [2] The appropriate quantifier-prefix is: $(\forall p)(\forall q)(Ar)$.
√ explicitly accepted   [3] The appropriate quantifier prefix is: $(Ap)(Aq)(Ar)$.
x explicitly rejected

[16] Note, however, that this specific feature of these rules does not exclude them from a proper and positive role in the logic of preference viewed in a wider perspective. Cf. the discussion of Sect. V below.

Several features of this tabulation warrant comment:

(i) It is noteworthy that the only really uncontested principles are numbers (1) and (2) (i.e., irreflexivity and transitivity).[17]

(ii) It is striking that the various authorities are so seriously at odds with one another after going beyond the just-indicated point of common departure.

(iii) It is interesting that so few of the plausible-seeming principles listed after number (12) are acceptable on any of the three accounts of the matter here under consideration.

All this, I believe, goes far toward showing undesirability of proceeding by intuition in the construction of an axiomatic theory for the rules of preference-logic. The advantages of the semantical approach come strikingly to the fore.

We now have a guide to the selection of preference-principles which safeguards us against the often paradoxical features of the deliverances of intuition. At the purely informal, intuitive level of understanding, a concept may well prove to be equivocal. In this case, it takes one form for which certain principles "obviously" hold, and also a second form for which other, equally "obvious" principles hold that are inconsistent with the former. The semantical approach protects us against this logically intolerable situation in which incompatible results confront us with equal plausibility.

Taking the semantical approach we can say that "we know what we are doing" in a far more thoroughgoing way than is possible with any axiomatic treatment. Although serious problems doubtless still remain to be resolved, there can be little doubt that the *semantical* – in contrast to the *axiomatic* – approach affords the most promising prospects for the development of the logic of preference, and that the best hopes for future progress in this field lie in this direction.

$$* \quad * \quad *$$

Chisholm and Sosa discuss two principles of the logic of preference which have been accepted by certain writers, but which they themselves reject. These principles are as follows:

	$P\sharp$	$P\star$
(R1) $\begin{cases} pPq \to {\sim}qP{\sim}p \\ {\sim}qP{\sim}p \to pPq \end{cases}$	$(+)$ $(+)$	$+$ $+$
(R2) $=$ (W3) above	$+$	$+$

---

[17] In this regard it deserves remark how matters fare with the preference measure $P\S$ based on the valuation of a proposition in terms of a probabilistically weighted mean of the possible worlds in which this proposition is true. (With $P\sharp$ all these weights are set equal. Cf. footnote 10 above.) Here principles (1) and (2) survive, but even such plausible principles as (3)–(6), acceptable for all the other modes of P-preference, will fail to hold.

Thus all of the preference principles rejected by Chisholm and Sosa are both $P\sharp$ and P^*-tautologies. The reasons for this divergence warrant brief consideration.

For specificity, let us focus attention upon (R1), with respect to which Chisholm and Sosa argue as follows:

> . . . although the state of affairs consisting of there being no happy egrets (p) is better than that one consisting of there being stones (q), the state of affairs that consists of there being no stones ($\sim q$) is not better, or worse, than that state of affairs consisting of there being no happy egrets ($\sim p$).

As this quotation brings out, Chisholm and Sosa do not deal with our (completely characterized) possible worlds, but with particular states of affairs (i.e., with p's and q's rather than (p & q)'s and (p & $\sim q$)'s). Moreover, they proceed on the basis of what might be called the "raw" or intrinsic propositional valuations, of the sort of which the following is a good example.

If it is the case that	then the resultant utility-value is
p	+4.0 units
$\sim p$	0.0 units
q	+0.5 units
$\sim q$	—1.0 units

And here it is certainly true, with respect to such "raw" valuations, that p's (first-order) preferability to q by no means guarantees not-q's preferability to not-p. But this fact does not conflict with our findings, which proceed on a quite different plane. For note that on our approach we would first transform the raw-valuations of the preceding scheme into valuations of alternative possible worlds:

Possible world	$\sharp$-valuation
w_1: p & q	+4.5 units
w_2: p & $\sim q$	+3.0 units
w_3: $\sim p$ & q	+0.5 units
w_4: $\sim p$ & $\sim q$	—1.0 units

And the propositional $\sharp$-valuations we would *then* derive – and thus the preferences that would be based upon them – would have a quite different structure, to wit:

Proposition	$\sharp$-value
p	+3.75 units
$\sim p$	—0.25 units
q	+2.50 units
$\sim q$	+1.00 units

And on *this* basis of assessment it would have to be the case that – as we have shown – p's preferability to q guarantees not-q's preferability to not-p. In summary, the intuitive ideas operative in the Chisholm-Sosa concept of

E

55

"intrinsic preferability" in no way conflict or involve incompatibilities with the procedures and results of our formal semantics.

Exactly the same line of analysis applies to the Chisholm-Sosa line of objection to von Wright's (W3):

$$pPq \leftrightarrow (p \ \& \sim q)P(\sim p \ \& \ q)$$

Their counter-example is of the type:

If it is the case that	then one is to get
p	$+3$
$\sim p$	0
q	$+1$
$\sim q$	-2

Clearly one prefers p's happening to q's (*i.e.*, prefers a 3-unit gain to a 1-unit gain). But one certainly does not prefer $(p \ \& \sim q)$'s happening (when one gets $+1$) to $(\sim p \ \& \ q)$'s happening (when one also gets exactly $+1$). But let us translate this "raw" valuation into our technical #-valuation *via* the consideration of the possible worlds:

Possible world	#-value
w_1: $p \ \& \ q$	$+4$
w_2: $p \ \& \sim q$	$+1$
w_3: $\sim p \ \& \ q$	$+1$
w_4: $\sim p \ \& \sim q$	-2

And now with respect to the derivative #-values, it is clear that we could not have

$$pP^{\#}q \ \ i.e., \ \ \frac{\#(w_1) + \#(w_2)}{2} > \frac{\#(w_1) + \#(w_3)}{2} \ \ i.e., \#(w_2) > \#(w_3)$$

without also concurrently having:

$$(p \ \& \sim q)P^{\#}(\sim p \ \& \ q) \ \ i.e., \#(w_2) > \#(w_3)$$

*   *   *

The proscription of contradiction-generating substitutions with respect to the #-measure requires further discussion. Consider, for example, the principle (acceptable both for $P^{\#}$ and $P^{\star}$):

$$(W3) \ \ pPq \rightarrow (p \ \& \sim q)P(\sim p \ \& \ q)$$

and let it be assumed that $\vdash p \rightarrow q$, so that we have

$$(W4) \ \ pPq \rightarrow cP(\sim p \ \& \ q) \ \ \ \ \ \ \ c = \text{a contradiction}$$

Now take a concrete example, letting

p = Having \$12 (*i.e.*, having at least \$12, that is, \$12 or more)

q = Having \$11 (*i.e.*, having at least \$11, that is, having \$11 or more)

Note that *this p is preferable to this q* on any presystematic understanding of the matter, and that, moreover, p entails q. Consequently, we would come to be committed by W4 to:

$$cP \text{ (Having exactly \$11)}$$

This consequence is clearly absurd. But it is not, in fact, a valid consequence of our logic of preference because one of the essential steps by which it was obtained involved a fallacious process of inference, to wit, a contradiction-generating substitution for the $\sharp$-measure.

It will be objected that the principle at issue (W3) holds not only for $\sharp$-preference, where we have insisted on excluding contradiction-generating substitutions, but also for $\star$-preference, where this restriction has been dropped. Consequently, so goes the objection, the indicated way out is not available. This objection is correct, so far as it goes, but it fails to realize that, because of the *technical* character of $\star$-preference, the entire difficulty at issue does not arise.

Let it be supposed, for the sake of simplicity, that \$20 is the maximum amount which, as a matter of the "practical politics" of the situation, is at issue (nothing would be affected if this were fixed at \$100 or \$1,000). Then we shall have it that:

$$\sharp(p) = \sharp(\$12 \text{ or more}) = \frac{12 + 13 + \ldots + 20}{9} = 16.0$$

$$\sharp(q) = \sharp(\$11 \text{ or more}) = \frac{11 + 12 + \ldots + 20}{10} = 15.5$$

$$\sharp(\sim p) = \sharp(\$11 \text{ or less}) = \frac{0 + 1 + 2 + \ldots + 11}{12} = 5.5$$

$$\sharp(\sim q) = \sharp(\$10 \text{ or less}) = \frac{0 + 1 + 2 + \ldots + 10}{10} = 5.0$$

As a consequence,

$$\star(p) = 16.0 - 5.5 = 10.5$$
$$\star(q) = 15.5 - 5.0 = 10.5$$

It is thus simply not the case with respect to the technical concept of $\star$-preference now at issue that p ("Having \$12 or more") is preferable to q ("Having \$11 or more"). The difficulty at issue falls to the ground because one of its essential premises fails to be true.

V. A MEASURE-THEORETIC PERSPECTIVE UPON THE LOGIC OF PREFERENCE

It is useful to look at our quantitative approach to the logic of preference from a somewhat different perspective. Let it be supposed that we have a family of propositions represented by the meta-variables 'α', 'β', 'γ', etc. These proportions are assumed to range over the set S, assumed to be closed under the familiar truth-functional connectives. Let there be a real-value measure μ with

$$\mu(\alpha)$$

defined over the set S, subject to the stipulation that equivalent propositions obtain the same μ-value, i.e., that:

$$\text{If } \vdash \alpha \leftrightarrow \beta, \text{ then } \mu(\alpha) = \mu(\beta).$$

Moreover, let it be supposed that our μ-measure is such as to satisfy the following additional condition:

$$\mu(\sim\alpha) = -\mu(\alpha)$$

(It should be observed that our measure $\star(\alpha)$ is, whereas $\#(\alpha)$ is not, of such a kind as to meet this last-named condition.) It may be remarked, moreover, that this condition has the consequence that:

$$\text{If } \mu(\alpha) = \mu(\sim\alpha), \text{ then } \mu(\alpha) = 0.$$

Now it is readily verified that if we stipulate a preference-relation P^μ in such a way that

$$\alpha P^\mu \beta \quad \text{iff} \quad \mu(\alpha) > \mu(\beta)$$

then wherever the μ-measure satisfies the aforementioned conditions, then P^μ must satisfy all of the Chisholm-Sosa axioms (as well as the first two von Wright axioms). It is also readily verified that, under the stipulated conditions, we must have it that P^μ must satisfy the Chisholm-Sosa rejected thesis:

$$\alpha P^\mu \beta \leftrightarrow \sim\beta P^\mu \sim\alpha$$

This way of approaching the matter at once systematizes our previous group of findings with respect to $P\star$.

* * *

It deserves remark that one further, additional stipulation upon the $\#$-measure serves, in effect, to transform $\#$ into a $\star$-type measure. This is the stipulation that the value of a tautology be 0:

$$(S) \quad \#(p \vee \sim p) = 0$$

For this amounts to saying that the value-sum across all the possible worlds is 0:

$$\#(w_1) + \#(w_2) + \ldots + \#(w_n) = 0$$

This establishes that

$$- \#(p) = \#(\sim p)$$

which is the crucial feature distinctive of the $\star$-measure in contrast to the unqualified $\#$ measure. Thus, given the added stipulation (S), $P^\#$ will also satisfy all $P\star$-tautologies, as well as all of the Chisholm-Sosa axioms (by the reasoning of the earlier part of this section). The stipulation (S) thus represents a unification between the two approaches we have primarily been concerned to develop here.

* * *

It is of interest to re-examine, in the light of our generalized measure-theoretic approach, some of the principles previously found unacceptable for $P^{\sharp}$ and $P^{\star}$. By way of example, let us return to the axiom (in the style of R. M. Martin)

$$(M2) \quad pP^{\mu}(q \vee r) \rightarrow (pP^{\mu}q \;\&\; pP^{\mu}r)$$

This now becomes

$$\mu(p) > \mu(p \vee q) \rightarrow [(\mu(p) > \mu(q)) \;\&\; (\mu(p) > u(r))]$$

or equivalently:

$$\mu(p \vee q) \geq \max [\mu(p), \mu(r)]$$

Thus any μ-measure that is a monotonically increasing function of its Boolean constituent will satisfy (M2). This condition, while unquestionably plausible for certain propositional measures (e.g. probability), is patently unsuitable for a measure of "goodness".

Again, consider the axiom

$$(M1) \quad (pP^{\mu}r \vee qP^{\mu}r) > (p \vee q)P^{\mu}r$$

This now becomes

$$[(\mu(p) > \mu(r)) \vee (\mu(q) > \mu(r))] \rightarrow \mu(p \vee q) > \mu(r)$$

or equivalently

$$\mu(p \vee q) \geq \min [\mu(p), \mu(q)]$$

This, of course, would also be guaranteed immediately by the previous condition.

VI. CONCLUSION

It has been the main aim of this paper to provide a systematically developed semantical theory for the logic of preference. Using as starting point the orthodox semantical notion of a "possible world" we have adopted the idea of a valuation-measure for such worlds as a determinant of preferabilities. This apparatus has been applied to appraise the acceptability of various preference-principles accepted on the basis of informal considerations by the several writers who have to date attempted to systematize the logic of preference. Our method has to some extent been able to reconcile the divergent approaches proposed in the literature. But in any case, sufficient evidence has, I trust, been provided to indicate the power and promise of the suggested line of approach.

VII. APPENDIX

Restricted vs. Unrestricted Quantification

When we consider the tautologousness of a preference-principle such as

$$pPq \rightarrow {\sim}qP{\sim}p$$

for a specific construction of P, such as $P^{\sharp}$ or $P^{\star}$, we must – as we saw in

Sect. III above – inquire into the style of universal quantifier that is to prevail over the variables involved. The purpose of this appendix is to explain and illustrate the sort of checking procedure involved in the type of tautology-testing that is at issue here.

Let us first consider the $P^{\sharp}$ interpretation of P:

$$(\text{I}) \quad pP^{\sharp}q \to \sim qP^{\sharp}\sim p$$

And let us begin by understanding this principle as asserted with respect to weak (i.e., restricted) quantification:

$$(\text{Ia}) \quad (Ap)(Aq)[pP^{\sharp}q \to \sim qP^{\sharp}\sim p]$$

Consider now an (arbitrary) index of merit measure $\sharp$ for the relevant possible worlds w_1, as follows:

Possible worlds	$\sharp$-values
w_1: p & q	a
w_2: p & $\sim q$	b
w_3: $\sim p$ & q	c
w_4: $\sim p$ & $\sim q$	d

Given our canonical interpretation of $P^{\sharp}$, (I) is now rendered as a relationship between arithmetical inequalities as follows:

$$\left(\frac{a+b}{2} > \frac{a+c}{2}\right) \to \left(\frac{b+d}{2} > \frac{c+d}{2}\right)$$

or equivalently

$$(b > c) \to (b > c)$$

The acceptability of this, its arithmetical transform, at once establishes the acceptability of (I) when construed as (Ia).

Let us next consider whether we can strengthen this to

$$(\text{Ib}) \quad (\forall p)(Aq)[pP^{\sharp}q \to \sim qP^{\sharp}\sim p]$$

that is – ask whether we can make arbitrary substitutions for 'p', putting for 'p' also formulas involving 'q'. We must in particular examine the result of putting in place of 'p' such replacements as:

$$q, \sim q, p \,\&\, q, p \,\&\, \sim q, p \lor q, p \lor \sim q$$

(In fact, this list must prove sufficient.) But now, when we put "p & q" for 'p' in (I), we obtain

$$(\text{II}) \quad pP^{\sharp}(p \,\&\, q) \to \sim(p \,\&\, q)P^{\sharp}\sim p$$

whose arithmetical transform is

$$\left(\frac{a+b}{2} > a\right) \to \left(\frac{b+c+d}{3} > \frac{c+d}{2}\right)$$

Since this is not a truth of arithmetic, we see that II is not a $\sharp$-tautology, and therefore leave it that (Ia) cannot be strengthened to (Ib).

But – on the other hand – can (Ia) be strengthened to

$$(\text{Ic}) \quad (Ap)(\forall q)[pP^{\sharp}q \to \sim qP^{\sharp}\sim p]?$$

Again let us examine the result of 'q'-substitutions. Consider putting "$p \vee q$" for 'q':

$$\text{(III)} \quad pP^{\sharp}(p \vee q) \to \sim(p \vee q)P^{\sharp}\sim p$$

The arithmetical transform of this $P^{\sharp}$-principle is

$$\left(\frac{a+b}{2} > \frac{a+b+c}{3}\right) \to \frac{d > c+d}{2}$$

which is clearly not a truth of arithmetic. Thus (III) is not a $P^{\sharp}$-tautology, and consequently we cannot strengthen (Ia) to (Ic). In the face of these findings, it now goes without saying that (Ia) cannot be strengthened to

$$\text{(Id)} \quad (\forall p)(\forall q)[pP^{\sharp}q \to \sim qP^{\sharp}\sim p]$$

Let us turn now to the $P^{\star}$-interpretation of our initial preference-principle:

$$\text{(IV)} \quad pP^{\star}q \to \sim qP^{\star}\sim p$$

Again, let us begin by understanding this principle as asserted with respect to weak (i.e., restricted) quantification

$$\text{(IVa)} \quad (\mathrm{A}p)(\mathrm{A}q)[pP^{\star}q \to \sim qP^{\star}\sim p]$$

This version of the principle yields the arithmetical transform.

$$[\star(p) > \star(q)] \to [\star(\sim q) > \star(\sim p)]$$

which, by the definition of the $\star$-measure, amounts to

$$([\sharp(p) - \sharp(\sim p)] > [\sharp(q) - \sharp\sim(q)]) \to ([\sharp(\sim q) - \sharp(q)] > [\sharp(\sim p) - \sharp(p)])$$

which, being of the form

$$(x > y) \to (-y > -x)$$

is a truth of arithmetic.

It remains to be seen whether (IVa) can actually be strengthened to

$$\text{(IVb)} \quad (\forall p)(\forall q)[pP^{\star}q \to \sim qP^{\star}\sim p].$$

Let us try the effect of some particular substitution, say "$p \& q$" for 'p'. Then (IVb) yields

$$\text{(V)} \quad (p \& q)P^{\star}q \to \sim qP^{\star}\sim(p \& q)$$

whose arithmetical transform is

$$\left[\left(a - \frac{b+c+d}{3}\right) > \left(\frac{a+c}{2} - \frac{b+d}{2}\right)\right] \to$$
$$\left[\left(\frac{b+d}{2} - \frac{a+c}{2}\right) > \left(\frac{b+c+d}{3} - a\right)\right]$$

which, being of the form

$$(x > y) \to (-y > -x)$$

is again a truth of arithmetic. So far so good. And the general fact that all substitution instances of

$$pP^{\star}q \to \sim qP^{\star}\sim p$$

are $p^{\star}$-tautologies is readily established – as follows: Regardless of the substitutions made in (IV), the result will take the form:

$$XP^{\star}Y \to \sim YP^{\star}\sim X$$

61

whose arithmetical transform will be

$$([\#(X) - \#(\sim X)] > [\#(Y) - \#(\sim Y)]) \to$$
$$([\#(\sim Y) - \#(Y)] > [\#(\sim X) - \#(X)])$$

which is readily seen – on analogy with the preceding – to be a truth of arithmetic.

It is thus clear that the preference-principle we have selected for examination,

$$pPq \to \sim qP \sim p$$

is unrestrictedly tautologous for P^*, but is only a restricted tautology for $P^\#$.

VIII. BIBLIOGRAPHY

ARISTOTLE (4th cent. B.C.). Aristotle. *Topics*, book iii. [For historical stage-setting.]

SCHWARZ (1900). Herman Schwarz. *Psychologie des Willens zur Grundlegung der Ethik*. Leipzig, 1900.

BROGAN (1919). A. P. Brogan. "The Fundamental Value Universal," *Journal of Philosophy, Psychology and Scientific Methods*, vol. 16 (1919).

SCHELER (1921). Max Scheler. *Der Formalismus in der Ethik und die materiale Wertethik*. Halle, 1921.

KATKOV (1937). Georg Katkov. *Untersuchungen zur Werttheorie und Theodizee*. Brünn, 1937.

KRAUS (1937). Oskar Kraus. *Die Werttheorien*. Brünn, 1937.

MOORE (1942). G. E. Moore. "A Reply to My Critics," in P. A. Schilpp (ed.), *The Philosophy of G. E. Moore*. Evanston, 1942.

HOUTHAKKER (1950). H. S. Houthakker. "Revealed Preference and the Utility Function," *Economica*, vol. 17 (1950).

ARROW (1951). K. J. Arrow. *Social Choice and Individual Values*. New York, 1951. [The classical treatment of the economists' approach to preference.]

DAVIDSON, McKINSEY, and SUPPES (1955). Donald Davidson, J. C. C. McKinsey, and Patrick Suppes. "Outlines of a Formal Theory of Value, I," *Philosophy of Science*, vol. 22 (1955).

HALLDÉN (1957). Sören Halldén. *On the Logic of 'Better'*. Uppsala, 1957 (Library of Theoria, no. 2).

LUCE and RAIFFA (1957). R. D. Luce and H. Raiffa. *Games and Decisions* (New York, 1957). [Presents the mathematicians' approach to utility and preference theory.]

KEMENY and SNELL (1962). J. G. Kemeny and J. L. Snell. *Mathematical Models in the Social Sciences* (Boston, 1962). [See ch. II on "Preference Rankings."]

ÅQVIST (1963). Lennart Åqvist. "Deontic Logic Based on a Logic of 'Better'," *Acta Philosophica Fennica*, vol. 16 (Helsinki, 1963), pp. 285–290.

MARTIN (1963). Richard M. Martin. *Intension and Decision*. Englewood Cliffs, N. J., 1963. [See ch. 2 on "Preference".]

VON WRIGHT (1963). G. H. von Wright. *The Logic of Preference*. Edinburgh, 1963. [The principal treatise on the subject.]

CHISHOLM (1964). R. M. Chisholm. "The Descriptive Element in the Concept of Action," *The Journal of Philosophy*, vol. 61 (1964).

BAYLIS (1965). Charles Baylis. "Tranquility is Not Enough," *Pacific Philosophy Forum*, vol. 3 (1965).

HOUTHAKKER (1965). H. S. Houthakker. "The Logic of Preference and Choice," in A. T. Tymieniecka (ed.), *Contributions to Logic and Methodology in Honor of J. M. Bochenski* (Amsterdam, 1965), pp. 193–207. [An attempt to draw together the interests of logicians and economists.]

JEFFREY (1965). R. C. Jeffrey. *The Logic of Decision* (New York, 1965).

CHISHOLM and SOSA (1966). Roderick M. Chisholm and Ernest Sosa. "On the Logic of Intrinsically Better," *American Philosophical Quarterly*, vol. 3 (1966).

A. COMMENTS ON N. RESCHER'S
"SEMANTIC FOUNDATIONS FOR THE LOGIC OF PREFERENCE"

ALAN ROSS ANDERSON

WITH PROFESSOR RESCHER'S informal discussion of the two modes of preference P^* and $P^\sharp$, I have no cavil whatever. It seems to me that the distinctions made are intuitively compelling, and do shed light on the differences between the approaches of VON WRIGHT (1963) (see bibliography at the end of this paper) on the one hand, and CHISHOLM AND SOSA (1966) on the other. Moreover, the semantical considerations have another advantage, especially if one is interested in formalizing the logic of preference, for reasons I shall mention briefly.

As is clear, there is a two-way street between syntax and semantics. When we consider classical propositional or functional calculus, it is of course true that syntax came first, in the work of Frege, and Whitehead and Russell; and that semantics came later in POST (1920), where (possibly with the help of Wittgenstein's *Tractatus*) the first modern completeness theorem for a logical calculus is proved, and GÖDEL (1930), which looks in retrospect like a natural generalization of Post's. And in fact, it has always seemed to me almost unbelievable that Whitehead and Russell should have set down a *complete* set of axioms and rules for the restricted predicate calculus, in the absence of any formal semantics to guide the choice of postulates.

But of course things can equally well go in the other direction; one might begin with semantical notions, outline their properties much as Rescher has done, and then look for an appropriate formalism which would (hopefully) be complete with respect to the semantics.

For the semantical systems Rescher considers, this is obviously a fairly large order, and I have no intention of trying to complete the job here. What I shall do rather is to try to take some preliminary steps in the direction of finding a formalism suitable to express some of the semantical notions concerning preference which Rescher has explained. In particular, I shall concentrate on his distinction between restricted and unrestricted quantification, first considering some difficulties which arise when one tries to formalize these notions, and then trying to see what can be done about them.

I

It might help to begin by making one or two elementary observations about the use of free variables and quantifiers.

Quantification in ordinary textbook treatments of elementary algebra is, as is well-known, ambiguous. If we see

$$x + 3 = 5$$

written down, we ordinarily take this as an invitation to find a number ("There exists a number") satisfying the condition stated. If we find

$$x + y = z$$

we are likely to be puzzled, since although there surely are triples of numbers satisfying the condition, we would be perplexed, in the absence of further information, as to what to *do* with this equation.

But when we come to an equation like

$$x + y = y + x,$$

our doubts leave us; surely what is meant is that for *every* assignment of values to the variables x and y, (given an appropriate range of variables, or "universe of discourse") this formula is true. And it is precisely this understanding of free variables, and the use of the word *"every"* just above, that motivates the introduction of quantifiers; so that, in more sophisticated languages, we write, instead of the formula above:

$$(\forall x)(\forall y)[x + y = y + x].$$

Now for some reason which I have never been able to fathom, there are some philosophers (Goodman, Martin, Quine, etc.) who feel that it is absolutely essential to make quantification explicit in cases like this, but who feel also that it is somehow *Wicked* in clearly parallel cases.

When one says

$$p \lor \sim p,$$

surely what is meant is that for *every* assignment of values to the variable p (given an appropriate range of variables, or "universe of discourse") this formula is true. And it is precisely this understanding of free variables, and the use of the word *"every"* just above, that motivates the introduction of quantifiers; so that, in more sophisticated languages, we write, instead of the formula above:

$$(\forall p)[p \lor \sim p]$$

My point is that quantifying over propositions, or properties, or truth-values, or what-have-you, never did anyone any harm – I don't think any propositions were ever hurt by having $(\forall p)$ stuck in front of their matrices – so the problems I want to raise have nothing to do with this issue. I will be more than happy to give Rescher quantification over propositions.

What I would like to worry about is rather how the axioms for Rescher's restricted and unrestricted quantification should work.

Now of course restricted quantification, *in the sense of* quantification over a restricted domain, is already familiar to us (see HAILPERIN (1957) for a comprehensive account). Here we are considering situations where we want to introduce notational innovations simply to avoid boredom. If in standard set theories we are interested in discussing ordinal numbers, for example, we get tired of writing

$$(\forall x)[\mathrm{Ord}(x) \supset \ldots x \ldots]$$

all the time, and instead introduce a special style of variable, say, lower case Greek letters, and write

$$(\forall \alpha)[\ldots \alpha \ldots]$$

to mean exactly what the preceding displayed formula means. Similarly we write

$$(\exists \alpha)[\ldots \alpha \ldots]$$

to mean the same as

$$(\exists x)[\mathrm{Ord}(x) \,\&\, \ldots x \ldots].$$

But of course this is not the kind of restricted quantification Rescher has in mind, though the terminology might misleadingly suggest that it is. And the fact that Rescher's distinction between restricted and unrestricted quantification is not the usual one is made clear by two facts:

(a) Variables are not used to indicate generality in the usual manner. So that

$$pP^{\sharp}q \to \sim(qP^{\sharp}p)$$

is unrestrictedly true (*i.e.*, every substitution instance is true, so we may universally quantify in the ordinary way), but

$$pP^{\sharp}q \to \sim qP^{\sharp}\sim p$$

is true only for *some* (specifiable) substitution instances; in this case free variables are being used in the idiosyncratic way which requires a distinction between $(\forall p)$ and (Ap).

(b) As is clear from the remarks at the end of Rescher's sect. IIIC, we are not using restricted quantification over a special domain, but rather over a domain which is relative to the formula in question.

$$(\forall p)(\ldots p \ldots) \to (\ldots q \ldots)$$

for every q, but

$$(Ap)(\ldots p \ldots) \to (\ldots q \ldots)$$

holds only when q is irrelevant to p.

But now syntactical difficulties arise. If we look at the matter from the point of view of Gentzen, then the last two formulas can be thought of as "elimination rules" (or the corresponding axioms) for the two universal quantifiers. And it seems clear that the corresponding introduction rule for A should be the usual one: from

$$(\ldots p \ldots)$$

to infer

$$(Ap)(\ldots p \ldots).$$

But it looks as if an introduction rule for $\forall$ would be intolerably complex, since in order to infer

$$(\forall p)(\ldots p \ldots)$$

we would have to examine every substitution instance of

$$(\ldots p \ldots)$$

with all possible propositions to which p is relevant. There may be some way of dealing with this problem within the usual framework of truth-functional or modal logic, though I don't know of one; however, there is an alternative non-classical approach which might possibly do the required trick.

II

We begin by considering a system of BELNAP (1960), called '**B**' (not for "Belnap," but for "basic implication"). It has variables and truth-functions, and a relation of entailment, symbolized by an arrow, as primitive; we let $A, B, C, \ldots$, range over truth-functional compounds of variables (*i.e.*, A, $B, C, \ldots$, have no arrows in them).

Axioms:

Entailment:	$A \rightarrow A$
Conjunction:	$(A \,\&\, B) \rightarrow A$
	$(A \,\&\, B) \rightarrow B$
Disjunction:	$A \rightarrow (A \vee B)$
	$B \rightarrow (A \vee B)$
Conjunction and Disjunction:	$A \,\&\, (B \vee C) \rightarrow (A \,\&\, B) \vee C$
Negation:	$A \rightarrow \overline{\overline{A}}$
	$\overline{\overline{A}} \rightarrow A$

Rules:

Entailment: (suffixing) from $A \rightarrow B$ and $B \rightarrow C$ to infer $A \rightarrow C$

                 (prefixing) from $A \rightarrow B$ and $C \rightarrow A$ to infer $C \rightarrow B$

Conjunction: from $A \rightarrow B$ and $A \rightarrow C$ to infer $A \rightarrow (B \,\&\, C)$

Disjunction: from $A \rightarrow C$ and $B \rightarrow C$ to infer $(A \vee B) \rightarrow C$

Negation: from $A \rightarrow B$ to infer $\overline{B} \rightarrow \overline{A}$.

This set of axioms and rules is redundant, but it does serve to show what is important for the purposes at hand. We shall not bother to develop formal properties of this system; what we shall do rather is simply state without proof some properties relevant to the present discussion (the proofs can be constructed easily from BELNAP (1960) or ANDERSON AND BELNAP (1962)). We first introduce Frege's assertion-sign, letting $\vdash A$ mean that A is provable in the system B, and then add a double arrow, so that $\vdash A \leftrightarrow B$ is to mean that both $\vdash A \rightarrow B$ and $\vdash B \rightarrow A$. The relevant observations are then as follows:

1. Only truth-functional compounds of variables may appear on the left or right of an arrow; i.e., no formulas of **B** have arrows nested. This fact

seems to accord with the semantics Rescher has in mind, since pPq is considered only when p and q are truth-functions.

2. If $\vdash A \leftrightarrow B$, then $\vdash (\ldots A \ldots) \leftrightarrow (\ldots B \ldots)$. This means that the system **B** is "extensional", in the sense that equivalence between truth-functions guarantees intersubstitutability. (Note: "equivalence" does *not* mean the truth-functional $\equiv$, but rather the double arrow.)

3. For every truth-functional A, there exists a disjunctive normal form $A_1 \vee \ldots \vee A_n$ such that $\vdash A \leftrightarrow (A_1 \vee \ldots \vee A_n)$.

4. For every truth-functional B, there exists a conjunctive normal form $B_1 \& \ldots \& B_m$ such that $\vdash B \leftrightarrow (B_1 \& \ldots \& B_m)$.

5. 2, 3, and 4 give us the result that for any truth-functional A and B, $A \rightarrow B$ may be rewritten equivalently as

$$(A_1 \vee \ldots \vee A_n) \rightarrow (B_1 \& \ldots \& B_m).$$

Hence $\vdash A \rightarrow B$ if and only if the formula just displayed is provable.

6. By repeated application of the *Rules* for conjunction and disjunction, it is clear that the formula displayed under 5 is provable just in case, for every i and j, we have

$$\vdash A_i \rightarrow B_j.$$

This means that the question of provability in **B** for $A \rightarrow B$ reduces to the question of provability of $A_i \rightarrow B_j$ for each i and j, *i.e.*, to the question as to whether a conjunction of atoms (variables or their denials) entails a disjunction of atoms.

7. This brings us to the point where classical theories of implication and the system **B** diverge, for up to this point everything has been valid for the arrow of **B**, and also for the horseshoe (of material implication) and the hook (of strict implication). Classically $A_i \rightarrow B_j$ is provable under any of three conditions:

(a) There is a contradiction on the left (*i.e.*, we have some atom and also its denial on the left); *e.g.*, $(A \& B \& \overline{A}) \rightarrow C$

(b) There is an excluded middle on the right (*i.e.*, we have some atom and also its denial on the right); *e.g.*, $A \rightarrow (B \vee C \vee \overline{B})$

(c) A_i and B_j share an atom; *e.g.*, $(A \& \overline{B}) \rightarrow (\overline{B} \vee C)$.

But in the system **B**, as in other stronger systems which take the notion of relevance seriously, only condition (c) suffices. That is, $\vdash A \rightarrow B$ if *and only if* A_i and B_j share an atom, for each i and j.

The reason for considering this system at such length is that it appears to provide the beginnings of a syntactical tool with which to treat Rescher's distinction between restricted and unrestricted quantification. As he points out in part C of sect. III, $P\star$ and $P\sharp$ coincide only when related propositions "represent *independent* propositions: propositions devoid of logical interconnections . . . ," and the system **B** looks like a way to get a handle on this condition, without sacrificing $\forall$ to $\wedge$.

III

By saying that **B** is a "beginning" I mean only that there is still a sharp difference between **B** (as syntax) and Rescher's semantical considerations: if propositional quantifiers are added to **B**, then the usual introduction rule for the universal quantifiers:

$$(\ldots p \ldots)$$
$$(\forall p)(\ldots p \ldots)$$

will be available. But there will still be a problem as to what to do syntactically with Rescher's quantifier (Ap).

It is precisely this problem which leads to the abandonment of the use of free variables to indicate generality. Because what needs to be said is that we can infer

$$(\ldots q \ldots)$$

from

$$(Ap)(\ldots p \ldots),$$

provided that q is irrelevant to p. But irrelevance, unlike relevance, does not have the substitution property ordinarily associated with free variables. When (in **B**) we write

$$\vdash (p \,\&\, q) \rightarrow (r \text{ v } s)$$

we don't mean that *every* substitution instance thereof is false, but only that some are, since $(p \,\&\, q) \rightarrow (q \text{ v } s)$ is a true substitution instance of the formula just displayed.

But if we introduce constants for propositions, as well as variables, we can extend the system **B** to a system I shall call **B*** in which the ordinary rules of universal generalization on variables still holds, but which seems adequate to Rescher's purposes. We add to the vocabulary of **B** some new letters, say, $a, b, c, \ldots$, from the beginning of the alphabet, and consider them as constants; i.e., they bear the same relation to the propositional variables as the ordinary Arabic numerals bear to variables in algebra. Then to the axioms of **B** we add the *denials* of all those formulas $A_i \ldots B_j$, involving constants only, in which the antecedent and consequent fail to share a (constant) atom. So that for example we will have in **B***

$$\vdash (p \,\&\, \bar{p}) \rightarrow (p \text{ v } \bar{p}),$$

and hence by the usual rule of generalization

$$\vdash (\forall p)[p \,\&\, \bar{p}) \rightarrow (p \text{ v } \bar{p})].$$

We would also have (to return to the example mentioned above) not only

$$\dashv (p \,\&\, q) \rightarrow (r \text{ v } s),$$

but also

$$\vdash \overline{(a \,\&\, b) \rightarrow (c \text{ v } d)};$$

though of course for obvious reasons we have neither

$$\vdash (\forall p)(\forall q)(\forall r)(\forall s)\overline{(p \,\&\, q) \rightarrow (r \text{ v } s)}$$

nor

$$\vdash (\forall a)(\forall b)(\forall c)(\forall d)\overline{(a \,\&\, b) \rightarrow (c \text{ v } d)}.$$

The latter formula fails because letters from the beginning of the alphabet are constants, not variables for quantification; and the former because the rejection sign "⊣" (fourth formula above) does not mean that *every* substitution instance of $(p \mathbin{\&} q) \to (r \mathbin{v} s)$ is false – only that *some* are.

In considering **B*** we first note that in **B** (also in **B***) we can derive the rules (for both variables and constants),

$$\frac{\vdash A \to (B \mathbin{\&} C)}{\vdash A \to B \text{ and } \vdash A \to C}$$

and

$$\frac{\vdash A \mathbin{v} B \to C}{\vdash A \to C \text{ and } \vdash B \to C}$$

where the long double line means "if and only if". By additional rules, and considerations which are exactly dual to those of 2-6 under sect. II, it can be made to follow that in **B***, if A and B are truth-functions of constants, then $\overline{A \to B}$ is provable just in case one of the $A_i \to B_j$ of sect. II fails to share an atom; i.e., just in case $\vdash \overline{A_i \to B_j}$ in **B***.

The additional rules can be expressed in the notation above (where A, B, and C are truth-functions of constants) as

$$\frac{\vdash \overline{A \to (B \mathbin{\&} C)}}{\vdash \overline{A \to B} \text{ or } \vdash \overline{A \to C}}$$

and

$$\frac{\vdash \overline{(A \mathbin{v} B) \to C}}{\vdash \overline{A \to C} \text{ or } \vdash \overline{B \to C}}$$

B* then gives us a formalization of what I take to be a plausible sense of "independence" as between truth-functional compounds of propositional constants: A and B will be independent just in case both $\overline{A \to B}$ and $\overline{B \to A}$ are provable in **B***.

Now the examples Rescher considers all have the form $A \to B$, where A and B are truth functions of formulas of the form pPq, where p and q are truth-functions of propositional letters. As examples consider those of his sect. III, pt. 4:

$$pP^{\sharp}q \to \sim(qP^{\sharp}q),$$
$$pP^{\sharp}q \to \sim qP^{\sharp}\sim p,$$
$$(pP^{\sharp}q \mathbin{\&} qP^{\sharp}r) \to pP^{\sharp}r.$$

The second of these fails, under the generality interpretation of free variables because, though (in some sense) true as it stands, it has a false substitution instance in

$$pP^{\sharp}(p \mathbin{v} q) \to \sim(p \mathbin{v} q)P^{\sharp}\sim p.$$

What I would like to propose, in the direction of clarifying the syntax of Rescher's restricted quantification, is to treat the p's and q's of this formula as truth-functions of constants, and use **B*** as the underlying calculus. Then the second axiom would look like

$$\overline{(p \to q} \ \& \ \overline{q \to p} \ \& \ (pP^{\#}q)) \to (\sim qP^{\#} \sim p),$$

answering (perhaps) to Rescher's requirement of independence of B from variables in $(\ldots p \ldots)$ for the inference from $(\mathsf{A}p)(\ldots p \ldots)$ to $(\ldots B \ldots)$

To quote him, "Thus it will only be in the special case of independent relata (essentially, those which do not share a common variable) that the two modes of preference will coincide." (I should note incidentally that the parenthetical remark will, I believe, not quite do for Rescher's purposes: certainly B and $\overline{B}$ are independent, in the sense that in general neither entails the other; but they do share a variable.)

If we rewrite Rescher's second axiom as above, then the generality-interpretation of free variables discussed in Sect. I above is restored, and we may conclude from the axiom (*via* the usual rules for universal quantification):

$$(\forall p)(\forall q)[\overline{(p \to q} \ \& \ \overline{q \to p} \ \& \ (pP^{\#}q)) \to (\sim qP^{\#} \sim p)],$$

thus dispensing with the odd "restricted quantifer" $(\mathsf{A}p)$. How much justice this does to Rescher's intent is for him to say; I simply hope that this is a step in the right direction.

BIBLIOGRAPHY

ANDERSON and BELNAP (1962). Alan Ross Anderson and Nuel D. Belnap, Jr. "Tautological Entailments," *Philosophical Studies*, vol. 13 (1962), pp. 9–24.

BELNAP (1960). Nuel D. Belnap, Jr. *A Formal Analysis of Entailment*. Technical report no. 7, Office of Naval Research, Group Psychology Branch, New Haven (1960).

CHISHOLM and SOSA (1966). Roderick M. Chisholm and Ernest Sosa. "On the Logic of 'Intrinsically Better'," *American Philosophical Quarterly*, vol. 3 (1966), pp. 244–249.

GÖDEL (1930). Kurt Gödel. "Die Völlstandigkeit der Axiome des logischen Funktionenkalküls," *Monatshefte für Mathematik und Physik*, vol. 37 (1930), pp. 349–360.

HAILPERIN (1957). Theodore Hailperin. "A Theory of Restricted Quantification," *Journal of Symbolic Logic*, vol. 22 (1957), pp. 19–35 and 113–129.

POST (1920). E. L. Post. "Introduction to a General Theory of Elementary Propositions," *American Journal of Mathematics*, vol. 43 (1920), pp. 163–185.

VON WRIGHT (1963). Georg Henrik von Wright. *Norm and Action*. London, Routledge and Kegan Paul (1963).

B. COMMENTS ON N. RESCHER'S
"SEMANTIC FOUNDATIONS FOR THE LOGIC OF PREFERENCE"

ROBERT ACKERMANN

PROFESSOR RESCHER's paper is an attempt to provide a semantical theory on the basis of which it becomes possible to pursue an impartial analysis of various conflicting theories (or logics) of preference which can be mined from the philosophical literature, or postulated on the basis of the proposed semantical theory. The formal results of the semantical theory leave little to quarrel with, but there may be considerable disagreement with Rescher's claim that his semantical foundations represent the best hopes for progress in understanding preference logics. I feel a vague dissatisfaction with this claim that I would like to explore in my comments. Perhaps these comments will provoke some remarks from Rescher as to the status of philosophical analyses of various preference concepts, for it seems to me that such analyses are required to give preference logics philosophical significance.

To begin with, it needs to be shown (and has not been shown) that there *is* a logic of preference of sufficient generality to make a formal semantical theory for preference logic an important philosophical desideratum. Perhaps the present position in preference theory is this. Various theories employed in decision theory, economics, and psychology incorporate preference principles which have the philosophical defect that they leave the significance of the preference notion to intuition. This is not terribly serious (witness the history of probability theory) insofar as we have a fair intuitive grasp of what we can say about our own considered preferences. At a general level, abstracting from the special circumstances of the specific theories, there are no demonstrable preference principles except (perhaps) those asserting the transitivity and asymmetry of preference. In saying this, I am fully aware that agents show intransitivities and symmetries in announced preferences, but any normative axiomatic theory of preference is justified in postulating transitivity and asymmetry on the grounds of intuitive puzzlement whenever these properties are violated by announced preferences.

The reason that other properties do not seem to hold at a very general level is not due directly to announced preferences which violate them, but to the more insidious fact that coherent preference rankings are usually tied closely to some purpose of the agent making the ranking. Let A and B stand for names of objects, activities, or whatever, and suppose that an agent announces a preference for A over B at one point, and then later a preference for B over A, apparently violating asymmetry. Apart from the possibility that he has made a mistake or has changed his mind, he may be entirely consistent if in each case he is discussing some different purpose or projected purpose with which he takes A and B to be involved. For example, many people prefer Cadillacs to Volkswagens for quietness of operation, and Volkswagens to Cadillacs for economy of operation. No inconsistency is involved.

This observation seems to be capable of generalization to a preference principle: If an agent prefers A to B in some circumstances, it is possible to describe circumstances in which the agent would prefer B to A. This principle seems true of preference even in those circumstances where preferences may not be involved with purpose. A woman glancing into a store window may say "I prefer that yellow dress to that green one," even though she may not have any inclination to purchase either, and is not dress shopping at all. It may be a matter of considerable delicacy to demonstrate that her indicated performance is unrelated to any purpose, but let us suppose that it is possible under the specific circumstances to do this. Even so, folklore makes it plain that circumstances can be described in which some purpose would cause her to prefer the green dress to the yellow dress. Apparent counterexamples, for example the fictional revenger who desires the death of someone *no matter what the consequences*, always seem to involve a lunatic agent, and may be dismissed.

Now because of the complex ways in which purposes may be related for an agent, this claim conflicts with the unguarded optimism of psychologists, philosophers, and decision theorists who have suggested that any agent can construct an arbitrarily large unified preference ranking with sufficient thought. But an agent with the generalized purpose of buying a car, to return to our earlier example, may have specific purposes in owning the car (business travel, transportation of children to school, etc.) for which no single car is preferable to all others. Using decision theory (or just plain hard thinking), he may ultimately be able to achieve a choice by means of a constructed preference ranking, but decision theory does not necessarily lead to a choice since such a ranking is not always available. In fact, many car buyers seem to be frustrated in the decision situation to where some random-like or "irrational" decision procedure is adopted apparently to achieve relaxation of the anxiety brought about by the lack of a unified preference ranking. Thus preference logics incorporating asymmetry of preferences may be applicable only under quite specific circumstances.

I confess the prospects of a philosophically interesting general analysis of preference seem rather gloomy if these considerations force us to consider transitivity and asymmetry as properties that will be true of preference rankings which are associated with intuitively rather specific circumstances. The gloom, of course, is cast by the notoriously slow progress in coming to some satisfactory philosophical analysis of human purpose. And as we have seen, transitivity and asymmetry are the most tractable of the preference properties that philosophers have considered.

Now suppose that some agent with a fairly specific purpose for constructing a ranking is able to determine a preference ranking with the properties of transitivity and asymmetry. Can any further claims be made about his ranking? It will be irreflexive, of course, but this follows from the usual definitions of transitivity and asymmetry. From the way in which such rankings are announced, it seems clear that the ranking may be taken as connected. (If utilities are permitted, they seem to reflect connectivity of all of the items admitted into the ranking.) But in the general case, no further properties seem to characterize such preference rankings.

The argument as to what constitutes the general case is not easy to make out. It seems reasonable to me to take Bayesian decision theory, which has a theory of preference associated with it, as capturing formally the general case to which foundational studies or philosophical analyses might be profitably directed.[1] Bayesian decision theory, which permits a variety of inferences about preferences, has a preference theory which is inextricably tied up with probability theory. If I can represent some object of preference as a proposition C which may be formally construed as the disjunction of two propositions A and B which are incompatible, then the preference ranking of C can be calculated from the rankings of A and B along with their probabilities.[2] It is fairly obvious that the involvement of probabilities makes things complicated, and in fact only the wanted properties of transitivity, asymmetry, irreflexivity, and connectivity can be asserted for a preference ranking in the general theory. Perhaps it is tempting to think that preference may be studied apart from probabilities in a foundational manner, with probability theory being considered an addition to the resulting fundamental preference theory in certain circumstances. This line of thinking seems to me to be mistaken in the sense that the preference principles which may be developed independently of probability assignments may all be represented as special cases of the preference rankings encountered in Bayesian decision theory, while the converse does not hold. If preference principles are developed independently of probabilities, the addition of probabilities results in the *loss* of principles rather than the addition of new ones, contrary to the usual line of development of foundational studies. The preference principles given for the preference operators explicitly considered in Rescher's paper reflect this fact, since many of them do not hold when various possible probability assignments are made to the propositions under consideration. Further, these principles reflect conditions which are hardly ever encountered in preference problems with philosophical (particularly ethical) significance.

---

[1] Bayesian decision theory has recently been treated in a novel and philosophically fascinating way by R. C. Jeffrey in his *The Logic of Decision* (New York, 1965).

[2] See Jeffrey, *op. cit.*, p. 70, for details. The incompatibility between A and B may be logical inconsistency, but if subjective probabilities are allowed, the conjunction of A and B will be incompatible in the appropriate sense if probability 0 is assigned to the conjunction. Jeffrey gives the detail of the appropriate calculations in his book.

It can be shown that the preference principles provided by Rescher's $P^{\sharp}$ and $P^{\star}$ operators (except for transitivity and asymmetry) must be dropped in this fashion to obtain the preference principles of Bayesian decision theory incorporating probabilities. In computing the preference value of propositions true in more than one state-description, Rescher's semantic foundations for these operators assume, in decision theory terms, that each state-description has equal weight, or formally, an equal probability assignment. This represents a very special case hardly ever encountered in decision theory or in real life. In particular, consider the preference principle $pPq \to \sim qP \sim p$ which has a true instantiation if P is replaced by $P^{\sharp}$ or $P^{\star}$ provided that p and q are fixed logically independent propositions. Let p represent "Cordelia will be dead by the Ides of March" and q represent "Cordelia will be dishonored by the Ides of March" where Cordelia is a Roman matron who prefers death to dishonor.[3] If Cordelia will kill herself if she is dishonored, the logically possible world where she is dishonored but not dead may be considered morally impossible in her preference considerations. Under the reading for p and q suggested, we may assign Rescher's merit measure as follows: $\sharp(p \sim \& q) = 0$, $\sharp(p \& q) = 1$, $\sharp(p \& \sim q) = 2$, and $\sharp(\sim p \& \sim q) = 3$. This assignment is surely conceivable given what we know about Roman virtue. Death is preferred to dishonor and honor to not being dead on both of Rescher's preference principles. However, on the assumption that the matron considers it impossible that she be dishonored but not dead by the Ides of March, it is clear on the assignment that in fact she will prefer not being dead to not being dishonored, since in the former case she will not have been dishonored and will be alive, and in the latter case she will also not have been dishonored but may be dead.

Examples like this strike at the heart of the difficulty with using state-descriptions of equal weight for providing semantical foundations for preference operators. In announcing preferences, we are usually announcing a relationship between two states of affairs such that at least one excludes the possibility of the other. It is not at all clear how this typical non-independence can be translated into state-descriptions, since the non-independence may typically be traced to some subjective characteristic of the agent, and is not a feature of the objective states of affairs presumably captured by state-descriptions which are assigned equal weight.

Rescher's characterization of $\sharp$ as an *intrinsic* measure of a possible world is not intuitively clear. The utility assignments permitted in decision theory are usually taken as equivalent under linear transformations, and this property preserves the preference behavior which utility theory is designed to make amenable to mathematical treatment. I find nothing in intuition to support the idea that possible worlds can be assigned *intrinsic*, as opposed

---

[3] This example is found in Jeffrey, *op. cit.*, p. 79. The formal computation solving the example is discussed in the text.

to some kind of *comparative*, preference values. The difficulty is compounded by Rescher's treatment of $P^{\#}$ and $P^{\star}$. For let p, q, and r be independent. Now pPq will hold if, say, the following assignment is made to two possible worlds: $\#(p\ \&\ \sim q) = 5$, and $\#(\sim p\ \&\ q) = 3$. The *intrinsic* nature of $\#$ leads one to suspect that some assignment to worlds (r) and $(\sim r)$ is possible such that exactly one of $\#(r) > \#(\sim r)$, $\#(r) = \#(\sim r)$, or $\#(r) < \#(\sim r)$ should hold. For any of these cases, the independence of p, q, and r would lead one to expect that the possible world $(p\ \&\ \sim q\ \&\ r)$ should be preferred to $(\sim p\ \&\ q\ \&\ r)$ when r is conjoined to the possible worlds given above. But Rescher permits the assignment $\#(p\ \&\ \sim q\ \&\ r) = 1$, $\#(\sim p\ \&\ q\ \&\ r) = 2$. It would seem that not all of the intuitive consequences of characterizing $\#$ as *intrinsic* and p, q, r, etc., as *independent* are captured in Rescher's $P^{\#}$ and $P^{\star}$ principles. This appears again in the announced contention that P^{w} preferability entails $P^{\star}$ preferability, as Preference Principle 10 ($pPq \rightarrow$ $[(p\ \&\ r)P(q\ \&\ r)\ \&\ (p\ \&\ \sim r)P(q\ \&\ \sim r)]$) is a P^{w} principle but not a $P^{\star}$ principle.

Rescher has himself provided an argument based on his semantical foundations against the von Wright preference operator. This objection is not new to decision theory, paralleling very closely as it does a standard objection to minimax strategies (as opposed to Bayesian strategies) in the decision theory literature. The minimax strategies can be argued for where certain probabilities are *unknown*, and their primary application is to certain estimation problems in statistical inference. Thus, given Rescher's example, p is preferable to q on the slightest confidence that w_5 is not the real world, and this may be represented by a suitable probability assignment. With no information about p, q, and r, however (particularly about their probabilities), it is very difficult to say what is or is not intuitively plausible.

Under what circumstances might preferences be contemplated in the complete absence of probabilities or detailed background. Well, someone might say to us, "Suppose you were in a department where the chairman . . . , etc., what would you do?" Where this comes up, we always (if we are really considering the problem, and not giving a dogmatic or offhand answer) want additional information, and circumstances have convinced me that projected preferences of this kind rarely work out satisfactorily in the complexity of an actual situation in which some estimated probabilities are important. All things considered, it seems to me that preference rankings are transitory affairs, invoked to solve particular problems in particular circumstances. Even apparently permanent preferences, like Beethoven to Bartok, can suffer under unusual circumstances. (One's neighbor plays one Beethoven record over and over at high volume on his new high fidelity equipment.) The permanence may not be so much in the preference as in the expectation that circumstances will remain normal. If all of this is true, the search for general semantical foundations of preference logics may be a quest provided by arbitrary philosophical manufacture. By contrast, the problem of satisfactorily relating preferences to purposes, desires, choices, picks, wants, wishes, etc., seems to present a budget of important philosophical analyses which has hardly been attacked.

C. REPLY TO COMMENTS

NICHOLAS RESCHER

A. *Reply to Professor Anderson's Comments*

PROFESSOR ANDERSON has proved himself to be the very model of the constructive critic who actually helps his target in getting over the rough spots on his road. From the logical point of view, the distinction between the two modes of general quantifiers ($\forall$ vs A), the second of which is of *restricted* universality in a nonstandard way, is the one strikingly unorthodox piece of machinery employed in the paper. Anderson's proposal for tidying up this nonstandard conception strikes me as ingenious and right-minded. I can see no reason for doubting that the quantificational machinery needed for the purposes I had in mind can be developed along the lines of Anderson's proposed construction.

B. *Reply to Professor Ackermann's Comments*

Various points must be made in reply to Professor Ackermann's comments:

1. "It needs to be shown that there is a logic of preference of sufficient generality to make a formal semantical theory for preference logic an important philosophical desideratum." Because of the long-recognized importance of the concept of preference in the practical reasoning and in the theory of rational choice, various philosophers and logicians have attempted to systematize the formal rules governing reasoning in this sphere. The semantical rationalization of such sets of rules seems to me to be an obviously desirable step.

2. *Why rest the semantical foundations upon the notion of a state description?* (1) It is a natural tactic for a theory of preference based upon a *propositional* preference operator; (2) it is a most plausible procedure when one bases preference upon propositional valuation-function (if the value of p is 1, and that of $\sim p$ is 0, and that of q is 1, and that of $\sim q$ is —1, and p and q are independent, then of course one gets

combination	value
$p \ \& \ q$	2
$p \ \& \ \sim q$	0
$\sim p \ \& \ q$	1
$\sim p \ \& \ \sim q$	—1

and so one can, in any such case, get to state-description values easily from an external starting-point); (3) there is good precedent in the literature of the subject (in Professor von Wright's work) for approaching the logic of preference from the direction of state-descriptions.

77

3. "No preference theory of widespread acceptance is available to guide the development of the semantic foundations." This perfectly true observation ought not, however, be permitted to prove a deterrent to the inquiry. It must, of course, influence the methodology: it points to the importance of exploring a variety of *alternative* approaches, as was in fact done. In the early stages of a science there is often no generally accepted theory – it is only after the examination and testing of a series of alternatives that a theory of widespread acceptance is attained. Our procedure is largely experimental in character: in concurrently developing a series of *alternative* systems with a view to facilitating a comparative assessment of their relative advantages and shortcomings.

4. "[The preference principles based on $P^{\sharp}$ and $P^{\star}$ dealt with] are more restrictive than the preference principles dealt with in decision theory." Two comments are in order: (1) The indicated preference principles are not "more restrictive" than those of the decision theorist, they are just *different*, and implement a variant concept of a measure of merit. (2) There is no reason whatever why the usual merit measure of Bayesian decision theory cannot be used to construct a preference-logic along the lines of our procedure. Indeed, just this is the object of our own proposal in footnote 17 (and cf. also footnote 10).

5. The Cordelia example, and what ensues "on the assumption that the Roman matron considered it impossible that she is to be dishonored but not dead." The objection trades on an equivocation of the phrase "considers it impossible." Presumably our Roman lady considers it eminently undesirable, indeed unthinkable (*nefas*), in such a way as to make for a very low measure of merit in the case. Were the situation not thus, and dishonor were an *actual impossibility*, so that the case can in fact be ruled out of consideration altogether, then the preference among the alternatives would of course be altered correspondingly. But this second prospect is an inherently implausible one in the indicated circumstances.

6. "The independence of p, q, and r, would lead one to suspect that the possible world (p & $\sim q$ & r) should be preferred to ($\sim p$ & q & r) [when $\sharp(p$ & $\sim q) = 5$ and $\sharp(\sim p$ & $q) = 3$]." But of course the independence at issue is the *logical independence* needed for the generation of genuinely alternative worlds, and not *independence in point of value considerations*. (Thus the relations $\sharp$ (p & $\sim q) = 5$ and $\sharp$ ($\sim p$ & $q) = 3$ arise — on our account — when $\sharp$ (p & $\sim q$ & $r) = 1$ and $\sharp$ ($\sim p$ & q & $r) = 2$, provided that also $\sharp$ (p & $q \sim r) = 9$ and $\sharp$ ($\sim p$ & q & $\sim r) = 4$. The "suspicion" at issue is thus simply not borne out for the [semi-technical] mode of preference that has been at issue throughout our deliberations.)

7. "Coherent preference rankings are usually tied quite closely to some purpose of the agent making the ranking. . . . People prefer Cadillacs to Volkswagens for quietness of operation and Volkswagens to Cadillacs for

economy of operation. No inconsistency is involved." The observation is true but harmless. The logic of preference deals with the abstract formal features generic to the notion of preference. No doubt in most applications we have to do, not with evaluating items in terms of their "preferability-in-general" but in terms of "preferability in point of economy," or "in point of reliability," or some other particular manner or mode. The object of a *logic of preference* is to elucidate the formal characteristics common to such particular manifestations of preference. Their variety does not indicate the infeasibility of the enterprise, any more than the fact that one pile contains more than another in point of stones and less than the other in point of pebbles indicates the impossibility of a theory of counting.

8. In summary, then, my conviction of the feasibility and fruitfulness of the enterprise of providing a semantical foundation for the logic of preference is not shaken by the considerations adduced by Professor Ackermann. No doubt, much remains to be done along these lines. But I cannot see any sufficient basis for claiming the enterprise is not worth while, let alone that it is in principle impossible.

III

THE LOGICAL FORM OF ACTION SENTENCES

DONALD DAVIDSON[1]

STRANGE GOINGS on! Jones did it slowly, deliberately, in the bathroom, with a knife, at midnight. What he did was butter a piece of toast. We are too familiar with the language of action to notice at first an anomaly: the "it" of "Jones did it slowly, deliberately, . . ." seems to refer to some entity, presumably an action, that is then characterized in a number of ways. Asked for the logical form of this sentence, we might volunteer something like "There is an action x such that Jones did x slowly and Jones did x deliberately and Jones did x in the bathroom, . . ." and so on. But then we need an appropriate singular term to substitute for 'x'. In fact we know Jones buttered a piece of toast. And, allowing a little slack, we can substitute for 'x' and get "Jones buttered a piece of toast slowly and Jones buttered a piece of toast deliberately and Jones buttered a piece of toast in the bathroom . . ." and so on. The trouble is that we have nothing here we would ordinarily recognize as a singular term. Another sign that we have not caught the logical form of the sentence is that in this last version there is no implication that any *one* action was slow, deliberate, and in the bathroom, though this is clearly part of what is meant by the original.

The present paper is devoted to trying to get the logical form of simple sentences about actions straight. I would like to give an account of the logical or grammatical role of the parts or words of such sentences that is consistent with the entailment relations between such sentences and with what is known of the role of those same parts or words in other (non-action) sentences. I take this enterprise to be the same as showing how the meanings of action sentences depend on their structure. I am not concerned with the meaning analysis of logically simple expressions in so far as this goes beyond the question of logical form. Applied to the case at hand, for example, I am not concerned with the meaning of "deliberately" as opposed, perhaps, to "voluntarily"; but I am interested in the logical role of both these words.

[1] I have profited from discussion with Daniel Bennett, Paul Grice, Sue Larson, David Pears, Merrill Provence, and David Wiggins. John Wallace and I talked on topics connected with this paper almost daily walking through the Odyssean landscape of Corfu during the spring of 1965; his contribution to the ideas expressed here is too pervasive to be disentangled. My research was supported by the National Science Foundation.

To give another illustration of the distinction I have in mind: we need not view the difference between "Joe believes that there is life on Mars" and "Joe knows that there is life on Mars" as a difference in logical form. That the second, but not the first, entails "There is life on Mars" is plausibly a logical truth; but it is a truth that emerges only when we consider the meaning analysis of "believes" and "knows." Admittedly there is something arbitrary in how much of logic to pin on logical form. But limits are set if our interest is in giving a coherent and constructive account of meaning: we must uncover enough structure to make it possible to state, for an arbitrary sentence, how its meaning depends on that structure, and we must not attribute more structure than such a theory of meaning can accommodate.

Consider the sentence:

(1) Jones buttered the toast slowly, deliberately, in the bathroom, with a knife, at midnight.

Despite the superficial grammar we cannot, I shall argue later, treat the "deliberately" on a par with the other modifying clauses. It alone imputes intention, for of course Jones may have buttered the toast slowly, in the bathroom, with a knife, at midnight, and quite unintentionally, having mistaken the toast for his hairbrush which was what he intended to butter. Let us, therefore, postpone discussion of the "deliberately" and its intentional kindred.

"Slowly," unlike the other adverbial clauses, fails to introduce a new entity (a place, an instrument, a time), and also may involve a special difficulty. For suppose we take "Jones buttered the toast slowly" as saying that Jones's buttering of the toast was slow; is it clear that we can equally well say of Jones's action, no matter how we describe it, that it was slow? A change in the example will help. Susan says, "I crossed the Channel in fifteen hours." "Good grief, that was slow." (Notice how much more naturally we say "slow" here than "slowly." But *what* was slow, what does "that" refer to? No appropriate singular term appears in "I crossed the Channel in fifteen hours.") Now Susan adds, "But I swam." "Good grief, that was fast." We do not withdraw the claim that it was a slow crossing; this is consistent with its being a fast swimming. Here we have enough to show, I think, that we cannot construe "It was a slow crossing" as "It was slow and it was a crossing" since the crossing may also be a swimming that was not slow, in which case we would have "It was slow and it was a crossing and it was a swimming and it was not slow." The problem is not peculiar to talk of actions, however. It appears equally when we try to explain the logical role of the attributive adjectives in "Grundy was a short basketball player, but a tall man," and "This is a good memento of the murder, but a poor steak knife." The problem of attributives is indeed a problem about logical form, but it may be put to one side here because it is not a problem only when the subject is action.

We have decided to ignore, for the moment at least, the first two adverbial modifiers in (1), and may now deal with the problem of the logical form of:

(2) Jones buttered the toast in the bathroom with a knife at midnight.

Anthony Kenny, who deserves the credit for calling explicit attention to this problem,[2] points out that most philosophers today would, as a start, analyze this sentence as containing a five-place predicate with the argument places filled in the obvious ways with singular terms or bound variables. If we go on to analyze "Jones buttered the toast" as containing a two-place predicate, "Jones buttered the toast in the bathroom" as containing a three-place predicate, and so forth, we obliterate the logical relation between these sentences, namely that (2) entails the others. Or, to put the objection another way, the original sentences contain a common syntactic element ("buttered") which we intuitively recognize as relevant to the meaning relations of the sentences. But the proposed analyses show no such common syntactic element.

Kenny rejects the suggestion that "Jones buttered the toast" be considered as elliptical for "Jones buttered the toast somewhere with something at some time," which would restore the wanted entailments, on the ground that we could never be sure how many standby positions to provide in each predicate of action. For example, couldn't we add to (2) the phrase "by holding it between the toes of his left foot"? Still, this adds a place to the predicate only if it differs in meaning from "while holding it between the toes of his left foot," and it is not quite clear that this is so. I am inclined to agree with Kenny that we cannot view verbs of action as usually containing a large number of standby positions, but I do not have what I would consider a knock-down argument. (A knock-down argument would consist in a method for increasing the number of places indefinitely.[3])

Kenny proposes that we may exhibit the logical form of (2) in somewhat the following manner:

(3) Jones brought it about that the toast was buttered in the bathroom with a knife at midnight.

Whatever the other merits in this proposal (I shall consider some of them presently) it is clear that it does not solve the problem Kenny raises. For it is, if anything, even more obscure how (3) entails "Jones brought it about that the toast was buttered" or "The toast was buttered" than how (2) entails "Jones buttered the toast." Kenny seems to have confused two different problems. One is the problem of how to represent the idea of *agency*: it is this that prompts Kenny to assign "Jones" a logically distinguished

---

[2] Anthony Kenny, *Action, Emotion and Will* (London, 1963), ch. VII.

[3] Kenny seems to think there is such a method, for he writes, "If we cast our net widely enough, we can make 'Brutus killed Caesar' into a sentence which describes, with a certain lack of specification, the whole history of the world." (*op. cit.*, p. 160). But he does not show how to make each addition to the sentence one that irreducibly modifies the killing as opposed, say, to Brutus or Caesar, or the place or the time.

role in (3). The other is the problem of the "variable polyadicity" (as Kenny calls it) of action verbs. And it is clear that this problem is independent of the first, since it arises with respect to the sentences that replace 'p' in "x brings it about that p."

If I say I bought a house downtown that has four bedrooms, two fireplaces, and a glass chandelier in the kitchen, it's obvious that I can go on forever adding details. Yet the logical form of the sentences I use presents no problem (in this respect). It is something like "There is a house such that I bought it, it is downtown, it has four bedrooms, . . ." and so forth. We can tack on a new clause at will because the iterated relative pronoun will carry the reference back to the same entity as often as desired. (Of course we know how to state this much more precisely.) Much of our talk of action suggests the same idea: that there are such *things* as actions, and that a sentence like (2) describes the action in a number of ways. "Jones did it with a knife." "Please tell me more about it." The "it" here doesn't refer to Jones or the knife, but to what Jones did – or so it seems.

". . . it is in principle always open to us, along various lines, to describe or refer to 'what I did' in so many different ways," writes Austin in "A Plea for Excuses."[4] Austin is obviously leery of the apparent singular term, which he puts in scare quotes; yet the grammar of his sentence requires a singular term. Austin would have had little sympathy, I imagine, for the investigation into logical form I am undertaking here, though the demand that underlies it, for an intuitively acceptable and constructive theory of meaning, is one that begins to appear in the closing chapters of *How to Do Things with Words.* But in any case, Austin's discussion of excuses illustrates over and over the fact that our common talk and reasoning about actions is most naturally analyzed by supposing that there are such entities.

"I didn't know it was loaded" belongs to one standard pattern of excuse. I do not deny that I pointed the gun and pulled the trigger, nor that I shot the victim. My ignorance explains how it happened that I pointed the gun and pulled the trigger intentionally, but did not shoot the victim intentionally. That the bullet pierced the victim was a consequence of my pointing the gun and pulling the trigger. It is clear that these are two different events, since one began slightly after the other. But what is the relation between my pointing the gun and pulling the trigger, and my shooting the victim? The natural and, I think, correct answer is that the relation is that of identity. The logic of this sort of excuse includes, it seems, at least this much structure: I am accused of doing b, which is deplorable. I admit I did a, which is excusable. My excuse for doing b rests upon my claim that I did not know that $a = b$.

Another pattern of excuse would have me allow that I shot the victim

4 John Austin, "A Plea for Excuses," in *Philosophical Papers* (Oxford, 1961), p. 148.

intentionally, but in self-defense. Now the structure includes something more. I am still accused of b (my shooting the victim), which is deplorable. I admit I did c (my shooting the victim in self-defense), which is excusable. My excuse for doing b rests upon my claim that I knew or believed that $b = c$. The additional structure, not yet displayed, would reveal the following as a logical truth: $x = c \rightarrow x = b$, that is, if an action is my shooting the victim in self-defense, it is my shooting the victim.

The story can be given another twist. Again I shoot the victim, again intentionally. What I am asked to explain is my shooting of the bank president (d), for the victim was that distinguished gentleman. My excuse is that I shot the escaping murderer (e), and, surprising and unpleasant as it is, my shooting the escaping murderer and my shooting of the bank president were one and the same action ($e = d$), since the bank president and the escaping murderer were one and the same person. To justify the "since" we must presumably think of "my shooting of x" as a functional expression that names an action when the 'x' is replaced by an appropriate singular term. The relevant reasoning would then be an application of the principle $x = y \rightarrow fx = fy$.

Excuses provide endless examples of cases where we seem compelled to take talk of "alternative descriptions of the same action" seriously, i.e., literally. But there are plenty of other contexts in which the same need presses. *Explaining* an action by giving an intention with which it was done provides new descriptions of the action: I am writing my name on a piece of paper with the intention of writing a check with the intention of paying my gambling debt. List all the different descriptions of my action. Here are a few for a start: I am writing my name. I am writing my name on a piece of paper. I am writing my name on a piece of paper with the intention of writing a check. I am writing a check. I am paying my gambling debt. It is hard to imagine how we can have a coherent theory of action unless we are allowed to say here: each of these sentences describes the same action. Redescription may supply the motive ("I was getting my revenge"), place the action in the context of a rule ("I am castling"), give the outcome ("I killed him"), or provide evaluation ("I did the right thing").

According to Kenny, as we just noted, action sentences have the form "Jones brought it about that p." The sentence that replaces 'p' is to be in the present tense, and it describes the result that the agent has wrought: it is a sentence "newly true of the patient."[5] Thus "The doctor removed the patient's appendix" must be rendered "The doctor brought it about that the patient has no appendix." By insisting that the sentence that replaces 'p' describe a terminal *state* rather than an *event*, it may be thought that Kenny can avoid the criticism made above that the problem of logical form

[5] Kenny, *op. cit.*, p. 181.

of action sentences turns up within the sentence that replaces 'p': we may allow that "The patient has no appendix" presents no relevant problem. The difficulty is that neither will the analysis stand in its present form. The doctor may bring it about that the patient has no appendix by turning the patient over to another doctor who performs the operation; or by running the patient down with his Lincoln Continental. In neither case would we say the doctor removed the patient's appendix. Closer approximations to a correct analysis might be "The doctor brought it about that the doctor has removed the patient's appendix" or perhaps "The doctor brought it about that the patient has had his appendix removed by the doctor." One may still have a few doubts, I think, as to whether these sentences have the same truth conditions as "The doctor removed the patient's appendix." But in any case it is plain that in these versions, the problem of the logical form of action sentences does turn up in the sentences that replace 'p': "The patient has had his appendix removed by the doctor" or "The doctor has removed the patient's appendix" are surely no *easier* to analyze than "The doctor removed the patient's appendix." By the same token, "Cass walked to the store" can't be given as "Cass brought it about that Cass is at the store," since this drops the idea of walking. Nor is it clear that "Cass brought it about that Cass is at the store and is there through having walked" will serve; but in any case again the contained sentence is worse than what we started with.

It is not easy to decide what to do with "Smith coughed." Should we say "Smith brought it about that Smith is in a state of just having coughed"? At best this would be correct only if Smith coughed on purpose.

The difficulty in Kenny's proposal that we have been discussing may perhaps be put this way: he wants to represent every (completed) action in terms only of the agent, the notion of bringing it about that a state of affairs obtains, and the state of affairs brought about by the agent. But many action sentences yield no description of the state of affairs brought about by the action except that it *is* the state of affairs brought about by that action. A natural move, then, is to allow that the sentence that replaces 'p' in "x brings it about that p" may (or perhaps must) describe an event.

If I am not mistaken, Chisholm has suggested an analysis that at least permits the sentence that replaces 'p' to describe (as we are allowing ourselves to say) an event.[6] His favored locution is "x makes p happen," though he uses such variants as "x brings it about that p" or "x makes it true that p." Chisholm speaks of the entities to which the expressions that replace 'p' refer as "states of affairs," and explicitly adds that states of affairs may be changes or events (as well as "unchanges"). An example

---

[6] Roderick Chisholm, "The Descriptive Element in the Concept of Action," *The Journal of Philosophy*, vol. LXI, No. 20, pp. 613–625. Also see Chisholm, "The Ethics of Requirement," *American Philosophical Quarterly*, vol. 1, no. 2, pp. 1–7.

Chisholm provides is this: if a man raises his arm, then we may say he makes it happen that his arm goes up. I do not know whether Chisholm would propose "Jones made it happen that Jones's arm went up" as an analysis of "Jones raised his arm," but I think the proposal would be wrong because although the second of these sentences does perhaps entail the first, the first does not entail the second. The point is even clearer if we take as our example "Jones batted an eyelash." In this case I think nothing will do but "Jones made it happen that Jones batted an eyelash" (or some trivial variant), and this cannot be called progress in uncovering the logical form of "Jones batted an eyelash."

There is something else that may puzzle us about Chisholm's analysis of action sentences, and it is independent of the question what sentence we substitute for 'p'. Whatever we put for 'p', we are to interpret it as describing some event. It is natural to say, I think, that *whole* sentences of the form "x makes it happen that p" also describe events. Should we say that these events are the *same* event, or that they are different? If they are the same event, as many people would claim (perhaps including Chisholm), then no matter what we put for 'p', we cannot have solved the *general* problem of the logical form of sentences about actions until we have dealt with the sentences that can replace 'p'. If they are different events, we must ask how the element of agency has been introduced into the larger sentence though it is lacking in the sentence for which 'p' stands; for each has the agent as its subject. The answer Chisholm gives, I think, is that the special notion of making it happen that he has in mind is intentional, and thus to be distinguished from simply causing something to happen. Suppose we want to say that Alice broke the mirror without implying that she did it intentionally. Then Chisholm's special idiom is not called for; but we could say "Alice caused it to happen that the mirror broke." Suppose we now want to add that she did it intentionally. Then the Chisholm-sentence would be: "Alice made it happen that Alice caused it to happen that the mirror broke." And now we want to know, what is the event that the whole sentence reports, and that the contained sentence does not? It is, apparently, just what used to be called an act of the will. I will not dredge up the standard objections to the view that acts of the will are special events distinct from, say, our bodily movements, and perhaps the causes of them. But even if Chisholm is willing to accept such a view, the problem of the logical form of the sentences that can replace 'p' remains, and these describe the things people do as we describe them when we do not impute intention.

A somewhat different view has been developed with care and precision by von Wright in his book *Norm and Action*.[7] In effect, von Wright puts action sentences into the following form: "x brings it about that a state

---

[7] Georg Henrik von Wright, *Norm and Action* (London, 1963).

where p changes into a state where q." Thus the important relevant difference between von Wright's analysis and the ones we have been considering is the more complex structure of the description of the change or event the agent brings about: where Kenny and Chisholm were content to describe the result of the change, von Wright includes also a description of the initial state.

Von Wright is interested in exploring the logic of change and action, and not, at least primarily, in giving the logical form of our common sentences about acts or events. For the purposes of his study, it may be very fruitful to think of events as ordered pairs of states. But I think it is also fairly obvious that this does not give us a standard way of translating or representing the form of most sentences about acts and events. If I walk from San Francisco to Pittsburgh, for example, my initial state is that I am in San Francisco and my terminal state is that I am in Pittsburgh; but the same is more pleasantly true if I fly. Of course, we may describe the terminal state as my having walked to Pittsburgh from San Francisco, but then we no longer need the separate statement of the initial state. Indeed, viewed as an analysis of ordinary sentences about actions, von Wright's proposal seems subject to all the difficulties I have already outlined plus the extra one that most action sentences do not yield a non-trivial description of the initial state (try "He circled the field," "He recited the *Odyssey*," "He flirted with Olga").

In two matters, however, it seems to me von Wright suggests important and valuable changes in the pattern of analysis we have been considering, or at least in our interpretation of it. First, he says that an action is not an event, but rather the bringing about of an event. I do not think this can be correct. If I fall down, this is an event whether I do it intentionally or not. If you thought my falling was an accident and later discovered I did it on purpose, you would not be tempted to withdraw your claim that you had witnessed an event. I take von Wright's refusal to call an action an event to be a reflection of the embarrassment we found follows if we say an act is an event, when agency is introduced by a phrase like "brings it about that." The solution lies, however, not in distinguishing acts from events, but in finding a different logical form for action sentences. The second important idea von Wright introduces comes in the context of his distinction between *generic* and *individual* propositions about events.[8] This distinction is not, as von Wright makes it, quite clear, for he says both: that an individual proposition differs from a generic one in having a uniquely determined truth value, while a generic proposition has a truth value only when coupled with an occasion; and that, that Brutus killed Caesar is an individual proposition while that Brutus kissed Caesar is a generic proposition, because "a person

[8] *Op. cit.*, p. 23.

can be kissed by another on more than one occasion." In fact the proposition that Brutus kissed Caesar seems to have a uniquely determined truth value in the same sense that the proposition that Brutus killed Caesar does. But it is, I believe, a very important observation that "Brutus kissed Caesar" does not, by virtue of its meaning alone, describe a single act.

It is easy to see that the proposals we have been considering concerning the logical form of action sentences do not yield solutions to the problems with which we began. I have already pointed out that Kenny's problem, that verbs of action apparently have "variable polyadicity," arises within the sentences that can replace 'p' in such formulas as "x brought it about that p." An analogous remark goes for von Wright's more elaborate formula. The other main problem may be put as that of assigning a logical form to action sentences that will justify claims that two sentences describe "the same action." A study of some of the ways in which we excuse, or attempt to excuse, acts shows that we want to make inferences such as this: I flew my spaceship to the Morning Star, the Morning Star is identical with the Evening Star; so, I flew my spaceship to the Evening Star. (My leader told me not to go to the Evening Star; I headed for the Morning Star not knowing.) But suppose we translate the action sentences along the lines suggested by Kenny or Chisholm or von Wright. Then we have something like "I brought it about that my spaceship is on the Morning Star." How can we infer, given the well-known identity, "I brought it about that my spaceship is on the Evening Star"? We know that if we replace "the Morning Star" by "the Evening Star" in "My spaceship is on the Morning Star" the truth-value will not be disturbed; and so if the occurrence of this sentence in "I brought it about that my spaceship is on the Morning Star" is truth-functional, the inference is justified. But of course the occurrence can't be truth-functional: otherwise, from the fact that I brought about one actual state of affairs it would follow that I brought about every actual state of affairs. It is no good saying that after the words "bring it about that" sentences describe something *between* truth-values and propositions, say states of affairs. Such a claim must be backed by a semantic theory telling us how each sentence determines the state of affairs it does; otherwise the claim is empty.

Israel Scheffler has put forward an analysis of sentences about choice that can be applied without serious modification to sentences about intentional acts.[9] Scheffler makes no suggestion concerning action sentences that do not impute intention, and so has no solution to the chief problems I am discussing. Nevertheless, his analysis has a feature I should like to mention. Scheffler would have us render "Jones intentionally buttered the toast" as "Jones made-true a that Jones-buttered-the-toast inscription." This cannot,

---

[9] Israel Scheffler, *The Anatomy of Inquiry* (New York, 1963). See especially pp. 104–105.

for reasons I have urged in detail elsewhere,[10] be considered a finally satisfying form for such sentences because it contains the logically unstructured predicate "is a that Jones-buttered-the-toast inscription," and there are an infinite number of such semantical primitives in the language. But in one respect, I believe Scheffler's analysis is clearly superior to the others, for it implies that introducing the element of intentionality does not call for a reduction in the content of the sentence that expresses *what* was done intentionally. This brings out a fact otherwise suppressed, that, to use our example, "Jones" turns up twice, once inside and once outside the scope of the international operator. I shall return briefly to this point.

A discussion of the logical form of action sentences in ordinary language is to be found in the justly famed ch. VII of Reichenbach's *Elements of Symbolic Logic*.[11] According to Reichenbach's doctrine, we may transform a sentence like

(4) Amundsen flew to the North pole

into:

(5) $(\exists x)(x$ consists in the fact that Amundsen flew to the North Pole). The words "is an event that consists in the fact that" are to be viewed as an operator which, when prefixed to a sentence, forms a predicate of events. Reichenbach does not think of (5) as showing or revealing the logical form of (4), for he thinks (4) is unproblematic. Rather he says (5) is logically equivalent to (4). (5) has its counterpart in a more ordinary idiom:

(6) A flight by Amundsen to the North Pole took place.

Thus Reichenbach seems to hold that we have two ways of expressing the same idea, (4) and (6); they have quite different logical forms, but they are logically equivalent; one speaks literally of events while the other does not. I believe this view spoils much of the merit in Reichenbach's proposal, and that we must abandon the idea that (4) has an unproblematic logical form distinct from that of (5) or (6). Following Reichenbach's formula for putting any action sentence into the form of (5) we translate

(7) Amundsen flew to the North Pole in May 1926

into:

(8) $(\exists x)(x$ consists in the fact that Amundsen flew to the North Pole in May 1926).

The fact that (8) entails (5) is no more obvious than that (7) entails (4); what was obscure remains obscure. The correct way to render (7) is:

(9) $(\exists x)(x$ consists in the fact that Amundsen flew to the North Pole and x took place in May 1926).

But (9) does not bear the simple relation to the standard way of interpreting

[10] Donald Davidson, "Theories of Meaning and Learnable Languages" in *Proceedings of the 1964 International Congress for Logic, Methodology and Philosophy of Science* (Amsterdam, 1965), pp. 390–391.

[11] Hans Reichenbach, *Elements of Symbolic Logic* (New York, 1947), §48.

(7) that (8) does. We do not know of any logical operation on (7) as it would usually be formalized (with a 3-place predicate) that would make it logically equivalent to (9). This is why I suggest that we treat (9) alone as giving the logical form of (7). If we follow this strategy, Kenny's problem of the "variable polyadicity" of action verbs is on the way to solution; there is, of course, no variable polyadicity. The problem is solved in the natural way, by introducing events as entities about which an indefinite number of things can be said.

Reichenbach's proposal has another attractive feature: it eliminates a peculiar confusion that seemed to attach to the idea that sentences like (7) "describe an event." The difficulty was that one wavered between thinking of the sentence as describing or referring to that one flight Amundsen made in May 1926, or as describing a kind of event, or perhaps as describing (potentially?) several. As von Wright pointed out, any number of events might be described by a sentence like "Brutus kissed Caesar." This fog is dispelled in a way I find entirely persuasive by Reichenbach's proposal that ordinary action sentences have, in effect, an existential quantifier binding the action-variable. When we were tempted into thinking a sentence like (7) describes a single event we were misled: it does not describe any event at all. But if (7) is true, then there is an event that makes it true. This unrecognized element of generality in action sentences is, I think, of the utmost importance in understanding the relation between actions and desires; this, however, is a subject for another occasion.

There are two objections to Reichenbach's analysis of action sentences. The first may not be fatal. It is that as matters stand the analysis may be applied to any sentence whatsoever, whether it deals with actions, events, or anything else. Even "$2 + 3 = 5$" becomes "$(\exists x)(x$ consists in the fact that $2 + 3 = 5)$." Why not say "$2 + 3 = 5$" does not show its true colors until put through the machine? For that matter, are we finished when we get to the first step? Shouldn't we go on to "$(\exists y)(y$ consists in the fact that $(\exists x)(x$ consists in the fact that $2 + 3 = 5)$"? And so on. It isn't clear on what principle the decision to apply the analysis is based.

The second objection is worse. We have:

(10) $(\exists x)(x$ consists in the fact that I flew my spaceship to the Morning Star)

and

(11) the Morning Star = the Evening Star

and we want to make the inference to

(12) $(\exists x)(x$ consists in the fact that I flew my spaceship to the Evening Star).

The likely principle to justify the inference would be:

(13) (x) $(x$ consists in the fact that $S \leftrightarrow x$ consists in the fact that $S')$

where 'S'' differs from 'S' only in containing in one or more places some singular term where 'S' contains another singular term that refers to the same thing. It is plausible to add that (13) holds if 'S' and 'S'' are logically equivalent. But (13) and the last assumption lead to trouble. For observing that 'S' is logically equivalent to "$\hat{y}(y = y \,\&\, S) = \hat{y}(y = y)$" we get

(14) $(x)(x$ consists in the fact that $S \leftrightarrow x$ consists in the fact that $(\hat{y}(y = y \,\&\, S) = \hat{y}(y = y)))$.

Now suppose 'R' is any sentence materially equivalent to 'S': then "$\hat{y}(y = y \,\&\, S)$" and "$\hat{y}(y = y \,\&\, R)$" will refer to the same thing. Substituting in (14) we obtain

(15) $(x)(x$ consists in the fact that $S \leftrightarrow x$ consists in the fact that $(\hat{y}(y = y \,\&\, R) = \hat{y}(y = y))$,

which leads to

(16) $(x)(x$ consists in the fact that $S \leftrightarrow x$ consists in the fact that $R)$ when we observe the logical equivalence of 'R' and "$\hat{y}(y = y \,\&\, R) = \hat{y}(y = y)$." (16) may be interpreted as saying (considering that the sole assumption is that 'R' and 'S' are materially equivalent) that all events that occur ($=$ all events) are identical. This demonstrates, I think, that Reichenbach's analysis is radically defective.

Now I would like to put forward an analysis of action sentences that seems to me to combine most of the merits of the alternatives already discussed, and to avoid the difficulties. The basic idea is that verbs of action – verbs that say "what someone did" – should be construed as containing a place, for singular terms or variables, that they do not appear to. For example, we would normally suppose that "Shem kicked Shaun" consisted in two names and a two-place predicate. I suggest, though, that we think of "kicked" as a *three*-place predicate, and that the sentence be given in this form:

(17) $(\exists x)(\text{Kicked}(\text{Shem, Shaun, } x))$.

If we try for an English sentence that directly reflects this form, we run into difficulties. "There is an event x such that x is a kicking of Shaun by Shem" is about the best I can do, but we must remember "a kicking" is not a singular term. Given this English reading, my proposal may sound very like Reichenbach's; but of course it has quite different logical properties. The *sentence* "Shem kicked Shaun" nowhere appears inside my analytic sentence, and this makes it differ from all the theories we have considered.

The principles that license the Morning Star-Evening Star inference now make no trouble: they are the usual principles of extensionality. As a result, nothing now stands in the way of giving a standard theory of meaning for action sentences, in the form of a Tarski-type truth definition; nothing stands in the way, that is, of giving a coherent and constructive account of how the meanings (truth conditions) of these sentences depend upon their structure. To see how one of the troublesome inferences now goes through, consider (10) rewritten as

(18) $(\exists x)(\text{Flew}(I, \text{my spaceship}, x) \& \text{To}(\text{the Morning Star}, x))$.
which, along with (11), entails

(19) $(\exists x)(\text{Flew}(I, \text{my spaceship}, x) \& \text{To}(\text{the Evening Star}, x))$.

It is not necessary, in representing this argument, to separate off the To-relation; instead we could have taken "Flew" as a four-place predicate. But that would have obscured *another* inference, namely that from (19) to

(20) $(\exists x)(\text{Flew}(I, \text{my spaceship}, x))$.

In general, we conceal logical structure when we treat prepositions as integral parts of verbs; it is a merit of the present proposal that it suggests a way of treating prepositions as contributing structure. Not only is it nice to have the inference from (19) to (20); it is also nice to be able to keep track of the common element in "fly to" and "fly away from" and this of course we cannot do if we treat these as unstructured predicates.

The problem that threatened in Reichenbach's analysis, that there seemed no clear principle on which to refrain from applying the analysis to every sentence, has a natural solution if my suggestion is accepted. Part of what we must learn when we learn the meaning of any predicate is how many places it has, and what sorts of entities the variables that hold these places range over. Some predicates have an event-place, some do not.

In general, what kinds of predicates do have event-places? Without pursuing this question very far, I think it is evident that if action predicates do, many predicates that have little relation to action do. Indeed, the problems we have been mainly concerned with are not at all unique to talk of actions: they are common to talk of events of any kind. An action of flying to the Morning Star is identical with an action of flying to the Evening Star; but equally, an eclipse of the Morning Star is an eclipse of the Evening Star. Our ordinary talk of events, of causes and effects, requires constant use of the idea of different descriptions of the same event. When it is pointed out that striking the match was not sufficient to light it, what is not sufficient is not the event, but the description of it – it was a *dry* match, and so on. And of course Kenny's problem of "variable polyadicity," though he takes it to be a mark of verbs of action, is common to all verbs that describe events.

It may now appear that the apparent success of the analysis proposed here is due to the fact that it has simply omitted what is peculiar to action sentences as contrasted with other sentences about events. But I do not think so. The concept of agency contains two elements, and when we separate them clearly, I think we shall see that the present analysis has not left anything out. The first of these two elements we try, rather feebly, to elicit by saying that the agent acts, or does something, instead of being acted upon, or having something happen to him. Or we say that the agent is active rather than passive; and perhaps try to make use of the moods of the verb as a grammatical clue. And we may try to depend upon some fixed phrase like "brings it about that" or "makes it the case that." But only a little thought will make it clear that there is no satisfactory grammatical test for verbs where we want to say there is agency. Perhaps it is a *necessary* condition of attributing agency that one argument-place in the verb is filled with a reference to the agent as a person; it will not do to refer to his body, or his members, or to anyone else. But beyond that it is hard to go. I sleep, I snore, I push buttons, I recite verses, I catch cold. Also others are insulted by me, struck by me, admired by me, and so on. No grammatical test I know of, in terms of the things we may be said to do, of active or passive mood, or of any other sort, will separate out the cases here where we want to speak of agency. Perhaps it is true that "brings it about that" guarantees agency; but as we have seen, many sentences that do attribute agency cannot be cast in this grammatical form.

I believe the correct thing to say about *this* element in the concept of agency is that it is simply introduced by certain verbs and not by others; when we understand the verb we recognize whether or not it includes the idea of an agent. Thus "I coughed" and "I insulted him" *do* impute agency to the person referred to by the first singular term, "I caught cold" and "I had my thirteenth birthday" do not. In these cases, we do seem to have the following test: we impute agency only where it makes sense to ask whether the agent acted intentionally. But there are other cases, or so it seems to me, where we impute agency only when the answer to the question whether the agent acted intentionally is "yes." If a man falls down by accident or because a truck knocks him down, we do not impute agency; but we do if he fell down on purpose.

This introduces the second element in the concept of agency, for we surely impute agency when we say or imply that the act is intentional. Instead of speaking of two elements in the concept of agency, perhaps it would be better to say there are two ways we can imply that a person acted as an agent: we may use a verb that implies it directly, or we may use a verb that is non-committal, and add that the act was intentional. But when we take the second course, it is important not to think of the intentionality as adding an extra doing of the agent; we must not make the expression that introduces intention a verb of action. In particular, we cannot use "intentionally brings it about that" as the expression that introduces intention for, "brings it about that" is in itself a verb of action, and imputes agency, but it is neutral with respect to the question whether the action was intentional as described.

This leaves the question what logical form the expression that introduces intention should (must) have. It is obvious, I hope, that the adverbial form must be in some way deceptive; intentional actions are not a class of actions, or, to put the point a little differently, doing something intentionally is not a manner of doing it. To say someone did something intentionally is to describe the action in a way that bears a special relation to the beliefs and attitudes of the agent; and perhaps further to describe the action as having been caused by those beliefs and attitudes.[12] But of course to describe the action of the agent as having been caused in a certain way does not mean that the agent is described as performing any further action. From a logical point of view, there are thus these important conditions governing the expression that introduces intention: it must not be interpreted as a verb of action, it is intentional, and the intentionality is tied to a person. I propose then that we use some form of words like "It was intentional of x that p" where 'x' names the agent, and 'p' is a sentence that says the agent did something. It is useful, perhaps necessary, that the agent be named twice when we try to make logical form explicit. It is useful, because it reminds us that to describe an action as intentional is to describe the action in the light of certain attitudes and beliefs of a particular person; it may be necessary in order to illuminate what goes on in those cases in which the agent makes a mistake about who he is. It was intentional of Oedipus, and hence of the slayer of Laius, that Oedipus sought the slayer of Laius, but it was not intentional of Oedipus (the slayer of Laius) that the slayer of Laius sought the slayer of Laius.

---

[12] These, and other matters directly related to the present paper, are discussed in my "Actions, Reasons and Causes," *Journal of Philosophy*, vol. 60 (1963), pp. 685–700.

A. COMMENTS ON D. DAVIDSON'S
"THE LOGICAL FORM OF ACTION SENTENCES"

E. J. Lemmon

I AGREE with nearly all Davidson's criticisms of others, and I am fairly persuaded by his own final analysis of action sentences. I would like to suggest, however, certain modifications of it which seem to me to be required if one is going to take seriously the element of time (or tense) in these sentences: an aspect of them which Davidson largely ignores. This will involve a very preliminary sketch of a new approach to tense-logic.

Let me begin by summarizing what I take to be the main conclusions of the paper. Consider

> (1) Jones buttered the toast slowly, deliberately, in the bathroom, with a knife, at midnight.

We are for the moment to ignore the adverbs "deliberately" and "slowly"; the first raises problems of intentionality, and the second is an attributive adverb – I shall come back to these at the end. We require an analysis of (1) satisfying at least the following two conditions: (i) it must be seen to entail such sentences as "Jones buttered the toast," "Jones buttered the toast with a knife," "Jones buttered the toast in the bathroom at midnight"; (ii) suitable identity-substitutions on (1) must be seen to be correct – for example, if Jones is (was?) the man in the iron mask, then (1) should entail "the man in the iron mask buttered the toast . . . ." A third quite natural demand, not mentioned by Davidson, would seem to be: (iii) (1) should entail "Jones *was* in the bathroom at midnight" and "the toast *was* in the bathroom at midnight." There could be doubt, however, about this condition. For what if Jones, outside the bathroom door, has a long knife with which he is buttering the toast just inside the bathroom? Or Jones is in the bathroom but the toast is just outside? Thus "Jones turned on the light in the bathroom" appears to entail "the light was in the bathroom" but not "Jones was in the bathroom." Place-phrases ("in the bathroom") sometimes qualify the whole action sentence, sometimes more closely one particular part (subject or object) of the sentence. Compare "Jones buttered the bread on the table" and its failure to entail "Jones was on the table." Again, I shall return to condition (iii) later.

If we analyze "Jones buttered the toast in the bathroom" in terms of a three-place butter-predicate, and "Jones buttered the toast" in terms of a two-place butter-predicate, the first of these three conditions will simply not be met, according to Kenny and, I think, also Davidson. While in a sense this is so, the suggestion that the difficulty is peculiar to action sentences or even event sentences is not correct. For example, in predicate calculus

"This is a horse's head" becomes "There exists a horse of which this is the head," in which "is the head of" is a dyadic relation; and this analysis precisely obscures the entailing of "This is a head," *unless* this means "This is something's head." And, just as we *can* say "This is a head" means "This is in the domain of the head relation," so we can say "Brutus killed" means "Brutus is in the domain of the kill relation" and "Caesar was killed" means "Caesar is in the converse domain of the kill relation." The difficulty is perhaps worse with event sentences because we appear to be able to tag on adverbial clauses more or less indefinitely. But I am not quite convinced that a conventional treatment will not here suffice; nor, I gather, is Davidson.

"Brought-it-about-that" analyses of action sentences, in the manner of Kenny, Chisholm, and von Wright, whatever merits for other purposes they may have, will not solve Davidson's problem; they merely push the problem one stage back. Of particular importance here, I think, are Davidson's comments on von Wright. Von Wright attempts to represent change sentences by sentences of the form "p at time t and then (or next) q at time $t + n$." If this analysis is correct, then change sentences find their place within an orthodox tense-logic for which a suitable semantic definition of "p is true at moment t" can be given. While the von Wright analysis seems useful in certain simple cases ("The door was closed" becomes "At time t it was not the case that the door is closed and then at time $t + n$ it was the case that the door is closed"), Davidson shows that it seems incapable of revealing the difference between "I walked from Stanford to Pittsburgh" and "I flew from Stanford to Pittsburgh," where the sentences concerning the initial and final states would be the same. I conclude from this that a tense-logic rich enough to draw the contrast requires, in addition to the semantic notion of truth *at* a moment t, the further notion of truth *over a period* of time. Crudely, we need a logic of time-*stretches* as well as of time-*moments*. For example, the sentence "He was mowing the lawn when I entered the garden" should mean something like "There is a period of time z earlier than now and a moment of time t within z such that *over z* 'he is mowing the lawn' is true and *at t* 'I enter the garden' is true." (Refinements later.)

Davidson's own analysis toward the end of the paper is given in terms of a different example, namely:

(2) I flew my spaceship to the Morning Star.

Davidson wants this to entail

(3) I flew my spaceship to the Evening Star

in view of the identity

(4) The Morning Star is the Evening Star

(condition (ii) above). His suggestion, reminiscent of but importantly different from Reichenbach's, is that we take (2) to mean

(5) $(\exists x)$(Flew (I, my spaceship, x) & To (the Morning Star, x)).

This entails

(6) $(\exists x)$(Flew (I, my spaceship, x)),

which is the analysis of "I flew my spaceship," so that condition (i) is met, and by the usual principle of extensionality further entails a suitable analysis of (3), so that condition (ii) appears to be met too. Going back to (1), we presumably obtain

(7) $(\exists x)$(Buttered (Jones, the toast, x) ; Within (the bathroom, x) & At (midnight, x) & $(\exists y)$(Knife (y) & With (y,x)))

(ignoring, of course, "slowly" and "deliberately").

First, a formal difficulty; then, perhaps, a more philosophical one. It does not seem to me that (2) and (4) *do* entail (3); not, at least, if the "is" in (4) is the true present tense. What is required to obtain (3) from (2) is more like "The Morning Star *was at that time* the Evening Star." Of course, it is reasonable to construe the "is" of (4) as being omnitemporal (or nearly so), in which case the inference is sound (or nearly so). But this only shows that the example chosen conceals what is a real difficulty. For consider

(8) The Morning Star is the first planet struck by a man-made missile. We do not want (2) and (8) to entail

(9) I flew my spaceship to the first planet struck by a man-made missile (though perhaps (2) and (8) do entail "I flew my spaceship to what was later to be the first planet . . ." at least if the date of the flight precedes the date of the landing of the Russian missile). Davidson's completely extensional analysis hides from view what we may call the referential opacity of tense. The whole matter of identity-substitution in tensed contexts is very obscure (try "What was Gaul is now France" in "Caesar conquered Gaul" and "France is a Republic"), and only one principle seems quite safe: if $F(a)$ is true at time t, and at that same time $a = b$, then $F(b)$ is true at time t.

The second difficulty, which will turn out to be related to the first, concerns the identity of events. Davidson's analysis requires existential quantification over events, or at least event-like entities, and he also suggests that we can (only?) make good sense of much of our talk about excuses if we suppose that numerically the same event (action) can be described in different ways. So it is natural to ask for the criteria for two events being the same – to use the usual misleading idiom. Now Davidson suggests one such criterion, when he writes, of my pointing the gun and pulling the trigger on the one hand and the bullet piercing the victim on the other; "it is clear that these are two different events, since one began slightly after the other." This implies that a necessary condition for the identity of events e_1 and e_2 is that they take place *over exactly the same period of time*. Let us accept this. It is clearly not a sufficient condition; something must be said about the *place at which* the events take place. Indeed, it appears that a further necessary condition for the identity of e_1 and e_2 is that they take place in the same place – we might even say "take the same place." Now there may be a sense of "event" in which even these two conditions taken together are still not sufficient for the identity of e_1 and e_2; and there is also, no doubt, a lot of obscurity, or at least vagueness, in the notion of the place at which events occur and the time during which they happen. None the less, I propose taking these two conditions as jointly necessary and sufficient for e_1 and e_2 being identical. (Davidson's remarks on excuses again suggest that he may be cautiously sympathetic toward this proposal.) This means that we may invoke a version of the identity of indiscernibles and identify events with *space-time zones*. Thus Jones's buttering the toast *is* a space-time zone whose boundaries are included in what we may call the bathroom-slice determined by the period (say) 11:55 P.M.–12:05 A.M.

Is an event a topologically continuous space-time zone? Perhaps usually; but it need not be. A battle may stop while the participants have tea, and later be resumed. And it could even be resumed in the next field but one, rather than in the same field. And I suppose the same meeting may be going on simultaneously in two spatially separate rooms, with telephonic communication between the participants. We must not, therefore, construe "space-time zone" too narrowly. It will, however, always make sense to say that a moment of time falls within the temporal stretch of the zone; I shall say then that moment t *belongs to* zone z. Thus to say that event e occurred at t will mean that t belongs (fairly centrally) to the zone z constituted by e. It will further always make sense to say, of a physical object o, or even of an entity such as a person p closely linked to a physical object o (his body), that a temporal slice of o is included wholly within a zone z; I shall say then that o (or p) is a *participant* in z (or the event e which constitutes z). Of course, a participant may weave into and out of an event; Jones may leave the bathroom for a moment to turn off the radio in the process of buttering the toast (he must, of course, leave off buttering the toast for that period, if this is to take place *in* the bathroom).

I suggest, then, that we *accept* in outline Davidson's existential quantifier analysis of event-sentences, but construe the range of the variables in it as space-time zones; but one further modification is called for. Instead of leaving the verb in the past (or future) tense, we transform it into the present tense (in the manner of tense-logic) and insert a "before (after) now" clause. Thus (6) becomes

(10) $(\exists z)(z$ is before now & Flies (I, my spaceship, z)).

We can even capture, roughly, the tense-difference between "I flew my spaceship (yesterday morning)" and "I have been flying my spaceship (all this morning)." The latter becomes

(11) $(\exists z)(z$ extends up to now & Flies (I, my spaceship, z)).

It is clear that this revision of Davidson's proposal has the same merits with respect to condition (i) for a proper analysis of event sentences as his own. What of identity-substitution, however? If we are to take seriously the difficulties I have mentioned, we must clearly relativize identity sentences to moments of time. Thus our pattern is: $a = b$ at t. Then "$a = b$ throughout z" will mean "for all t belonging to z $a = b$ at t." Our principle of tense-extensionality will accordingly read

(12) If $F(a,z)$ and $a = b$ throughout z, then $F(b,z)$.

This will only license the inference from (2) to (3) without qualification if the Morning Star was the Evening Star throughout the period of the flight. Though not all the difficulties concerning identity-substitution in tensed contexts are hereby met, it seems possible that some development along these lines may lead to a satisfactory fulfillment of condition (ii) above.

Now for condition (iii), that (1) should be seen to entail "Jones was in the bathroom." We might argue as follows:

(13) If $F(a,z)$, then a is a participant in z.

"Butter (Jones, the toast, z)" entails that Jones and the toast are participants in z. Further

(14) If Within (p, z), then for all a such that a is a participant in z, then in (p,a,z).

In other words, if zone z is included within a place (the bathroom) p, then any participant in z is in p at some time during z. If the analysis of (1) includes at least

(15) $(\exists z)(z$ before now & Butter (Jones, the toast, z) & Within (the bathroom, z)),

then by (13) and (14) we may conclude

(16) $(\exists z)(z$ before now & In (the bathroom, Jones, z))

– Jones was in the bathroom. Now (14) would seem to be a geometrical truth, for suitable definitions of "Within," "In," and "Participant." What is clearly problematic is (13). If Jones is thinking about the toast in the bathroom, the toast need not be a participant in the event in the sense in which I am using this notion. It seems to me, therefore, likely that the question of the satisfaction of condition (iii) for particular cases will usually rest on the plausibility of (13) for particular choices of F. If F is buttering, (13) is very likely true.

Let us illustrate further how these devices can be employed to analyze different tenses. "Jones is buttering the toast" becomes

(17) $(\exists z)($now belongs to z & Butter (Jones, the toast, z)).

"Jones was buttering the toast when I entered the bathroom" becomes

(18) $(\exists z)(\exists t)(z$ before now and t belongs to z & Butter (Jones, the toast, z) & Enter (I, the bathroom, t)).

"Jones will have buttered the toast before I enter the bathroom" becomes

(19) $(\exists z)(\exists t)($now before z and t after z & Butter (Jones, the toast, z) & Enter (I, the bathroom, t)).

I am sorry not to have a full-grown logic of space-time zones to present. But it would clearly require (at least) a proper logical development of the

4-dimensional part-whole relation, and this I am quite unclear how to do. My hope is that, within such a framework, we can really do some justice to the tense distinctions marked in various languages (for example, as I have hinted, the extended or continuous tenses as opposed to the simple tenses, and the distinctions between perfect, imperfect, and pretorit, which are largely ignored in orthodox tense-logic), as well as to the logic of certain temporal adverbs – "before," "during," "after," "when," "as soon as," "while," "once."

It will be seen that I agree with Davidson in treating action sentences as part of the general problem raised by event sentences, though I link this problem more closely than he does with the problem of developing a sufficiently rich tense-logic. I should like to conclude with a couple of observations concerning "slowly" and "deliberately," which will lead back to the more specific question of action sentences.

Concerning "slowly buttered": Kenny (*Action, Emotion, and Will*, ch. 8) distinguishes verbs into three classes, static verbs, performance verbs, and activity verbs (that between performance verbs and the rest seems close to Jespersen's distinction between conclusive and non-conclusive verbs – see O. Jespersen, *Essentials of English Grammar*, 1933, pp. 249–250). Static verbs lack a continuous present tense, and their simple present is not frequentative: "understand," "know," "love," "perceive," etc. The main distinction between performance verbs and activity verbs is that, for performance verb φ, if *a* is φ-ing then *a* has *not* φ'd, while for activity verb φ, if *a* is φ-ing then *a* has φ'd. If I am building the house, I have not built it; but if I am weeping, then I have wept. (This distinction is perhaps not as sharp as one might wish: it is rather that if I am weeping then I have *been weeping* – "I have wept" may suggest that the weeping is recently finished; but then if I am building I also have *been building*.) Another contrast is that activities *go on for* a time while performances *take* time. "How long did it take you to weep (laugh, keep the secret, enjoy the play?" is odd by contrast with "How long did it take you to build the house (wash your hair, discover the truth)?" (It is worth remarking that "play the piano" and "walk" are activity verbs but "play the Pathétique" and "walk to the pub" are performance verbs.) Kenny concludes that only performance verbs can be qualified by "slowly" and "quickly." Now, though it is true that all Kenny's performance verbs can be qualified by "slowly," it is not the case that none of his activity verbs can be so qualified. One can weep slowly, laugh slowly, talk slowly, and stroke slowly, though not live at Rome or keep a secret slowly. On the other hand, it does seem to be true that the *sense* of the adverb in these latter cases is quite different from its sense as applied to performance verbs. Roughly, in the latter cases it is an adverb of manner (compare "his speech was slow and deliberate," or "he buttered the toast with slow, deliberate strokes"), while in the former cases it means "it took

101

a long time for . . . to be completed." Now "butter" is a performance verb
in Kenny's sense. Bearing in mind Davidson's observation concerning the
attributive nature of "slowly," we might therefore analyze "Jones slowly
buttered the toast" as

(20) ($\exists z$)(z before now & Butter (Jones, the toast, z) & z is a long zone
for a buttering).

But now what of "Jones *was slowly buttering* the toast"? It is tempting to
take "slowly" *here* as an adverb of manner. However that might be, a new
contrast and a new difficulty come to light. The first sentence, unlike the
second, entails that the toast *got buttered* ("You'll never guess what happened;
I found Jones buttering the toast in the bathroom; of course, I stopped him
at once"). Here is an entailment that neither Davidson's analysis nor mine
seems to catch; and it appears to depend on "butter" being a performance
verb rather than an activity verb.

Concerning "deliberately buttered": of course, "deliberately" may be an
adverb of manner too. Where, however, it means something close to
"intentionally," Davidson suggests that, rather than introduce some phrase
like "brought it about that" (which could erroneously suggest that some
extra action – an act of the will – was performed), we introduce the explicitly
referentially opaque "it was intentional of x that." I am again in sympathy
with this suggestion; what is unclear is how to combine it with the earlier
suggestions.

In the first place, presumably we have to *date* "it was intentional of x
that"; yet it may not always be clear *how* to date it. I suppose that in the
case of "Jones buttered the toast intentionally" what we want is

(21) ($\exists z$)(z before now & Butter (Jones, the toast, z) & Intentional
(Jones, z) that Butter (Jones, the toast, z)).

Or does the intentionality zone for Jones begin a little before his buttering
zone? A further problem arises in (21): does the second conjunct follow
from the third? In other words, are we to use "It was intentional of x that
p" in such a way that it entails that p? Note that in any case "Jones didn't
butter the toast intentionally" will have to be analyzed as "Jones buttered
the toast but it was not intentional of Jones that Jones buttered the toast."
It seems all round a little easier to use "intentional of x that p" in such a
way that it does not entail that p – in other words, in such a way that p
describes what x meant to achieve (if anything) rather than what he *did*
achieve. Then "Jones buttered the hairbrush thinking it was the toast"
might be

(22) ($\exists z$)(z before now & Butter (Jones, the hairbrush, z) & Intentional
(Jones, z) that Butter (Jones, the toast, z)),

to which we could, if desired, add the conjunct "Not intentional (Jones, z)
that Butter (Jones, the hairbrush, z)."

Thirdly, and sadly, the "intentional" construction seems to offer no help with notoriously opaque action verbs like "seek," "hunt," "want," "think about." Thus Oedipus might have been seeking the slayer of Laius even though Laius, unknown to Oedipus, was still alive. We might try, for "Oedipus is looking for the slayer of Laius," some such analysis as "Oedipus is . . . and it is intentional of Oedipus that Oedipus catches the slayer of Laius," where . . . is to be filled in by some (non-intentional) description of Oedipus' behavior. There are, however, two snags. First, one can look for the slayer of Laius in so many different ways that the . . . seems incapable of adequate completion. Second, and perhaps less important, the second clause of the analysis requires very careful dating – Oedipus now intends that there is a future time at which it is true that he catches the slayer of Laius.

However, Davidson did not go into these matters in his paper, so that I shall say no more about them here.

B. COMMENTS ON D. DAVIDSON'S
"THE LOGICAL FORM OF ACTION SENTENCES"

HECTOR-NERI CASTANEDA

PROFESSOR DAVIDSON'S essay is both clear and persuasive. His critique of earlier views on the logical form of statements about actions is devastating and conclusive. His own suggested view is exciting and worthy of refinement. Thus, I am casting away the traditional role of the commentator as a critic of argument or thesis, and joining forces with Davidson in order to develop further his exciting view on the logical form of action sentences.

1. *Data and Desideratum.* The basic data for Davidson's account of the logical form of action sentences are the following facts:

D1. Actions and events are spoken of as entities, indeed, as sorts of particulars with properties and principles of individuation and indentification.

D2. *The Kenny point*: Actions seem to be relations having a multiple polyadicity. For instance, the action of flying seems to be dyadic in (P) "Davidson flew his spaceship," triadic in (Q) "Davidson flew his spaceship to the Moon," tetradic in (R) "Davidson flew his spaceship to the Moon away from Mars," etc.

D3. A larger polyadic action statement entails a shorter one which is a part of it. For example, R above entails Q and Q entails P.

D4. Actions statements (or sentences) are extensional and conform to Leibniz' principle of substitution of identicals.

D5. An element that when added to an n-adic action statement yields an $(n + 1)$-adic statement is not itself a statement, or a propositional function that only needs quantification to yield a statement. Thus, there is no statement "to the Moon" or "There is an event (action) to the Moon" which is entailed by "Davidson flew his spaceship to the Moon."

Davidson's desideratum is to analyze action sentences (or statements) so that not only D1–D4 are satisfied, but so that the entailments mentioned in D3 can be exhibited as a matter of the logical form of the sentence (or statement). This is a great program, but D5 should also be accounted for.

2. *Davidson's Theses.* A good deal of Davidson's theory comes through a discussion of examples. Thus, I am not completely sure as to the exact statement of all the principles behind his discussion. One of his examples is this:

(1) I flew my spaceship to the Morning Star

He analyzes it as:

(1a) $(\exists x)$ (Flew (I, my spaceship, x) & To (the Morning Star, x)).

Clearly, (1) entails

(2) I flew my spaceship,

which is analyzed as

(2a) $(\exists x)$ (Flew (I, my spaceship, x)).

And (1a) does entail (2a) as a matter of mere logical form, thus satisfying Davidson's desideratum.

These examples and Davidson's discussion suggest that his view is made up by the following theses:

T1. *The Reichenbach thesis*: Action sentences of the form "*Y* did . . ." or "*Y* ed . . ." are implicitly existential quantifications over events.

T2. The basic structural core of an action is (i) a relation between an agent, and an event, if the action is intransitive, and (ii) a relation among an agent, a patient or accusative of the action, and an event, if the action is transitive, i.e., has an object, as in example (1) above.

T3. The expressions that formulate an increase in the polyadicity of an action statement are at bottom conjunctive sentential functions attributing properties to the event which is the action in question.

T4. Prepositions express relations of their own and must be segregated from verbs: "we conceal logical structure when we treat prepositions as integral parts of verbs . . . it is also nice to be able to keep track of the common element in 'fly to' and 'fly away from' and this of course we cannot do if we treat these as unstructured predicates" (p. 20).

T5. Thesis T1—T4 apply also to sentences about events.

T6. But an action sentence includes a reference to an agent: "Perhaps it is a *necessary* condition of attributing agency that one argument-place in the verb is filled with a reference to the agent as a person."

Davidson concludes his paper with two theses on intentionality:

T7. The adverb "intentionally" and the adjective "intentional" when applied to actions do not formulate a conjunctive sentential function of the type mentioned in T3, but are actually sentential operators more perspicuously put as "it was intentional of . . . that —," where the blank "—" is to be occupied by an action sentence of the type characterized in T1–T4.

T8. The agent mentioned in the expression filling the blank ". . ." referred to in T7 is again mentioned in the core conjunct which appears in the sentence filling the blank "—". This duplication "may be necessary in order to illuminate what goes on in those cases in which the agent makes a mistake about who he is" (p. 23).

Of these theses I accept T1, T3, T6, and T7 just as they are here formulated and I accept modified versions of T2, T5, and T8, which I shall introduce; I reject T4 altogether, and I shall formulate additional theses.

3. *Separation of Agents and Patients*. Consider a variation of Davidson's example:

(3) I flew to the Morning Star.

This entails:

(4) I flew.

By datum D3 and Davidson's desideratum and theory, (3) and (4) should be analyzed as:

(3a) $(\exists x)$ (Flew(I,x), &)(To(the Morning Star, x)),   and

(4a) $(\exists x)$ (Flew(I, x)).

Clearly, (3a) and (4a) exhibit the entailment of (4) by (3) as a purely formal entailment. But (3a) and (1a) above do not exhibit the entailment of (3) by (1) as a purely formal one; similarly, (2a) and (4a) do not exhibit the entailment of (4) by (2) as a purely formal one. Thus, Davidson's theory has to be modified in order fully to satisfy his desideratum.

An obvious suggestion is to give up part (ii) of thesis T2, and separate the agent from the patient. To this effect we revise Davidson's analyses of (1) as follows:

(1b) $(\exists x)$ (Flew(I,x) & Flew(my spaceship,x) & To(the Morning Star,x)), and

(2b) $(\exists x)$ (Flew(I,x) & Flew(my spaceship,x)).

Now all the above entailments are purely formal.

Clearly, (1) is exactly the same statement as

(1') My spaceship was flown by me to the Morning Star.

The action described and characterized in (1) is exactly the same as the action described and characterized in (1'). Similarly, (2) is exactly the same statement as

(2') My spaceship was flown by me.

Just as (2) entails (4), (2') entails

(5) My spaceship was flown.

By Davidson's theory as already modified in (2b), we should analyze (5) as

(5a) $(\exists x)$(Flew(my spaceship,x)).

This is entailed, formally, by (2b). Yet, this is not satisfactory. Here we can tell that my spaceship is a patient, or an object, or an accusative of an act of flying, not its agent, because we can look back up to (2) and (2b). But we need an analysis of (5) that can stand on its own feet. The situation can be corrected by the simple device of putting the event or action variable 'x' to the left of the agent, and to the right of every other object or person involved in the action or event in question. Thus, we revise the analyses of (1), (2), (3), and (5) as follows:

(1c) $(\exists x)$(Flew(I,x) & Flew(x,my spaceship) & To(x,the Morning Star));

(2c) $(\exists x)$Flew(I,x));

(3c) $(\exists x)$(Flew(I,x) & To(x,the Morning Star));

(5c) $(\exists x)$(Flew(x,my spaceship)).

The theory at the present stage does not only satisfy Davidson's desideratum more fully, but also improves his thesis T6 in that, even without a restriction of the substituents for the agent position, it definitely marks out the role of the agent in the logical structure of an action.

Now, there are actions that involve several agents, i.e., have teams of agents acting as teams. Compare, for example:

(11) Anthony and Bill won (each his own game), and

(12) Anthony and Bill (making up a team) won.

The discussion of the preceding examples suffices to find a symbolization of (11), namely:

(11c) $(\exists x)(\text{Won}(\text{Anthony},x))$ & $(\exists x(\text{Won}(\text{Bill},x))$.

But (12) does not entail "Bill won." (Of course, we can, as sometimes we probably do, use "win" in the sense of "sharing in winning". In this sense of "win" (12) allows a symbolization of the form of ((11c).) The proper analysis of (12) seems to be

(12a) $(\exists x)(\text{Won}(\text{Anthony}, \text{Bill}, x))$.

But (12a) fails to make it a formal matter that the order in which the agents enter in the winning relationship is inessential. Since this is true of all actions having teams of agents, a more adequate formalization is one that shows the lack of order for all such actions. Furthermore, *the action of winning seems to have the same polyadicity regardless of the number of members in a team.* That is, the relationship of winning holds between the team and the event of winning, period. Thus, instead of (12a), the analysis of (12) seems to be either

(12b) $(\exists x)(\text{Won}(\text{Anthony-Bill},x))$,

where the hyphen indicates a Goodman-type of summation of individuals, or

(12c) $(\exists x)(\text{Won}(\{\text{Anthony, Bill}\},x))$,

where the braces indicate the set whose members are listed or described within them.

There are also actions which take teams of accusatives, e.g., beating Jones and Smith, where each may truthfully say "We lost," but not "I lost." Here again the analysis of the action should involve a dyadic relation between an event and a sum individual or set.

For the sake of uniformity we can re-analyze (1)–(5) as involving the unit sets $\{I\}$ and $\{$my spaceship$\}$, instead of myself and my spaceship. Inasmuch as an object a is different from the unit set whose only member is a, but does not seem different from the sum of individuals whose only summand is a, it may be argued that we should employ sums of individuals and not sets in the analysis of action statements. But here we leave this ontological issue open.

At any rate, I propose to modify Davidson's thesis T2 to

T2'. The basic structural core of an action is a dyadic relation from a set or sum of agents to the event which is the action. If the action is transitive, then there is another core conjunct consisting of the same dyadic relation as before holding from the event in question to a set or sum of accusatives.

We also have a new thesis:

T3a. If an expression of those mentioned in T3 attributes a relation, then this is a relation from the event which is the action in question to some object, or person, or set (or sum) of persons or objects, *not* the other way around.

4. *Prepositions and Verbs.* Again consider

(1) I flew my spaceship to the Morning Star.

By datum D5 above, (1) does not entail

(6) There was a to the Morning Star,

for the simple reason that there is no such statement (or proposition as (6)). Yet by Davidson's original analysis of (1) as well as by the modified analysis we have suggested, there should be such statement as (6), or

(6a) $(\exists x)$ (To(Morning Star,x)), or

(6c) $(\exists x)$ (To(x,Morning Star)).

For clearly, (1a) should formally entail (6a), and (1c) should formally entail (6c).

Conceivably someone might reply as follows: there is no such thing as datum D5; ordinary language simply fails to have the means of formulating statements (6a) or (6c); thus, we must not say that (1) fails to entail a statement adumbrated by (6), but only that although it entails such statement, the latter cannot be formulated without the auxiliary symbolism, such as is used in (6a) and (6c).

I confess that this line of reasoning perplexes me beyond limit. I just don't know what to do with it. But it seems to me that expressions like (6) do not formulate statements because prepositions do not refer to just one well-specified relation. For instance, the preposition "to" and the phrase "to the Morning Star" may express very different relations depending on the verb that precedes them. This is the case in "Gaskon pointed to the Morning Star," "Privatus dedicated his poem to the Morning Star," "Frege referred to the Morning Star," and "A Roman gave the name 'Venus' to the Morning Star." In all these cases we have verbs denoting actions, so that even restricting ourselves to such verbs we are unable to get one well-specified relation *To*, or *To*-the-Morning-Star.

I conclude, therefore, that Davidson's thesis T4 is false, but since this thesis is really peripheral to the spirit of his view, our disagreement on this point is rather a small one.

On the other hand, (1) and (3) entail

(7) There was a flight (flying) to the Morning Star.

Likewise,

(8) I flew away from Mars

entails

(9) There was a flight (flying) away from Mars.

This suggests that in order to satisfy Davidson's desideratum of making the entailments involved in the variable polyadicity of action statements a matter of logical form, the proper thing to do is to consider the verbs and the prepositions linking those verbs to nominal expressions as forming *one* predicate. In this vein, I propose to analyze (1), (3), (7), (8), and (9) as follows:

(1d) $(\exists x)$ (Flew(I,x) & Flew (x,my spaceship) & Flying-to (x, the Morning Star));

(3d) $(\exists x)$ (Flew(I,x) & Flying-to(x,the Morning Star));

(7d) $(\exists x)$ (Flying-to(x,the Morning Star));

(8d) $(\exists x)$ (Flew(I,x) & Flying-away-from(x,Mars));

(8d) $(\exists x)$ (Flying-away-from(x,Mars)).

This proposal does justice to datum D5, accords very well with the theses already discussed, and satisfies Davidson's desideratum. Briefly, and in general:

T4'. Let w be a preposition, n a nominal expression, and Ving a gerundial form of an action verb V'. Let S be a sentence, or clause, whose main verb is a form of V'. Let S formulate an action statement A. Let S' be a sentence formulating an action statement A', which results from increasing the polyadicity of S. Let S' be the concatenation of S and w and n. Then the prepositional phrase $\ulcorner w,n \urcorner$ is to be analyzed as the conjunctive sentential function $\ulcorner(\text{Ving-}w(x,n))\urcorner$.

5. *Essential Quality of Actions*. It is clear that each one of the statements (1)–(9) entails

(10) There was a flight (flying).

The natural symbolization is:

(10e) $(\exists x)(\text{Flying}(x))$, or $(\exists x)(\text{Flight}(x))$.

This analysis has, however, the initial drawback that it prevents the entailment of (10) by (9) from conforming to the formal pattern characteristic of Davidson's theory. Here, however, abandoning dyadic predicates in favor of monadic predicates just won't do. Thus, I propose to formulate a special principle that will make the entailment from any one of (1)–(9) to (10) a matter of logical form, namely:

T4a. Let Ving, V', w, and n be as in T4'. Let V'' be a personal form of the verb V'. Let α be a constant or variable ranging over events. Let β be either a set (or sum) of agents or a set (or sum) of accusatives. Then a statement or statement function formulated by $\ulcorner(V''(\beta,x)\urcorner$ or $\ulcorner(V''(x,\beta)\urcorner$ or by $\ulcorner(\text{Ving-}w(x,n))\urcorner$ entails the corresponding statement or statement function formulated by $\ulcorner(\text{Ving}(\alpha))\urcorner$.

Note that the naturalness of the form of the entailments described in T4a would have been precluded had we adopted T4.

6. *Events and Actions*. As Davidson very nicely and correctly points out, the first difference between events and actions is that the latter are events that have agents. This is precisely what he formulates in theses T5 and T6. Now from our discussion of theses T2 and T4 it follows that T5 needs some revision. The natural revision is this:

T5'. A mere, i.e., non-action event differs from an action in that the former lacks the conjunctive component consisting of a dyadic relation from the set (or sum) of agents to the event. But a mere event may have accusatives.

Compare the following sentences:

(21) The river carried Smith's corpse;

(22) Paul carried Smith's corpse.

Obviously, both sentences can make the same type of statement, if Paul is an inanimate object or a person whose behavior is not meant to be different from that of an inanimate object. But more often than not "Paul" is used as a name of a person. In such a case, (21) will merely assert that a non-action event has taken place, and it should be analyzed as

(21e) $(\exists x)(\text{Carried}(x,\text{the river-Smith's corpse}))$,

using the sum analysis of the accusatives.

On the other hand, (22) will be used to make an action statement whose logical form is

(22e) $(\exists x)(\text{Carried}(x,\text{Paul})\ \&\ \text{Carried}(x,\text{Smith's corpse}))$.

Finally, I agree with Davidson that the slot in action predicates to the left of the event variable (or constant, for that matter) must be filled with individual signs ranging over or referring to persons. That is, I accept Davidson's thesis T6 as formulated.

7. *Intention.* Davidson is, it seems to me, absolutely correct in holding thesis T7. There is only one thing that I am not clear about. When Davidson introduces the formula "It was intentional of x that p," he seemed to me on the first reading of his paper to be claiming that from it one can derive that p. If this is the case, we surely need another prefix of the form, perhaps, "x intended that" to be prefixed to action sentences as finally characterized here, where the inference to such sentences is invalid. I regard this as the more fundamental of the two prefixes, but I am sure that there is no disagreement with Davidson here. In the sequel I shall consider the two prefixes as just differentiated.

Concerning thesis T8 there is a bit of disagreement. Davidson's examples to justify, or illustrate, T8 are:

(31) It was intentional of Oedipus (and of the slayer of Laius) that Oedipus sought the slayer of Laius,

(32) It was not intentional of Oedipus (or of the slayer of Laius) that the slayer of Laius sought the slayer of Laius.

I grant that a double reference to the agent has to be made in statements about intentional action. But neither (31) nor (32) tells us the whole, or the principal part of the story. Both (31) and (32) are derivative. *The primary type of intentions in the case of action are first-person intentions.* The primary type of intentions are those which are embodied in our decisions to act, which are necessarily of the form "I shall do such and such." Even syntax reveals this fact by making the basic construction of "I intend" to be one in which this expression is followed by an infinitive, whose subject is the very same pronoun 'I'. No doubt, constructions like "I intend that he does it" are possible, but they seem to be abbreviations of something like "I intend to see (make sure) that he does it."

Neither (31) nor (32) ascribes to Oedipus (or the slayer of Laius) the possession or the lack, respectively, of a first-person intention. In this regard they contrast with

(33) It was intentional of Oedipus [the slayer of Laius] that he (himself) sought the slayer of Laius.

I have argued elsewhere[1] that the use of "he (himself)" as in (33) is an irreducible use. I have called it the *"he" of self-consciousness* as well as *the primary quasi-indicator "he*" corresponding to the first-person*. Quasi-indicators are pronouns used in *oratio obliqua* to ascribe indexical references to someone; in this case we attribute to Oedipus references by means of the first-person indicator. I have no space or time to rehearse my arguments here, but I want to call attention to two features of the use of "he (himself)." On the one hand, even though (33) is a singular sentence, i.e., one without quantifiers, "he (himself)" cannot be replaced by its antecedent "Oedipus" without risk of falsehood. On the other hand, if "it is intentional of *x* that . . ." is used so that from the statement it helps to formulate one can derive that the action mentioned in the sentence filling the blank ". . ." was performed by *x*, then one infers something slightly, but importantly, different from the statement formulated by the sentence filling the blank ". . .". Suppose, for example, that from (33) one can derive:

(34) he sought the slayer of Laius.

The curious thing is that the "he" of (34) is merely a proxy for "Oedipus" (or "the slayer of Laius"). The sentence (34) is itself incomplete, so that the complete statement of the conclusion requires that we read "Oedipus" (or "the slayer of Laius") for "he." Yet, the statement "Oedipus [or the slayer of Laius] sought the slayer of Laius" is not the one expressed by the subordinate clause of (33). For surely, Oedipus may have failed to know that he himself was the slayer of Laius, or that he himself was Oedipus. To greater emphasis, while the subordinate clause of (33) ascribes to Oedipus a first-person reference to himself, (34) does not.

In brief, I propose to substitute the following thesis for T8:

T8'. The primary statements of intention (or intentional action) are formulated in sentences of the form ⌜it is intentional of β that φ⌝ or ⌜β intends that φ⌝, where β is a name of a person or a variable ranging over persons, and φ is an action sentence satisfying all the preceding theses so far adopted, except that φ has an occurrence of the primary quasi-indicator "he*" in the agent position.

---

[1] In " 'He': A Study in the Logic of Self-Consciousness," *Ratio* (forthcoming) and in "Indicators and Quasi-indicators," *American Philosophical Quarterly*, vol. 4 (1967) pp. 85–100.

Naturally, there may be other occurrences of quasi-indicators in φ, and some of them raise very serious problems of analysis. But for this I can only refer here to the papers mentioned in footnote 1.

We must accept third-person intentions, like those formulated in Davidson's examples (31) and (32). For one thing, we must be able to formulate the intentions of a given member of a team concerning the team's actions. But I shall leave this matter open here. And I shall also leave open the proper analysis of what may be called *a team's intentions*. These are expressed in sentences of the form ⌜it is intentional of β_1–. . .–β_n that φ⌝, or ⌜it is intentional of $\{\beta_1, \ldots, \beta_n\}$ that φ⌝, or ⌜β–$_1$ . . .–β_n intends that φ⌝ or⌜$\{\beta_1, , \ldots, \beta_n\}$ intends that φ⌝, or it ⌜is intentional of α that φ⌝, or ⌜α intends that φ⌝, where each β_i is an expression referring to persons and α is an expression referring to a team. All these statements, it seems to me, are of the same kind as, or of a kind intimately related to the kind of, the statements Wilfrid Sellars has referred to as formulation of intentions in the *we*-mode.[2] But by saying this I am not committing myself to Sellars' analysis of "ought" in terms of we-intentions. These are all exciting questions that must be left open here.

I said that Davidson's (31) "It was intentional of Oedipus that Oedipus sought the slayer of Laius" is derivatively true. It is derivatively true at least in accordance with Sophocles' tragedy, since by this tragedy (31) was true simply because: both it was intentional of Oedipus that he himself (= he*)sought the slayer of Laius, and Oedipus knew that he* was Oedipus.

8. *Conclusion.* Davidson's proposed theory on the logical form of action statements (sentences) is a brilliant account of data D1–D4. His theory has a high degree of initial adequacy. This adequacy is enhanced by allowing the minor modifications suggested above. That enables it not only to account for datum D5, but to account jointly for all data D1–D5.

---

[2] W. Sellars, "Imperatives, Intentions, and 'Oughts'," in H-N. Castaneda and G. Nakhnikian (eds.), *Morality and the Language of Conduct* (Detroit, 1963), pp. 202–206.

C. COMMENTS ON D. DAVIDSON'S
"THE LOGICAL FORM OF ACTION SENTENCES"

RODERICK M. CHISHOLM

I AM GRATEFUL for this opportunity to reply to Professor Davidson's observations about my own theory of action. I am happy to do so, for I think that my theory, on the whole, is consistent with his and indeed that the two theories may supplement each other.[1]

I had proposed that we take as undefined "He made it happen that p in the endeavor to make it happen that q" or, for short, "Mp,q." We should assume, among other things, (1) that "Mp,q" implies p and (2) that "Mp,q" implies "$M(Mp,q),q$." The locution expresses the concept of agency, for it refers to the person as cause. *He* makes something happen and in so doing he makes it happen that he makes that something happen. And the locution is intentional; for although "Mp,q" implies p, it does not imply q. The agent may make it happen that p in the endeavor to make it happen that q and yet not make it happen that q.[2]

The following definitions may now be introduced: "He *undertakes or endeavors* to make p happen" for "$(\exists q)(Mq,p)$"; "He *makes it happen* that p" for "$(\exists q)(Mp,q)$"; and "He is *successful in making it happen* that p" for "Mp,p." Undertaking p does not imply making p happen, and making p happen does not imply undertaking p. But successfully making p happen implies undertaking p and making p happen. Undertaking p, given assumption (2), implies making it happen that one undertakes p, but it does not imply successfully undertaking p or undertaking to undertake p.

The examples to which Davidson refers in connection with my views require a further distinction between directly and indirectly undertaking. A man undertakes p *indirectly* if there is some q such that he undertakes to make q cause p; he undertakes p *directly* if he undertakes p but not indirectly. "Jones raised his arm," in the usual sense of this expression, could now be interpreted as telling us, not only that Jones made it happen that his arm went up, but also that he undertook directly to make it happen and that he was successful. Analogously for "He batted an eyelash" and his making it happen that his eye closed and opened quickly. "Alice broke the mirror intentionally" will tell us that Alice successfully made it happen that the mirror is broken; and "Alice broke the mirror but not intentionally" will tell us that although she made it happen that the mirror is broken she didn't undertake to make it happen.

---

[1] An improved version of the theory to which he refers may be found in "Freedom in Action," in Keith Lehrer, ed., *Freedom and Determinism* (New York, 1966), pp. 11–44.

[2] Quantified formulae may replace the letters 'p' and 'q' in the ways I suggested, above, in commenting on Professor von Wright's paper.

There is no "act of will" involved in this account. Our assumptions do imply that whenever a man does something freely then there is something he is thereby endeavoring or undertaking to do. But undertaking, as we have said, does not imply undertaking to undertake. I assume that the *person* makes certain events happen and hence that agents as well as events may be causes. I suspect that if there is any disagreement with Davidson, it pertains to this latter point. But how are we to render "He made it happen that p" in terms merely of relations among events?

D. REPLY TO COMMENTS

Donald Davidson

Speaking of a topic closely related to ours, John Austin said, "I owe it to the subject to say, that it has long afforded me what philosophy is so often thought, and made, barren of – the fun of discovery, the pleasures of co-operation, and the satisfaction of reaching agreement." The extent of the agreement reached in the exchange recorded here is gratifying; but even more important to me is the sense that we were engaged in a common and creative enterprise. Austin gives the credit to his subject; I am more inclined to say that it was my cosymposiasts that made the occasion so rewarding.

First I would like to discuss some of the main points in John Lemmon's comments.

A. *Reply to Lemmon on Tenses:* My goal was to get clear about the logical form of action sentences. By action sentences I mean sentences *in English* about actions. At the level of abstraction on which the discussion moved, little was said that would not apply to sentences about actions in many other languages if it applied to sentences in English. The ideal implicit in the paper is a theory that spells out every element of logical form in every English sentence about actions. I dream of a theory that makes the transition from the ordinary idiom to canonical notation purely mechanical, and a canonical notation rich enough to capture, in its dull and explicit way, every difference and connection legitimately considered the business of a theory of meaning. The point of canonical notation so conceived is not to improve on something left vague and defective in natural language, but to help elicit in a perspicuous and general form the understanding of logical grammar we all have that constitutes (part of) our grasp of our native tongue.

In exploring the logical form of sentences about actions and events, I concentrated on certain features of such sentences and neglected others. One feature I totally neglected was that of tense; Lemmon is absolutely right in pointing out that some of the inferences I consider valid depend (in a standard way we have become hardened to) on fudging with respect to time. The necessity for fudging shows that we have failed to bring out a feature of logical form.

I accept the implication that my own account was incomplete through neglect of the element of tense, and I welcome Lemmon's attempt to remedy the situation. I am very much in sympathy with the methods he apparently thinks appropriate. Logicians have almost always assumed that the demonstrative element in natural languages necessarily resists serious semantic treatment, and they have accordingly tried to show how to replace tensed expressions with others containing no demonstrative feature. What recommends this strategy to logicians (the elimination of sentences with variable truth values) also serves to show that it is not a strategy for analyzing the sentences of English. Lemmon makes no attempt to eliminate the demonstrative element from his canonical notation (substituting "before now" for the past tense is a way of *articulating* the relation between the different tenses of the same verb, not of eliminating the demonstrative element). At the same time, he obviously has in mind that the structure he introduces must lend itself to formal semantic treatment. It is simply a mistake, Lemmon correctly assumes, to think that sentences with a demonstrative element resist the application of systematic semantic analysis.

B. *Reply to Lemmon on Identity Conditions for Events:* If we are going to quantify over events and interpret singular terms as referring to events, we need to say something about the conditions under which expressions of the form "$a = b$" are true where 'a' and 'b' refer, or purport to refer, to events. This is a difficult and complex subject, and I do not propose to do more here than comment briefly on some of Lemmon's remarks. But I think he is right to raise the issue; before we decide that our general approach to the analysis of event sentences is correct, there must be much more discussion of the criteria for individuating and identifying events.

Lemmon is surely right that a necessary condition for the identity of events is that they take place over exactly the same period of time. He suggests, very tentatively, that if we add that the events "take the same place," then we have necessary and sufficient conditions for identity. I am not at all certain this suggestion is wrong, but before we accept it we shall need to remove two doubts. The first centers on the question whether we have adequate criteria for the location of an event. As Lemmon realizes, his principle (13) that if $F(a,z)$ then a is a participant in z, cannot be true for every F (take 'F' as "took place a thousand miles south of" and 'a' as "New York"; we would not, presumably, say New York participated in every event that took place a thousand miles south of New York). Incidentally, this seems to show that Lemmon's condition (iii) is not a *general* condition that an analysis of logical form should satisfy. In any case, how do we deal with examples like this: if a man's arm goes up, the event takes place in the space-time zone occupied by the arm; but if a man raises his arm, doesn't the event fill the zone occupied by the whole man? Yet the events may be identical. If a man drives his car into his garage, how much of the garage does the event occupy? All of it, or only the zone occupied by the car? Finally, if events are to have a location in an interesting sense, we need to see what is wrong with the following argument: if an event is a change in a certain object, then the event occupies at least the zone occupied by the object during the time the event takes place. But if one object is part of another, a change in the first is a change in the second. Since and object is part of the universe, it follows that every event that is a change in an object takes place everywhere (throughout the universe). This argument is, I believe, faulty, but it must be shown to be so before we can talk intelligibly of the location of events.

The second doubt we must remove if we are to identify events with space-time zones is that there may be two different events in the same zone. Suppose that during exactly the same time interval Jones catches cold, swims the Hellespont, and counts his blessings. Are these all the same event? I suspect there may be a good argument to show they are; but until one is produced, we must suspend judgment on Lemmon's interesting proposal.

C. *Reply to Castaneda on Agent and Patient:* Castaneda very usefully summarizes the main points in my paper, and raises some questions about the principles that are implicit in my examples. My lack of explicitness has perhaps misled him in one respect. It is not part of my program to make all entailments matters of logical form. "$x > y$" entails "$y < x$", but not as a matter of form. "x is a grandfather" entails "x is a father," but not as a matter of form. And I think there are cases where, to use Castaneda's words, "a larger polyadic action statement entails a shorter one which is a part of it" and yet this is not a matter of logical form. An example, perhaps, is this: "I flew my spaceship" may entail "I flew," but if it does, it is not, I think, because of the logical form of the sentences. My reason for saying this is that I find no reason to believe the logical form of "I flew my spaceship" differs from that of "I sank the Bismarck," which does not entail "I sank" though it does happen to entail "The Bismarck sank." A comparison of these examples ought to go a long way to persuade us that simple sentences containing transitive verbs do not, as a matter of logical form, entail sentences with intransitive verbs. Putting sentences in the passive will not radically change things. If I sank the Bismarck, the Bismarck was sunk and the Bismarck sank. But "The Bismarck was sunk" and "The Bismarck sank" are not equivalent, for the second does not entail the first. Thus even if we were to accept Castaneda's view that "The Bismarck was sunk" has a logically intransitive verb, the passivity of the subject remains a feature of this verb distinguishing it from the verb of "The Bismarck sank." Thus there is no obvious economy in Castaneda's idea of indicating the distinction between agent and patient by position in verbs of action. There would be real merit, however, in keeping track of the relation between "The Bismarck was sunk" and "The Bismarck sank," which is that the first entails the second; but Castaneda's notation does not help with this.

Castaneda would have us put "The King insulted the Queen" in this form:

($\exists x$)(Insulted (the King, x) & Insulted (x, the Queen))

What is this relation, that relates a person and an event or, *in the same way,* an event and a person? What logical feature is preserved by this form that is not as well preserved, and less misleadingly, by

($\exists x$) (Insulted (the King, x) & Was insulted (the Queen, x))

(i.e. "There was an event that was an insulting by the King and of the Queen")? But I remain unconvinced of the advantages in splitting transitive verbs up in this way. The gain is the entailment of "My spaceship was flown" by "I flew my spaceship"; the loss becomes apparent when we realize that "My spaceship was flown" has been interpreted so as not to entail "Someone flew my spaceship."

D. *Reply to Castaneda on Prepositions:* My proposal to treat certain prepositions as verbs does seem odd, and perhaps it will turn out to be radically mistaken. But I am not quite convinced of this by what Castaneda says. My analysis of "I flew my spaceship to the Morning Star" does entail "($\exists x$) (To (the Morning Star, x))," and Castaneda turns this into words as "There was a to the Morning Star." But I think we can do better: "There was an event involving motion toward the Morning Star" or "There was an event characterized by being to (toward) the Morning Star." Castaneda himself proposes "flying-to," which shows he understands the *sort* of verb I have in mind. But of course I don't like "flying-to" as an unstructured predicate, since this breaks the connection with "walking-to" and its kin. Castaneda complains, of my use of plain "to," that there are many different senses of "to," depending on the verb it is coupled with. Let us suppose we understand this difficulty, with its heavy dependence on the concept of sameness of relation. I shall meet Castaneda half-way by introducing a special form of "to" which means "motion-toward-and-terminating-at"; this is more general than his "flying-to" and less general than my former, plain, "to." And I assume that if Castaneda understands "($\exists x$) (flying-to (the Morning Star, x))" he will understand "($\exists x$) (Motion-toward-and-terminating-at(the Morning Star, x))," for this verb differs from his merely in degree of generality. Taking this line will save us from Castaneda's T4' to which I would object since it deals with syntactic structure for which no semantic interpretation has been given. A similar remark goes, I am sorry to say, for the ingenious T4a. I hope Castaneda finds a way to echo T4a in a semantic theory, for it deals with an interesting problem. As things are, I think the difficulty for Castaneda could be put: how can we use T4a to state the truth conditions for sentences in the form of (10)?

E. *Reply to Castaneda on Intention:* First Castaneda makes the point, also made by Lemmon, that I would have done well to make basic a notion of intention that does not imply that what is intended is done. I think they are right in this.

Castaneda then goes on to claim that my analysis of "Oedipus intentionally sought the slayer of Laius" as "It was intentional of Oedipus that Oedipus sought the slayer of Laius" is faulty because the first sentence might be true and the second false if Oedipus failed to know that he was Oedipus. Castaneda suggests that to correct the analysis, we should put "he (himself)" for the second occurrence of "Oedipus." In my opinion, Castaneda is right both in his criticism and in his correction. There is, as he maintains, an irreducibly demonstrative element in the full analysis of sentences about intentions, and my proposal concealed it.

Perhaps I should remark here that I do not think it *solves* the problem of the analysis of sentences about intention to put them in the form of "It was intentional of x that p"; such sentences are notoriously hard to bring under a semantical theory. I view putting such sentences in this form as a first step; the problem then looks, even with Castaneda's revision, much like the problem of analyzing sentences about other propositional attitudes.

F. *Reply to Chisholm on Making Happen:* I am happy to have Chisholm's careful comments on the section of my paper that deals with his views; he has made me realize that I had not appreciated the subtlety of his analysis. It is not clear to me now whether, on the issues discussed in my paper, there is any disagreement between us. Let me formulate the questions that remain in my mind as I now understand them.

I assume that since he has not attempted an analysis of event sentences generally, and the 'p' in "He made it happen that p" refers to an event, Chisholm does not dispute my claim that he has not solved the main problems with which I deal in my paper. The question is rather whether there are any special problems in his analysis of action and agency. The first difficulty I raised for Chisholm was whether he could produce, in a reasonably mechanical way, for every sentence of the form "He raised his arm" or "Alice broke the mirror" another sentence of the form "He made it happen that p" or "Alice made it happen that p" where 'p' does not have the agent as subject. Chisholm shows, I think, that there is a chance he can handle "He raised his arm" and "Alice broke the mirror" except, perhaps, in the case where intention is not involved at all, and this is not under discussion. The cases I would now worry about are rather "He walked to the corner," "He carved the roast," "He fell down," or "The doctor removed the patient's appendix." In each of these examples I find I am puzzled as to what the agent makes happen. My problem isn't that I can't imagine that there is some bodily movement that the agent might be said to make happen, but that I see no way *automatically* to produce the right description from the original sentence. No doubt each time a man walks to the corner there is some way he makes his body move; but of course it does not follow that there is some one way he makes his body move every time he walks to the corner.

I   119

The second difficulty I raised for Chisholm concerned the question whether his analysis committed him to "acts of the will," perhaps contrary to his own intentions. It is clear that Chisholm does not *want* to be committed to acts of the will, and that his analysis does not *say* that there are acts of the will but I believe the question can still be raised. It can be raised by asking whether the event said to occur in "Jones made it happen that his arm went up" is the same event or a different one from the event said to occur in "Jones's arm went up." It seems to me Chisholm can avoid acts of the will only by saying the events are the same. He is free to say this, of course, and then the only objection is terminological. And "Jones's arm went up" would then be, when it was something Jones made happen, a description of an action.

At the end of his reply, Chisholm conjectures that I may not agree with him that agents may be causes. Actually I see no objection to saying that agents are causes, but I think we understand this only when we can reduce it to the case of an event being a cause; and here I do disagree with Chisholm. He asks how we are to render "He made it happen that p" in terms merely of relations among events. If the problem is that of giving the logical form of action sentences, then I have made a suggestion in the present paper. If the problem is to give an *analysis* of the concept of agency using other concepts, then I am not sure it can be done. Why must it be possible?

IV

THE LOGIC OF ACTION — A SKETCH

Georg Henrik von Wright

1. In my paper I shall sketch a formal theory which I propose to call the Logic of Action. A first attempt to construct such a theory was made in my book *Norm and Action* (especially ch. IV). The present system is a further elaboration and generalization of some ideas in the book. But it also contains essential modifications of my earlier views. A major difference of a formal nature is that the new system dispenses with the two operators '*d*' and '*f*' (for "doing" and "forbearance" respectively).

2. What is it to act? Perhaps an answer which covers all cases cannot be found. But an answer which captures an important type of action is this: To act is intentionally ("at will") to *bring about* or to *prevent* a *change* in the world (in nature). On this definition, to forbear (omit) action is either to leave something *unchanged* or to *let* something *happen*.

Action (on the above view) is thus of two kinds. We can call them *productive* action and *preventive* action. To them correspond two types of forbearance (omission). Thus we get a division of acts and omissions in four elementary types.

In the sequel the word "act" ("acting," "action") will be so used that it refers, not only to productive or preventive interference with the world, but also to forbearance.

3. To give an account of action, we must first be able to give an account of change. (A logic of action may be said to presuppose a logic of change.)

What is a change? A preliminary answer is that a change is a transformation of *states*. A change takes place when a state of affairs *ceases* to be or *comes* to be. When a state *continues* to be, the world is unchanged with regard to this state. It is convenient, however, to use the word "change" so that it includes also non-changes, *i.e.*, immediate progressions in time with the same initial and end-state.

The notion of a state of affairs is thus basic to the notion of change. I shall not attempt to answer here the question what a state (of affairs) is. I shall confine myself to the following observation:

One can distinguish between states of affairs in a *generic* and an *individual* sense. Individually the same state, *e.g.*, that the sun is shining in Pittsburgh on 18 March 1966 at 10 A.M., obtains only once in the history of the world.

Generically the same state, *e.g.*, that the sun is shining, can obtain repeatedly and in different places. Of the two senses, the generic seems to me to be the primary one. An individual state is, so to speak, a generic state instantiated ("incarnated") on a certain occasion in space and time.

In the sequel "state" will always be understood in the generic sense. As schematic descriptions of generic states we shall use the symbols $p, q, r, \ldots$, or such letters with an index-numeral.

4. Let us assume that the total state of the world on a given occasion can be completely described by indicating for every one of a finite number n of states $p_1, \ldots, p_n$ whether it obtains or does not obtain on that occasion. A description of this kind is called a *state-description*. As is well known, the number of possible total states is 2^n if the number of ("elementary") states is n. We can arrange them in a sequence and refer to them by means of state-descriptions: $s_1, \ldots, s_{2^n}$.

A world which satisfies the above assumption could be called a Wittgenstein-world. It is the kind of world which Wittgenstein envisaged in the *Tractatus*. I shall not here discuss the (important) ontological question, whether our real world *is* a Wittgenstein-world, or not. The answer is perhaps negative. But nobody would deny, I think, that, as a simplified model of "a world," Wittgenstein's idea is of great theoretical interest – and state-descriptions of great practical importance. Our study of changes and actions will throughout employ this model.

5. We shall further assume that time is a discrete medium of "time-points" ("moments," "occasions") in a linear order. We introduce a symbol 'T', to be read "and next." For the purpose of forming expressions 'T' functions exactly as the truth-connectives.

"$s_i T s_j$" says that the total state of the world is now s_i and next (at the next moment) s_j. If we write out the state-descriptions in terms of the underlying (elementary) states $p_1, \ldots, p_n$ we can, by comparing them, tell exactly in which features the world will change and in which it will remain unchanged, when "time passes" from the present moment to the next.

Consider m successive occasions in time. If for every one of them we indicate which total state of the world obtains on that occasion, we get a complete description of how the world changes (and does not change) over that interval of time. Such a description we shall call a *change-description* or *history* of the world of *length m*. It is easy to see that the number of possible histories of length m of a world which is "composed" of n elementary states, is 2^{mn}. We can order them in a sequence, $h_1, \ldots, h_{2^{mn}}$.

We need not here discuss the ontological question, whether time *is* discrete or continuous. It will be agreed, I think, that change-descriptions of finite length are in any case of considerable interest and value as simplified models of (stretches of) a world's history.

6. The logic of change which we need for our logic of action is essentially

a formal theory of the connective 'T' ("and next"). The rudiments of this theory are contained in my book *Norm and Action* (ch. ii, sects. 7–10). A fuller systematic presentation is found in my paper "And Next" (*Acta Philosophica Fennica*, vol. 18, 1965, pp. 293–304).

The vocabulary of the logic of change is the vocabulary of propositional logic (PL) enriched by the connective 'T'. The axioms are those of PL *and* the following four axioms:

A1. $(p \vee qTr \vee s) \leftrightarrow (pTr) \vee (pTs) \vee (qTr) \vee (qTs)$.
A2. $(pTq) \& (pTs) \rightarrow (pTq \& s)$.[1]
A3. $p \leftrightarrow (pTq \vee \sim q)$.
A4. $\sim(pTq \& \sim q)$.

Inference in the calculus proceeds through substitution, detachment, and replacement of expressions by provably equivalent expressions.

The calculus of the connective 'T' is a decidable theory. Any given expression of the calculus can be transformed into a normal form from which is immediately seen, whether it is a theorem of the T-calculus, a necessary truth in the logic of change, or not.

7. In the T-calculus we can describe changes (and non-changes) – from one moment to the next and over a certain period of time. But we cannot with this instrument describe actions (and omissions). Why this is so, is not difficult to see:

Assume that there is one agent in our world. Assume further that of this world it is first true that p and then that $\sim p$. Can we, from this information, conclude anything about the rôle of the agent in respect to this change? Obviously not. But if we are given the additional information that, had this agent not interfered with the world, this change would not have taken place, then we can conclude that he *brought about* the change, *i.e.*, destroyed the state p. And if we are told that, had this agent not been in the world, the change would nevertheless have occurred, then we can conclude that the agent *let* the change happen, *i.e.*, let the state p vanish.

Generally speaking, for a description of action in terms of states and transformations (changes), three items are required:

(*a*) First, we must be told the state in which the world is at the moment, when action is initiated. I shall call this the *initial* state.

(*b*) Secondly, we must be told the state, in which the world is, when action has been completed. I shall call it the *end*-state.

(*c*) Thirdly, we must be told the state, in which the world would be, had it not been for the presence of agency in it, or, as I shall also say, "independently of the agent."

---

[1] This axiom was originally stated in the form of an equivalence $(pTq) \& (rTs) \leftrightarrow (p \& rTq \& s)$. The implication from $(p \& rTq \& s)$ to $(pTq) \& (rTs)$, however, is provable from the other axioms. The implication from $(pTq) \& (rTs)$ to $(p \& rTq \& s)$ again is provable from the present $A2$ with the aid of the other axioms.

The state (*b*), the end-state, can also be spoken of as the *result* of the action.

The states (*a*) and (*c*) taken together may be said to constitute the *acting-situation* or, as it could also be called, *opportunity* of action. For example: If the world is initially in the state *p* and would remain in this state independently of an agent, then there is an opportunity for either destroying this state or letting it continue. If again the world is in the same initial state but would change to the state ~*p* independently of an agent, then the situation offers an opportunity either for preventing this state from vanishing or for letting it vanish.

States (*a*), (*b*), and (*c*) together determine the *nature of the action*. In other words the nature of the *action* is determined jointly by the opportunity and the result.

8. The relativity of action to an opportunity can also be spoken of as the *counterfactual* element involved in action. Every description of an action contains, in a concealed form, a counterfactual conditional statement. When we say, *e.g.*, that an agent opened a window, we imply that, had it not been for the agent's interference, the window would, on that occasion, have remained closed. When we say that an agent prevented a door from closing, we thereby intimate that "otherwise" (*i.e.*, had it not been for the agent) the door would have closed on that occasion.

Counterfactual conditional statements are connected with notorious difficulties. Because of the presence of a counterfactual element in action, a logic of action cannot skip these difficulties completely. But I think that, fortunately, we need not here dig deep into the problems of counterfactual conditionals. I propose to deal with the matter in the following way:

I introduce a symbol '*I*'. It is a binary connective. Expressions formed with its aid will be called *I*-expressions. To the left and right of (a not-iterated) '*I*' stand schematic descriptions of (generic) states of affairs. The description to the left of '*I*' is, in the *I*-expression, asserted to hold true of a world in which there is a certain agent. The description to the right holds true of the world which would be, if from the world which is we remove (in thought) the agent.

This "experiment of thought" calls for some comments. The "removal" of the agent does not mean the removal (in thought) of his *body*. The physical presence of the agent may have a causal influence on the world which is not at all connected with his actions. His physical absence would then make a difference to the world, – but *this* difference does not tell us anything about his actions. The "removal" of the agent is the removal (in thought) of whatever *intentions* he may have. It is, therefore, the removal of him *qua agent*.

One could substitute for this experiment of thought one in which the contrast is between a world in which the agent is present physically and a world from which he is absent physically. Then the comparison of the states would tell us for which changes and not-changes the agent, through his presence, is *causally responsible*. This class of changes (and not-changes) includes, but is not necessarily included in, the class of changes (and not-changes) for which he is responsible also *qua agent*.

I shall maintain, without further argument, that the formal rules which govern the behavior of the connective 'I' are exactly the same as those of the connective 'T'. Both connectives could be called "co-ordinators of worlds". 'T' co-ordinates the world which *is* now and the world which *will be* next. 'I' co-ordinates the world *as it is* with an agent in it and the world which *would be*, if there were no agent.

T-expressions and I-expressions may become combined (with the aid of truth-connectives or 'T' or 'I') to TI-expressions. The axiomatic system of TI-expressions will be called the TI-calculus. For present purposes a full description of this calculus and a discussion of formal problems connected with it (normal forms, tests of theoremhood, etc.) is not needed.

9. The TI-calculus gives us the means which we need here for a schematic description of action as the bringing about and preventing of changes. The general form of a description of action is "$-T(-I-)$", where the blanks are filled by molecular compounds of PL in terms of the same set of propositional variables. A description of this general form says that the world initially is in a certain state *and next* is in a certain second state *instead of* being in a certain third state. Given the three states, we can by comparing them "read off" the rôle of the agent in the context of these transformations. All three states, or any two of them, may be identical.

Consider an elementary state p and its negation-state $\sim p$. There are in all 8 ($= 2^3$) different possible ways, in which one can fill the blanks in "$-T(-I-)$" with $\sim$"p" or "p": $pT(pIp)$, $pT(pI\sim p)$, ..., $\sim pT(\sim pI\sim p)$. The first TI-expression is a schematic description of the action (strictly speaking, non-action) which we should call "letting a state continue," the second of the action called "preventing a state from vanishing," ..., and the eighth of the action called "letting a state remain absent." I shall refer to the 8 cases as *the eighth elementary modes of act and forbearance*. (Cf. *Norm and Action*, ch. iii, sect. 7–8.)

Consider a set of two or more variables $p,q,$ ... and three state-descriptions s_k, s_j, and s_i in terms of the members of this set. From $s_iT(s_jIs_k)$ we can now "read off" a compound of acts and/or omissions which are attributable to the agent (on the occasion in question). It is convenient to refer to such a compound as a *course* or *pattern of action* or as a *total action*. For example: "p & $\sim qT(\sim p$ & $qI\sim p$ & $\sim q)$" describes the course of action which an agent chooses when he *lets* one of two states *vanish* and *produces* the other.

n (elementary) states determine 2^n possible total states of the world and

$2^n \times 2 \times^n 2^n$ or 2^{3n} possible total actions (for a certain agent on a certain occasion). For $n = 1$, this gives us the eight elementary modes of action mentioned above.

10. We can use the connective 'T' to form chains of descriptions of action stretching over a succession of occasions: $-T((-I-)T((-I-)T \ldots)) \ldots$ We shall consider only the case, when the blanks are filled by state-descriptions in terms of the same set of n elementary states. We then "read off" from the expression a succession of courses of action taken by a certain agent on a sequence of successive occasions. It is convenient to call such a succession a *life* and its description a *biography*. By the *length* of the life we understand the number of moments in our discrete time which the description covers. (This is the number of occurrences of 'T' in the biography increased by 1.)

By the rules of our TI-calculus, an expression of the type we call a *biography* entails an expression of the type we called above a *history*. The latter is a succession of total states through which the world actually passes. A history tells us what actually *happens* in the world, in which there is an agent. But it does not tell us what the agent *does*, which courses of action he chooses at the successive stages of his life's journey, in short: how he lives. To know this we must know, not only how the world actually changes, but also how it would have changed from one occasion to the next, had it not been for the agent.

If the number of possible total *states* of the world (at any given time) is 2^n, then the total number of possible *histories* of the world of length m is 2^{mn}, and the total number of possible *lives* of this length is $2^{(2m-1n)}$. We can order the lives into a sequence $l_1, \ldots, l_2 (2m-1)n$.

For $m = 1$, the last expression becomes equal to 2^n. A state-description describes a "momentary" life, one could say. In this life nothing *happens*. Therefore there is also no room for action in it.

For $m = 2$ and $n = 1$, the formula for the number of possible lives assumes the value 8. These possible lives are the elementary modes of action themselves. They could also be called "minimal lives."

For $m = 3$ and $n = 2$, the formula assumes the value 2^{10} or 1024. In a world "composed" of only two elementary states, say p and q, and stretching over only three successive moments, no less than 1024 lives are possible for an agent. Then it should be remembered, however, that the course of a life depends, not only upon the action of the agent, but also upon the course (moves) which nature would take (make) independently of him. (Cf. below Sect. 12.)

Assume that all places but the penultimate one in the schema $-T((-I-)T (-I-))$ are filled by a state-description. These state-descriptions, taken together and in the proper order, may be said to determine a *life-situation*. An agent's life-situation at any given stage of his life's journey is thus determined, one could say, by his total life behind him *and* by what would be nature's next move independently of him. This notion of a life-situation is a generalization of our previous notion of an acting-situation. (Sect. 7.)

11. Our logic of action, so far, considers only the presence of *one* agent in the world. We can, however, generalize the theory to cases when there are two, three, or more agents. Then our theory of action becomes a theory also of the *interaction* of agents.

I shall here, in barest outline, indicate how this extension of the theory is accomplished.

Let there be two agents, *a* and *b*, in the world. To tell what each of them has done on a given occasion, we must know: First, the initial state of the world; secondly, the actual subsequent end-state of the world with the two agents in it; thirdly, the end-state which would have obtained had *a* been alone in the world; fourthly, the hypothetical end-state, had *b* been alone; and fifthly, the hypothetical end-state, had there been no agent at all in the world. Let, for example, the five states be, in order: $p \& q$, $\sim p \& \sim q$, $\sim p \& q$, $p \& \sim q$, and $p \& q$. By comparing them we "read off" that *a* destroys the first state and lets the second vanish (thanks to the activity of *b*), and that *b* destroys the second state and lets the first vanish (thanks to the activity of *a*). If we replace the second state-description above by "$\sim p \& q$," then the comparison would tell us that *a* destroys the first state and *prevents b* from destroying the second, and that *b* lets the first state vanish (thanks to the activity of *a*) and lets the second state remain (because prevented by *a* from destroying it).

12. I shall here discuss only the *fragment* of the logic of action which is a theory of biographies (lives) *of one agent*. Such a biography, it will be remembered, is a symbolic expression of the form $-T((-I-)T((-I-)T \ldots .)) \ldots$ where the blanks are filled by state-descriptions in terms of the same set of variables $p_1, \ldots, p_n$ and the dots indicate a finite number of repetitions of the pattern $((-I-)T$ and an equal number of closing brackets. The biography describes a succession of stages through which the world passes. But it also describes the agent's actions (and omissions) since it tells us, too, how the world would have been but for him. A biography of one agent is compatible with the existence of other agents in the world. But the contributions of those other agents appear, in the biography, merely as *changes* (and not-changes) "in nature." We cannot tell which *actions* those other agents performed. For, we are not told what would have happened but for those agents. Since other agents do not appear in the biographies *as agents*, we can also characterize the case which we are now considering as the case of an agent *"alone with nature."*

13. I now introduce a new ingredient into our theory. It is a modal operator '*M*', to be read "it is possible that." An expression consisting of '*M*' followed by an action-description or a biography says that a certain action or life *is possible*.

For example: $M(p \ \& \ qT(p \ \& \ \sim qI \sim p \ \& \ q))$ says that it is possible that a certain agent on a certain occasion prevents the state p from vanishing but destroys the state q.

The possibility of a certain action or life may be said to depend on two factors. It depends first of all upon the agent's *ability*, upon what he *can do* in the various action-situations. But it also depends upon which action-situations are possible in nature, upon the opportunities for action which nature will "allow." We can speak of this factor as *determinism*.

In our above example: The possibility that $p \ \& \ qT(p \ \& \ \sim qI \sim p \ \& \ q)$ requires, not only that the agent *can* prevent the one state from vanishing and destroy the other, but also that nature may provide him with an opportunity of exercising his ability, *i.e.*, that it is possible that the two states obtain and that the first one would vanish and the second one remain, if it were not for the agent.

Of the logical laws governing the modal operator we shall here only assume that they are (at least as strong as) those of the modal system M (of von Wright) or T (of Feys).

14. Let 't' be short for the disjunction of all state-descriptions $s_1, \ldots,$ s_{2n}. And let us assume that $M(s_i T(tIs_j))$. This means: we assume that the acting-situation, which is determined by the two total states of the world in question, is possible.

Consider now the function "$M(s_i T(-Is_j))$." We divide the class of 2_n state-descriptions in two sub-classes. The first consists of those state-descriptions which satisfy the function, *i.e.*, which turn it into a (sentence expressing a) true proposition when inserted in the argument-place. The second consists of those state-descriptions which dissatisfy the function. The assumption that $M(s_i T(tIs_j))$ warrants that the first class is not empty.

This partitioning of the class of state-descriptions pictures the agent's ability in the acting-situation under consideration. It tells us exactly what he can and what he cannot do, more specifically: which courses of action he can and which he cannot choose, in this situation.

An acting-situation is a limiting case of a life-situation. (Cf. Sect. 10.) We can apply the above procedure of dividing the class of state-descriptions in two sub-classes to all situations which may arise in the course of a life (of finite length m). In this way we get a complete inventory of all courses of action which are in the agent's power at the various possible stages on his life's journey. In general, his possibilities of action at each stage will be different, depending upon how he has acted in the past, *i.e.*, depending upon the life he has behind himself at that stage.

We can picture the possibilities in the form of a topological tree ("life-tree") as follows:

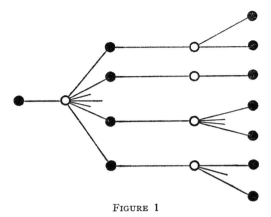

FIGURE 1

Life-tree in a deterministic universe.

Let a filled circle represent the total state of the agent's world when he, so to speak, embarks upon his life's journey. From it a line goes to an empty circle representing the total state in which the world would be next, if it were not for the agent. From the empty circle lines lead to as many filled circles as there are total states to which the agent can take the world (and/or let it change). (Each triple consisting of the first filled circle, the empty circle, and one of these last filled circles represents a course of action which is open to the agent.) From every one of the filled circles the tree continues to one empty circle representing the next total state which the world would assume, if it were not for the agent. From the empty circles there are again lines to one or several filled circles picturing the agent's abilities in the new acting-situation. And so forth.

15. Two limiting cases of the partitioning of the class of state-descriptions call for special attention.

One is when *all* state-descriptions satisfy the function. In this case the agent can take the world to any total state he may want it to be in, "steer the course of nature" completely according to his own wishes. When the maximum number (2^n) of courses of action are open to an agent, we could call him *omnipotent*.

Example: Let the function be "$M(p \mathbin{\&} qT(\text{-}Ip \mathbin{\&} \sim q))$," and the satisfying state-descriptions "$p \mathbin{\&} q$," "$p \mathbin{\&} \sim q$," "$\sim p \mathbin{\&} q$," and "$\sim p \mathbin{\&} \sim q$." In this situation the agent can either let the first state continue and prevent the second from vanishing *or* let the first state continue and the second vanish *or* destroy the first state and prevent the second from vanishing *or* destroy the first state and let the second vanish.—Note that if he chooses the second course he "does" nothing, but simply leaves nature free to take its own course independently of him.

The second extreme case occurs, when only *one* state-description satisfies the function. In this case the agent has no choice. He is *impotent* or *powerless*. If one takes the view that the possibility of choice is essential to action (and omission) one would have to refuse the name of a "course of *action*" to that which happens on such an occasion.

Impotence can be of two kinds. The one is, when the only state-description which satisfies "$M(s_i T(-Is_j))$" is the state-description s_j itself. This means that the intentions of the agent make no difference to what happens. The agent is there, but he is doomed to be completely passive. He can do nothing to produce a change which actually does not take place or to prevent a change which independently of him happens. We may call this case (forced) *passivity*.

The other kind of impotence occurs when the satisfying state-description is different from 's_j'. Then the intentions of the agent make a difference to what happens in the world, but this difference is not a result of the choice of the agent. The agent has no choice, and yet he does something to produce or prevent a change. This case I shall classify as *compulsion* ("forced action").

Let the number of state-descriptions which satisfy the function be μ. ($1 < \mu < 2^n$.) One can regard the fraction $\dfrac{\mu - 1}{2^n - 1}$ as a measure of the *degree of freedom* of the agent in the acting-situation determined by s_i and s_j. For $\mu = 2^n$ this measure equals 1 (= omnipotence). For $\mu = 1$ it is 0 (= impotence).

16. Assume that 'p_k' occurs either in *all* the μ state-descriptions which satisfy the function "$M(s_i T(-Is_j))$" or in *no one* of them (*i.e.*, "$\sim p_k$" occurs in all). Then the state p_k is (completely) *out of control* of the agent. His choice of a course of action will not affect the course of nature with regard to this state. An elementary state will be said to be *within the control* of the agent (in a given acting-situation), when it is not (completely) out of the agent's control.

Given the state-descriptions which satisfy the function "$M(s_i T(-Is_j))$" we can thus divide the class of elementary states, of which the total states of the world are "composed," in two sub-classes. The one consists of those elementary states which are within the control of the agent, and the other of those which are out of his control.

If again we take the view that possibility of choice is essential to action and omission, we should have to describe the various *courses of action* which are open to an agent in a given acting-situation in terms only of those elementary states which are within his control. Let the number of these elementary states be ν ($\nu < n$). It is easy to see that the maximum value of μ is 2^ν. When μ attains its maximum, we shall say that the agent has *complete* control of the elementary states (in his control). He can then produce or suppress these states, let them be or let them change in every combination which the action-situation allows. When μ is less than the maximum, some *combinations* of acts and omissions with regard to the ν elementary states are beyond the agent's power, although the ν states *individually* are in his control.

Example: Let the world be "composed" of three elementary states p, q, and r. Let μ be 3, and let the total states in question be $p \ \& \sim q \ \& \ r$, $\sim p \ \& \ q \ \& \ r$, and $\sim p \ \& \sim q \ \& \ r$. Then the state r is out of control of the agent. p and q are within his control. ν thus has the value 2. 2^ν now equals 4. $4 > 3$. This inequality reflects the fact that p and q, although within the control of the agent, are *not completely* in his control. He can see to it that one of the states is present and the other absent, or that both are absent. But he cannot act in such a way that they are both present.

The division of total states of the world into a part over which the agent has no control at all and another over which he has a higher or lower degree of control is of importance to the study of the notion of consequences of action. We shall not, however, embark upon this study here.

17. We have so far assumed that, at any given moment of a history (life), there is one, and one only, total state of the world which would be true of the next moment, if it were not for the (presence of the) agent. This means that we assume that the course of the world (nature), disregarding possible interferences on the part of a certain agent, is *strictly determined*.

This assumption, however, may become challenged. The question may be raised, whether *ontically* the course of the world is strictly determined. Some may wish to defend an affirmative answer. This aspect of the question of determinism need not concern us here. Nobody would deny, however, that there is a lesser or higher degree of "*epistemic* indeterminism" in the world, *i.e.* that the course of events cannot always be uniquely *foretold* (foreseen) from any given moment to the next. Sometimes, maybe, we can foresee exactly what will happen, if we do not interfere with the world (act). But sometimes we have to count with several alternative developments, independently of *our* action. In the second case our possibilities of action too will, in general, be different depending upon which of the alternative courses the world independently of us would take. It is feasible to think that the more remote from the *present* moment the acting-situation is, which we are contemplating, the more uncertainty will there be (for us) as to the independent course of the world in this future situation.

18. Let 't' again be short for the disjunction of all state-descriptions. We assume that Ms_i, *i.e.*, we assume that it is possible that the world now is in a certain total state. By the laws of the TI-calculus, "Ms_i" is equivalent with "$M(s_i T(tIt))$."

Consider now the function "$M(s_i T(tI\text{-}))$." We use this function for a partitioning of the class of state-descriptions into those which satisfy and those which do not satisfy the function. Our assumption that $M(s_i T(tIt))$ warrants that there is at least one satisfying state-description.

That a state-description, say 's_j', satisfies the function means that it is possible that there is an acting-situation which is determined by the pair of state-descriptions 's_i', 's_j'. That two state-descriptions, 's_j' and 's_k', satisfy the function means that it is possible that the total state of the world s_i *would*, if it were not for the agent, change to the total state s_j, but also possible that it *would*, if it were not for the agent, change to s_k. The phrase "it is possible that" can be understood in several different ways. *One* way of understanding it is as an expression of "epistemic indeterminism." Then it means that we cannot tell exactly how the world would change independently of the agent, and, therefore, have to count with several alternatives. This, incidentally, is a very common and perfectly natural use of the phrase "it is possible that."

If only *one* state-description satisfies the function "$M(s_i T(tI\text{-}))$," I shall say that the course of the world (nature) is *determined* relative to the initial state s_i. Instead of the phrase "relative to the initial state s_i," it is sometimes convenient to use the expression "in the point s_i."

If *all* 2^n state-descriptions satisfy the function, I shall say that the course of the world (nature) is *completely indetermined* in the point s_i.

Let μ be the number of state-descriptions which satisfy the function. The fraction $\dfrac{\mu - 1}{2^n - 1}$ we could call a measure of the degree of freedom (or indeterminism) of the world. For $\mu = 1$ this degree is 0. This means (rigid) determinism. For $\mu = 2^n$ this degree is 1. This means complete indeterminism.

19. We can apply the above procedure for obtaining a partitioning of the class of state-descriptions to any function of the general form "$M(l_i T(tI\text{-}))$," where "l_i" is the biography of a possible life of some length m (of the agent under consideration). In this way we obtain a complete inventory of the degree to which the course of the world is determined (and indetermined) at each stage in every possible life of the agent.

The topological tree of possible lives ("life-tree") can be embellished so that it pictures, beside the alternative courses of action open to the agent in every acting-situation, also the alternative acting-situations which may arise, independently of the agent, at every stage of his life's journey. To indicate that we have to count with several possible acting-situations on a given occasion, we connect the filled circle representing the state of the world on that occasion with several empty circles. The life-tree now has the following shape:

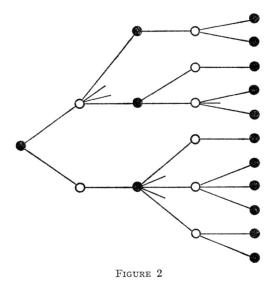

FIGURE 2

Life-tree in an indeterministic universe.

When a filled circle is connected with only one empty circle to its immediate right, this indicates that the course of the world, at that point, is completely determined. When an empty circle is connected with only one filled circle to its immediate right, this indicates that the agent has no freedom of choice but has to act under constraint or is doomed to passivity.

20. The notion of ability or *can do* with which we have so far been dealing signifies ability so to say in its "naked form," subject only to the restrictions imposed by the laws of nature (including the limits of man's innate capabilities of growth and learning). Within this broad concept of ability (*can do*) one can distinguish a narrower concept. When, in this narrower sense, we say of an agent that he *can do* or that *it is possible* for him to do a certain thing, we mean that his doing of this thing will not violate a set of rules (norms) or conditions such as, for example, the rules of a certain legal order or moral code. This is a common and natural use of the expressions "can do" and "it is possible to do." Very often, when we raise the question: *can* we do this? what we are asking is: does the law, or our conscience, or the moral code of our society *permit* this? When the answer is that we *cannot* do this, that it is impossible to do it, what is meant is often that the law, or our conscience, or the moral code *forbids it*.

The concept of possibility within the limits of natural law (including the laws of "human nature") we have denoted by 'M'. The concept of possibility within the limits of a normative order we shall denote by 'P'. It seems plausible to regard 'P' as the narrower concept in the sense that the

133

expression "$P(—)$" entails the expression "$M(—)$," when the blanks in both expressions are filled by the same description of an action or a life. To accept this relation between 'P' and 'M' is tantamount to accepting a (rather strong) version of the well-known principle which is usually formulated in the words "ought implies can."

We shall assume that the logical laws which govern 'P' are the same as those which govern 'M' with *one* important exception. This exception is that the *ab-esse-ad-posse-* principle, which holds for 'M', does not hold for 'P'. That an agent does a certain act or lives a certain life is proof that he *can do* this without "breaking" the laws of nature. But it is no proof that he can do this without violating a normative order.

The logical study of the permissibility of actions (and lives) from the point of view of a normative order is also called *deontic logic*. Deontic logic originated as an offshoot of modal propositional logic. Its proper place seems to me to be within the frame of a (modal) Logic of Action.

21. In its original form, deontic logic was a formal system which can be sketchily described as follows:

The vocabulary of the system is that of PL enriched with the symbol 'P'. Its well-formed formulas (P-expressions) are expressions of PL preceded by 'P' and truth-functional compounds of such expressions. Its specific axioms (in addition to the axioms of PL) are:

> *A*1. $Pp \lor P{\sim}p$.
>
> *A*2. $P(p \lor q) \leftrightarrow Pp \lor Pq$.

The inference rules are those of substitution, detachment, and extensionality (*i.e.*, interchangeability of provably equivalent PL-expressions in the P-expressions).

The question of interpreting (understanding the meaning of) P-expressions caused trouble from the beginning. The correct reading of "Pp" is "it is permitted that p," where 'p' represents an arbitrary state of affairs. But this is an uncommon and unnatural form of expression which stands in need of further explication. One way of explicating it is to say that it means "it is permitted to act in such a way that the state of affairs that p comes about as a result of action." For this expression I propose the following "formalization" in the logic of action: "$P(tT(pIt)$" where 't' is short for the tautology "$p \lor {\sim}p$" (or any other tautology of PL). The permission, thus "formalized," specifies only the *result* of the permitted action but not the acting-situation. The permitted *action* will be different, depending upon the nature of the acting-situation. If p is and would remain but for the agent, the permitted action is to let p continue. If p is but would vanish, if it were not for the agent, the permitted action is to prevent p from vanishing. If p is not but would originate, if it were not for the agent, the permitted action is to let p come about. And if p is not and would not come to be but for the agent, the permission is to let p remain absent. The formula "Pp" of the "old system" of deontic logic may thus be said to contain in a concealed form no less than four different types of permission.

A permission which specifies only the result of action and leaves the action-situation (entirely) unspecified I shall call *unconditional* or *absolute*. Deontic logic in its original form thus is a logic of unconditional permission (prohibition and obligation).

When translated into the language of our logic of action, $A1$ above becomes a principle to the effect that at least one of the eight elementary modes of action is (necessarily) permitted. $A2$ says that a permission to act in such a manner that one or the other of two states results from the action is equivalent to a permission to act in one of the various possible ways (modes of action) which result in one or the other of these two states. Both principles are valid in our logic of action, if we accept the view of the laws governing 'P' and 'M', which we mentioned in sect. 20.

It is convenient to call a permission (prohibition, obligation) *conditional* (or *hypothetical*) if it specifies (partly or wholly), not only the result of the permitted action, but also the (acting-)situation in which we are permitted to produce this result. For example: "$P(p \ \& \ qT(\sim pIp))$" expresses a permission to destroy the state of affairs p if it obtains together with the state of affairs q.

Within the (deontic) logic of action, the theory of absolute permissions (prohibitions, obligations) becomes a limiting case of a general theory of permissions (prohibitions, obligations). There are no special axioms which are distinguishing of absolute or of hypothetical permissions.

Permissions of elementary actions or of courses of action may be regarded as limiting cases of permissions of such sequences of actions and courses of action which we call *lives*. In its most general form deontic logic is a theory of *possible lives* (ways of living) under a normative order. This possibility of generalizing deontic logic adds, in my opinion, considerably to its philosophic interest.

22. Deontic logic is the logical study of acts from the point of view of their permissibility. By prohairetic logic we shall understand the logical study of acts from the point of view of their preferability. Prohairetic logic is the core of a general logic of value concepts.

It is a useful approach to prohairetic logic to view it as another extension of the logic of action (and lives). Consider the picture of a life-tree in sect. 19. The filled circles, to which there is a connection from a given empty circle, may become assessed from the point of view of their preferability or degree of "betterness" (to the agent himself, but also to other subjects). The empty circles again, indicating the possible courses of an indeterminate nature, may be considered from the point of view of their probability.

These two points of view may then be combined for purposes of ranking in order of preferability the various sequences of choices of a course of action which make up a life.

Assume that the probabilities could be evaluated numerically. The sum of the probabilities, associated with the empty circles to which there is a connection from a given filled circle, is 1. (It is certain that the world will continue *somehow*, although we do not know exactly *how*.) The *product* of the probabilities which lie on the same branch of the tree I shall call the *realizability-measure* (R) of the corresponding life. It is the probability that the agent will actually be able to live this life, if he consistently (*i.e.*, in every acting-situation when there is an opportunity) follows its path. In the case of strict determinism (from one acting-situation to the next), the realizability-measure is 1.

Assume that the preferabilities too could be evaluated numerically. By the *total value* (V) of a life I shall understand the sum of the preferability-values associated with the filled circles on the branch of the tree which is a picture of this life.

By a *life-plan* ("way of living") we shall mean any directive (or sequence of directives) for the choice of a course of action at each of the successive stages which together make up a whole life. An example would be the rule always to choose the (a) course which ranks best among the possible courses of action which are within the agent's ability in the various acting-situations. (It is by no means certain that by following this directive the agent will harvest a life of maximum total value.) Given the realizability-measure and total value of each life on the tree it is possible to calculate the *expected value* of any given life-plan. This value is the sum of the products $R \times V$, for all lives which conform to the life-plan under consideration.

The value-theoretic problems which here emerge within the logic of action are closely related to problems in game theory and decision theory. I do not think that the logic of action, as such, provides a useful instrument for dealing with problems in game or decision theory. It is rather the case that methods which have been developed within the theories of games and decisions may be fruitfully applied to the theory of action. And the conceptual connections which are seen to exist between these various fields of study are interesting in themselves.

The logic of action, when enriched with the notions of permission and preference (and concepts definable in their terms), seems to me ideally suited as a frame for restating and treating ideas and problems connected with utilitarian ethics. Reformulating the utilitarian ideas within the logic of action will help us to a clearer insight into the meaning of the various brands of utilitarianism which there are. The preliminary task of making clear their meaning must be accomplished if we are ever to be in a position finally to assess their plausibility or truth.

136

A. COMMENTS ON VON WRIGHT'S "THE LOGIC OF ACTION"

RODERICK M. CHISHOLM

I SHALL restrict myself to two general criticisms and to one observation about the kind of work that is yet to be done if we are to build upon the foundations that Professor von Wright has laid. I feel, as I am sure the rest of you do, that his paper is a philosophical contribution of first importance and that it is not necessary to comment upon each of the many valuable things that are to be found in it.

1. My first critical comments pertain to what von Wright says about the counterfactual element involved in action. He says: "When we say, e.g., that an agent opened a window, we imply that, had it not been for the agent's interference, the window would, on that occasion, have remained closed." Suppose that, unknown to the agent, there is an automatic device set to open the window on that particular occasion; and suppose further that the agent, as he reaches toward the window, inadvertently turns off this device and at the same time opens the window himself. On this occasion, the agent opened the window, but it is not true that, without his interference, the window would have remained closed. I suggest, therefore, that von Wright's statement be modified in this way:

"When we say, e.g., that an agent opened a window, we imply that there is an event p such that (1) had it not been for the agent's interference p would not have occurred and (2) p is a sufficient causal condition for the window's being open." We could say that p is a sufficient causal condition for q provided (a) p occurs but not later than q and (b) it is a law of nature that if p occurs then q occurs.

In his book *Norm and Action* (London, 1963, pp. 44–45), von Wright considered the possibility "that two persons at the same time shoot a third, and that each shot individually would have killed him." He there said, correctly it seems to me, that we should say of the two agents that "*both* did it, not 'jointly,' but 'individually'." Yet we cannot say of either agent, individually, that without *his* interference the victim would have continued living. The modified formula that I have just proposed, however, does apply to each agent individually. (The first assassin, say, shot the victim through the stomach and the second shot him through the heart; it is a law of nature that if a man is shot through the stomach, in the way in which this victim was shot, then he will die, and similarly for being shot through the heart.)

I think that what von Wright says in his lecture about the interaction of two agents also requires supplementation in this way, for as it stands it does not seem to me to be correct. He envisages two interacting agents, a and b, such that: (1) p & q is the initial state of the world on the occasion of their interaction; (2) $\sim p$ & $\sim q$ is the end state resulting from their interaction; (3) $\sim p$ & q is the end state which would have obtained had a been alone in the world; (4) p & $\sim q$ is the end state which would have obtained had b been alone; and (5) p & q is the end state which would have obtained had neither a nor b been in the world. von Wright says we may infer from this situation that it was a, and not b, who destroyed the first state p, and that it was b, and not a, who destroyed the second state q. Suppose, however, that p is the state of it not being the case that a has a haircut and q that of it not being the case that b has a haircut, and that a and b are two barbers each of whom allows his hair to be cut by the other but would do it himself if he were alone. In this case, von Wright's five formulae could be satisfied in the way that he describes but with the roles of the agents reversed.

2. My second critical comment is of a rather different sort. von Wright says that the proper place for deontic logic is "within the frame of a (modal) logic of action." I think that this is true, but I find a kind of inconsistency in von Wright's attitudes on this point, for he seems to view deontic logic psychologistically and modal logic non-psychologistically. A psychologistic interpretation of modal logic would be one that interpreted "Np" as, say, "I believe very strongly that p," or "The scientists of our culture circle are firmly wedded to the hypothesis that p," or "The hypothesis that p is the one that will never be revised, no matter what." On such an interpretation of modal logic, there is, of course, no guarantee that the usual axioms for the modal operator 'N' will be true.

A psychologistic interpretation of deontic logic, similarly, would interpret "Pp" as "p is permitted" thus implying that p is permitted *by* someone or other, or by the laws, or by the state. But here, too, there is no guarantee that the usual axioms will be true. If deontic logic is concerned with "man-made law", as von Wright suggests, we have no guarantee that the law will not be such as to forbid p and also to forbid not-p, or that it will not be such as to permit p v q while forbidding p and forbidding q. But if we read "Pp" non-psychologistically as "It is not morally (or ethically) wrong that p," then presumably von Wright's axioms for deontic logic will be true. (Similar remarks apply, *mutatis mutandis*, to prohairetic logic. If for example, "pPq" means that someone prefers p to q then we cannot be sure that 'P' designates a transitive relation, but if it means that p is preferable to q, or better than q, then we can.)

3. von Wright says that "to act is to bring about . . . a change in the world" (for simplicity I omit preventive action and forbearance). A complete logic of action would make this formula more specific in two ways. (1) Bringing about a change in the world is always a matter of bringing about a change in some *thing x*, or some collection of things x. Hence "He brings it about that p" will always imply a statement of the form "There is an x such that he brings it about that x is F." And (2) to act is always to *endeavor*

to bring it about that there is some change (again, for simplicity, I omit preventive action and forbearance). The changes that a man *does* bring about need not be those that he endeavors to bring about.

To accommodate these two features of action, we might be tempted to take as our basic action formula "There is an x such that he endeavors to bring it about that x is F." But this will not guarantee us that, on those occasions when a man acts but does not succeed in what he is endeavoring to do, there is all the same *some* change that he brings about. The simplest adequate basic locution would seem to be "He makes it happen that x is F (and does so) in the endeavor to make it happen that y is G" which could by symbolized as: "$M(Fx),Gy$." Quantifiers could be inserted in the following ways:

$$(\exists x) (\exists y) [M(Fx),Gy]$$
$$(\exists y) [M(\exists x) (Fx),Gy]$$
$$(\exists x)M(Fx),(\exists y) (Gy)$$
$$M(\exists x) (Fx),(\exists y) (Gy).$$

With this device, I think, we might be able to throw light on some of the intentional questions that Professor von Wright has not yet taken up.

B. COMMENTS ON VON WRIGHT'S "THE LOGIC OF ACTION"

John Robison

My comments on Professor von Wright's paper will not be of a general or programatic sort. Suffice it to say that the project of investigating what might be termed "the logical features of action" is one which I fully endorse and I look forward to seeing the further results of von Wright's studies in this connection. What I propose to do here is to offer some comments, hopefully helpful, on a few particular passages, with respect to their philosophical interest and importance, for the development of a logic of action and a logic of change.

1. Von Wright says, correctly I think, that a fully developed logic of action requires a logic of change, where change is construed as a transformation of states. In this connection, it is useful to note that the sense of "change" here characterized by von Wright is very broad, for as he says "It is convenient . . . to use the word 'change' so that it includes also non-changes, *i.e.*, immediate progressions in time with the same initial and end-state." Given this sense of "change" and the four special axioms governing the logic of change, we have the result that to say the world is not now being overrun by unicorns and next is not being plagued by centaurs is to give a true account, partial though it may be, of how the world is changing. I think it will be agreed that this is a wider than usual sense of "change" and one might raise the question of why and how such an extended sense is useful or required for a logic of change which is to underlie a logic of action.

2. Von Wright indicates that the present study is concerned with states of affairs as conceived of in a generic, as opposed to an individual, sense. I must confess that I am not fully clear on the nature of this distinction between states of affairs conceived of generically and individually. We are told that "An individual state is, so to speak, a generic state instantiated ('incarnated') on a certain occasion in space and time." As an example of an individual state we have "that the sun is shining in Pittsburgh on 18 March 1966 at 10 A.M." and as an example of a generic state we have "that the sun is shining." Now, when we assume that "the total state of the world on a given occasion can be completely described by indicating for every one of a finite number n of (generic) states $p_1, \ldots, p_n$ whether it obtains or does not obtain on that occasion" are we allowing that such a state description may include both p and $\sim p$? Simply with respect to whether or not the sun is shining (a generic state), it would seem that a complete world description might include both "the sun is shining" and "the sun is not shining." My suspicion is that what is to count as the reference of "the total state of the world on a given occasion" will somehow

bar such state descriptions as might include both p and $\sim p$, but I am not clear just how this will come about without resorting to individuating these generic states, thereby conceiving of them in an individual sense.

3. Professor von Wright suggests that if we assume (1) that there is one agent in our world, (2) that of this world it is first true that p and then that $\sim p$, and (3) that had this agent not interfered with the world, this change would not have taken place, then we can conclude that this agent brought about the change. What seems lacking here is some specification of the respect in which the agent interfered with the world, where this interference is somehow productive of the change in question and not merely an accompaniment of the change. Otherwise, this would seem to be inadequate as a sufficient basis for attributing acts to specific agents, in that it would not in general distinguish between acting and being acted upon or between acting and simply being present. Of course, considerable care must be taken in spelling out the appropriate conditions of interference, lest the explication of that notion reduce the claim in effect to something like: if the agent present in the world somehow effected the change from p to $\sim p$, then we can conclude that the agent brought about that change.

For example, suppose that the world is in state S and that there is an agent in the world. Then it will be true that the world is "(S while x φ's)." Now, assume that the world changes to "$\sim (S$ while x φ's)." While this change could not have occurred had not x interfered with the world by φ-ing, we could not conclude in general that the agent brought about the change. From the fact that the world changes from being populated by elephants while Jones wades in the river to it is not the case that the world is populated by elephants while Jones wades in the river would not normally enable us to conclude anything about what Jones brought about, even though it is true that the world could not have so changed had not Jones been wading in the river. This change, after all, could have been brought about by any number of things other than Jones, such as the extinction of the world, or the extinction of the world's elephants, of the extinction of Jones, or even the sudden drying up of the river. Again, Jones's being killed by a bolt of lightning is part of a change in the world which requires that Jones be an active part of the world, but it would not be the sort of thing that we would normally count as something brought about by Jones.

Similar comments apply to "p & $\sim q$ T ($\sim p$ & q I $\sim p$ & $\sim q$)" as describing "the course of action which an agent chooses when he *lets* one of two states *vanish* and *produces* the other." For example, "It is now raining but not snowing on John and next it is not raining but is snowing on John instead of neither raining nor snowing on John" would not normally be taken as telling us anything about what John chose or about what he did.

4. So much for the thesis that from the three assumptions indicated we can conclude what an agent brought about. A related, but weaker, claim

also seems not to characterize sufficiently the acting situation. This claim is to the effect that to say an agent brought about a change implies the third of the above assumptions, viz., that had the agent not interfered with the world the change would not have occurred. This involves what von Wright calls the "counterfactual element" in action. He says, "When we say, e.g., that an agent opened a window, we imply that, had it not been for the agent's interference, the window would, on that occasion, have remained closed. When we say that an agent prevented a door from closing, we thereby intimate that 'otherwise' (i.e., had it not been for the agent) the door would have closed on that occasion." This seems too strong. Imagine that the doorbell rings, setting off a furious scramble by three children to open the door. They race to the door, each striving to be the first there and admit the visitor. Suppose Robert wins the race by a mere fraction of a second and opens the door. Surely, we should then say that Robert opened the door, even though it is false that had it not been for the agent's interference the door on that occasion would have remained closed, for there is every reason to suppose that one or the other of the two remaining children would have taken great pleasure in opening the door.

5. With respect to the interaction of agents, von Wright considers the case when we are given that there are two agents, a and b, and that the world in fact changes from p & q to $\sim p$ & $\sim q$, whereas $\sim p$ & q would have obtained as the end state had a been alone, p & $\sim q$ would have obtained as the end state had b been alone, and p & q would have obtained as the end state had neither agent been in the world. From this, we may say that "a destroys the first state and lets the second state vanish (thanks to the activity of b) and that b destroys the second state and lets the first vanish (thanks to the activity of a). If we replace the second state description above by '$\sim p$ & q', then the comparison would tell us that a destroys the first state and *prevents* b from destroying the second, and that b lets the first state vanish (thanks to the activity of a) and lets the second state remain (because prevented by a from destroying it)." Now suppose that a is a farmer in Iowa, b is a king of France, and neither has any knowledge of or contact with the other. Then, for appropriate values of p and q, the above schema could be satisfied, but it would seem strange to suppose that the Iowa farmer let the French situation change or that the French king let the Iowa situation change or that either prevented the other from doing something.

6. One final point. Von Wright proposes to read "$P(p$ & q T $(\sim pIp))$" as a conditional permission to destroy the state of affairs p if it obtains together with the state of affairs q. A question which might now be raised is whether or not such a statement is to be taken as implying "$P(p$ & q & r T $(\sim pIp))$." This question has already received attention in the literature and so I shall only offer the comment here that such an implication

142

might well be considered unacceptable as a partial characterization of the ordinary senses of conditional permission. There are many acts which are conditionally permitted, but rarely, if ever, is the statement of conditions so complete as to provide a fully sufficient set of conditions for that act's being permitted.

C. REPLY TO COMMENTS

GEORG HENRIK VON WRIGHT

A. *Reply to Professor Chisholm's Comments*

I SAID in my paper that if a state of affairs p is a result of action, then p would not have been there, on the occasion in question, had it not been for the intentions of the agent. Professor Chisholm now considers a case, when the agent's interference with the world makes inoperative a cause of p which *would* have been operative had he *not* interfered. Chisholm seems to think that this case constitutes a genuine counterexample to my attempted formulation of the counterfactual element involved in an action, and he helpfully suggests a new formulation. I find the case described by Chisholm very interesting and very puzzling. But I am not sure that it constitutes a counterexample to my original position. Chisholm's example, it seems to me, tacitly presupposes *two* successive occasions for doing something. Must we not say that the agent in Chisholm's example *first* (inadvertently) turned off the device set to open the window, and *then* opened the window himself? It seems to me that unless we allow for this temporal succession between what the agent does inadvertently and what he does intentionally, we cannot say truly that the device was turned off and therefore not operative *on the occasion* when the action took place. Or am I mistaken?

The conclusion which Chisholm draws from the example of the two barbers is, I think, not entirely correct. The conclusion which can become extracted from a comparison of the five state-descriptions is that a has *his* hair cut and that b has *his* hair cut. These actions ("having one's hair cut") we impute to the agents on the basis of the comparison. Whether the two barbers cut their hair themselves or let the other barber do this, cannot be concluded from inspecting the state-descriptions in question. But this is due to the poverty of the descriptions which we feed into the calculus – and not to a shortcoming of the calculus itself.

Concerning Chisholm's second comment – I do not want to view deontic (and prohairetic) logic *exclusively* in what Chisholm calls the "psychologistic" way, although some less happy formulations of my thoughts may have suggested this. But I would wish to *include* this view too in my conception of deontic (and prohairetic) logic. I would, in other words, claim that the principles of deontic logic are valid also for a man-made law (normative order). A lawgiver, who prohibits both of two contradictory modes of action to one and the same subject on one and the same occasion, contradicts himself, I would maintain, in much the same way as a man does, who affirms at once both p and not-p. And I would say the same of a person, who on one and the same occasion professes to prefer, *intrinsically*, p to q and q to r and yet not to prefer p to r. What this person professes are not ("real") *preferences* – and what the self-contradicting lawgiver issues are not ("real") *prohibitions*. This, admittedly, is a linguistic move – we are here legislating about the meaning of "preference" and "prohibition" – but the move seems to me both legitimate and useful.

With Chisholm's constructive suggestions I am in complete agreement. My only worry is that they would complicate the formal calculus considerably. The axioms would have to be revised – and as a consequence the questions of completeness and decidability would assume a new aspect.

B. *Reply to Professor Robison's Comments*

1. I do not think that there is a genuine disagreement between Professor Robison and myself on this point. The issue seems to me to be purely terminological. I agree that it is, not only unnatural, but also illogical to call a not-change a "change." But when changes are being treated as ordered pairs of states of affairs, it is convenient to include in the treatment, as a limiting case, pairs in which the first and the second member are the same state.

2. I agree with Robison that the distinction between generic and individual states of affairs is problematic. An individual state is spatio-temporally fully specified. A generic state can be generic in the spatial and individual in the temporal component; or *vice versa*; or it can be generic in both components. A description of the total state of the world must, of course, not contain both p and not-p. Therefore, if we let "the world" embrace the whole of space, any generic state of affairs p, the presence or absence of which may be a characteristic of the world, must be individualized in the spatial component. p could then be, e.g., the state that *it is raining in Pittsburgh*. If, on the other hand, we confine "the world" to a specified location ("point") in space, the states of affairs which characterize it need not be individualized in either component. p could now be, e.g., the state that *it is raining*.

3. There are two ways in which one can handle, within the framework of my logic of action, the case of the children who are anxious to let the visitor in. The first is to subdivide the occasion in question. Then the occasion, when Robert opens the door, is being regarded as a different occasion from the one when the second in the race reaches the goal. This seems to me a perfectly legitimate move. But one can also let the occasion remain temporally undivided and view the case as an action of multiple agents – on the pattern suggested in sect. 11 of my paper. Then we should say that Robert opened the door and thereby *prevented* his siblings from doing the

145

same, since his opening of the door destroyed the opportunity for them to open it. But had it not been for Robert, one or the other of his siblings would, on that very occasion, have opened the door.

4. The objection is ingenious. But I think it is satisfactorily met by what I say in sect. 16 about the division of the elementary states in such which are outside the control of the agent and such which are in his control – and about the necessity of redescribing the courses of action in terms of those states only over which the agent has control. The reason, why the farmer in Iowa cannot rightly be said to *let* the King of France do this or that (nor *vice versa*), is that states of affairs in France are, on the whole, out of control of farmers in Iowa (and *vice versa*). This will have to be taken into account in the (re)description of the courses of action of the farmer in Iowa and of the King of France.

5. The answer to Robison's question is as follows: "$P(p \& qT(\sim pIp))$" entails – by virtue of A1 and the Rule of Extensionality and the distributivity of the deontic operator – the *disjunction* "$P(p \& q \& rT(\sim pIp))$ v $P(p \& q \& \sim rT(\sim pIp))$." This is in order. But "$P(p \& qT(\sim pIp))$" does not entail the two disjuncts individually, which would be objectionable.

THE FORMAL ANALYSIS OF NORMATIVE SYSTEMS

ALAN ROSS ANDERSON

PREFACE (1966)

THE ESSAY published below was written in 1955, largely, as is explained in the 1956 preface below, as a result of stimulation by Omar K. Moore. I am also grateful to a host of others, and my indebtedness to G. H. von Wright and A. N. Prior will be evident on every page.

In the course of the years since 1955, I have changed my attitude toward strict "implication" as an analysis of "if . . . then –"; it no longer seems to me to work. For an expression of this view see footnote 1 of Anderson 1962. References here made to, e.g., "Anderson 1962" are to the supplementary bibliography appended to the bibliography of 1955 for the essay below; it contains all relevant items published since 1955 known to me. I should add that I have benefited a great deal from inspection of an unpublished bibliography of writings on deontic logic compiled by Ernest Sosa, and also from the list of "Ouvrages cités" in Kalinowski 1965 and the bibliography of Rescher 1966. I have intended to include in the supplementary list only those works which had a clear bearing on *formal* [mathematical] logic dealing with normative systems – no attempt has been made to consider the literature concerned with more informal aspects of such systems. Myra Nassau was extremely helpful in compiling the supplementary bibliography.

The most promising analysis of implication for the purposes at hand is probably that of the system R of *relevant implication,* which is based on work of Church 1951 (or as an alternative) the system E of *entailment,* based on Ackermann's "strenge Implikation" of 1956. A detailed formal analysis of the differences between the system E of entailment, or the system R of relevant implication, on the one hand, and standard systems of modal logic on the other, can be found in various writings by Belnap and myself; for a reasonably comprehensive bibliography see the works cited in Anderson 1963. But the present essay could not be rewritten from the point of view which I now espouse without totally rewriting the whole thing; and since the 1955 essay has been fair game for criticism (see, e.g., Prior 1958, or Nowell-Smith and Lemmon 1960, or Kalinowski 1965), I have decided to let it stand as it was. The *real* truth of the matter will come later.

University of Pittsburgh   A. R. A.
June 1966

PREFACE (1956)

THE RESULTS contained in this *Report** grew out of small-group investigations currently being conducted by Professor Omar Khayyam Moore. More specifically, the normative structures developed by small groups in the process of solving problems, constitute an important aspect of Professor Moore's experiments. A review of the literature on the logical structure of normative systems convinced us that new analytic tools were urgently required for the description and analysis of these structures. The primary motivation for constructing the logical systems to be discussed here was the hope that they would fulfill this need.

Although it is quite obvious that small groups do develop normative systems, and that formal analysis might well contribute to the understanding of these systems, there seemed to be no compelling reasons to restrict attention to this area of application. It appears that the systems to be described are applicable to any normative systems whatever, within the limits noted in Sect. X. For this reason the results have been presented in the most general way possible, in the hope that they may prove of use to investigators in a variety of behavioral disciplines. The aim of generality has led to the consideration of "normative systems" without restriction to cases of small groups, and since many questions concerning norms have been traditionally placed under the rubric of philosophy, we have felt free to touch on philosophical matters where relevant.

An attempt has also been made to make this *Report* self-contained, in the sense of providing enough background material so a reader unfamiliar with the techniques of symbolic (or mathematical) logic will find the report intelligible. This material is contained in Sect. I; readers acquainted with modern logic might prefer to begin with Sect. II or III.

A word should be said about the anticipated use of the formal systems developed here. An attempt will be made to use these conceptual tools in the interpretation of data drawn from experiments carried on under this contract. It seems reasonable to suppose that such attempted applications will both stimulate further formal research and suggest directions for subsequent empirical investigations.

I should like to express my gratitude to the Philosophy Seminar at Johns Hopkins University, and especially to Professor Victor Lowe, for an opportunity to discuss the fundamental ideas of this *Report* at a meeting in May 1956. To Professor A. N. Prior (of Canterbury University College, Christchurch, N.Z.) I am much indebted for stimulating and suggestive correspondence, and for the opportunity to see a prepublication copy of his

*This paper was first circulated in 1956 as a Technical Report presenting a part of a research program on Problem Solving and Social Interaction sponsored at Yale University by the Office of Naval Research, Group Psychology Branch (Contract No. SAR/Nonr-609(16). Principal Investigator: Omar Khayyam Moore.)

forthcoming *Time and Modality* (Oxford, 1957). To my colleague Professor Moore, whose researches provided the initial impetus leading to the results described below, I am especially grateful. And I owe particular thanks to Ruth Garnand Moore for the care and competence exercised in the preparation of the manuscript.

Yale University   A. R. A.
November 1956

CONTENTS

Section		Page
I.	Preliminaries	151
II.	Deontic Extensions of Alethic Modal Logic	167
III.	Reduction of Deontic Logic to Alethic Modal Logic	174
IV.	The System OM	178
V.	The Deontic Status of Impossible and Necessary Propositions	181
VI.	Commitment	183
VII.	Miscellaneous Theorems	186
VIII.	Iterated Deontic Modalities	189
IX.	Restriction of Deontic Modes to Contingent Propositions	196
X.	Adequacy of the Systems OX	200
	Bibliography	206
	Supplementary Bibliography	210

I. Preliminaries

The purpose of this *Report* is to present a number of new systems of symbolic logic, which are intended (as one of their principal applications) to shed light on the logical structure of *normative systems*, as currently studied by social scientists. These logical systems are proposed as "explications" or "rational reconstructions"[1] of a variety of normative concepts (including *obligation, permission, prohibition*, and *commitment*), in the sense of providing a rigorously defined formalism, intended to reflect in a clear and unambiguous way certain features (presumably the more important features) of the corresponding vague, intuitive ideas of common sense. Such notions as mores, folkways, norms, sanctions, etc., are also amenable to the analysis provided by the systems considered; and it will be contended (see Sect. X) that the propositional content of substantive systems of ethics and positive law can be adequately formalized with the help of logical systems presented here. Notions of "consistency"[2] and "completeness" of sets of norms can also be given a clear explication.

From a purely expository point of view, our main aim is to interest social scientists in the techniques and results of modern symbolic logic, as having a direct and immediate bearing on their own problems. Symbolic logic has been applied in a number of empirical disciplines, including biology, neurology, psychology, anthropology, sociology, economics, descriptive linguistics, computing-machine design, and actuarial statistics.[3] But the surface has barely been scratched, and there are strong reasons to suppose that the conceptual tools of modern logic may be of still more extensive use in the behavioral sciences. The normative concepts mentioned above, for example, are in common and constant use among social scientists, and such light as formal analysis can shed on their logical structure should be of value, if only for conceptual clarification.

In view of the foregoing considerations, the fundamental ideas of the logistic method have been treated at somewhat greater length than would otherwise be necessary. All the formal theorems are "translated" into English, and in the first three sections there are a number of examples showing in detail how formal proofs may be constructed. Checking proofs, and providing proofs omitted, will of course demand familiarity with techniques of modern logic, but an appreciation of the ideas behind the formalism can be gained without a detailed study of the formal proofs.

---

[1] For a discussion of the motivation and techniques of "explication," as here understood, see, e.g., Carnap [24] ch. I and Appendix J, or Hempel [39] ch. I. (Numbers in square brackets refer to entries in the bibliography at the end of this *Report*.)

For a discussion of this point see A. R. Anderson and Moore [13].

[3] For examples of such applications, see Moore and S. B. Anderson [59], [60], and [61], and the numerous references there given; also S. B. Anderson [14], [15], and [16], Fitch and Barry [35] and Galanter [36].

Omission of the more technical portions of this *Report* need not impair an understanding of those ideas for which social scientific interest is claimed (though needless to say, a full understanding of the power and scope of modern logic will not be attained by cursory study).

From a purely formal point of view, the systems discussed here are of transparent simplicity; still, they are not altogether devoid of logical and philosophical interest. For example, formal systems of deontic logic[4] (i.e., the logic of obligation and permission), and the logic of imperatives,[5] have to date been regarded as autonomous, requiring special assumptions of their own, distinct from the axioms of truth-functional or alethic modal systems (i.e., logics of possibility and necessity). In Sect. III it is shown that deontic propositional logic requires no specifically deontic assumptions, but may be regarded simply as a branch of alethic modal logic.

Evidence for the adequacy of the reconstructions, *qua* reconstructions, can at best be merely persuasive, since the intuitive common-sense ideas to be explicated, not being clearly and unambiguously defined, do not admit of rigorous handling. Such evidence as the writer has been able to adduce will be indicated briefly in Sect. X, following the presentation of the formal systems proper. The remainder of this section will consist of an explanation of the formal notation, together with an outline of the logical machinery presupposed in the sections to follow.

Checking formal proofs will require some familiarity with the two-valued truth-functional calculus of propositions,[6] and the elements of alethic modal logic.[7] (These formal systems will be couched here in the parenthesis-free notation of Łukasiewicz,[8] which we have adopted in part for typographical

---

[4] The term "deontic" in this context seems to be due to Mally, who discusses "deontik Logik" in [56], 1926. It was recoined in English by Broad in 1950; see von Wright [79].

[5] For formal systems of deontic logic, see Mally [56], von Wright [79] and [80] ch. V, Prior [69] pp. 220–229 and [71] Appendix D, Feys [31], Kalinowski [45], Becker [18] and Castañeda [25]. For formal systems of imperative logic see Hofstadter and McKinsey [41], Menger [57], and Bohnert [20].

[6] Expositions of this calculus are to be found in any standard elementary textbook on symbolic logic, for example Copi [27] or [28], Lewis and Langford [48], Prior [69] or Quine [72], to mention only a few. The most comprehensive account is given in Church [26]. Prior [69] is especially to be recommended to readers of this *Report*, since it is the only introductory text now in print which makes extensive use of the logistic notation adopted here.

For a formulation which reflects in a particularly perspicuous way the motivating ideas for the two-valued propositional calculus, see Fitch [34] ch. 2 (especially section 10.20). Fitch's formulation in terms of "subordinate proofs" can be shown to be equivalent to the two-valued calculus, and has the additional advantage of providing almost automatically the motivation for the construction of proofs.

[7] The standard source for information on alethic modal logic is Lewis and Langford [48]. An account is also given in Prior [69] (using the notation adopted here). For an alternative, see von Wright [80] (and, for correction of a few errors, the review, A. R. Anderson [1]).

[8] Due originally to Łukasiewicz in 1929 (see [49] p. 78). For other accounts see Prior [69], Church [26], p. 38 and Copi [28], pp. 253–254. A detailed set of instructions for manipulating the parenthesis-free notation will be found in Moore [58].

reasons.) Certain of the fundamental ideas of these systems are sketched below.

I.1. *The two-valued calculus of propositions*

As notation for this calculus we use variables '*p*', '*q*', '*r*', '*s*', ..., understood as ranging over propositions or sentences,[9] and logical constants (or "operators," or "connectives") '*N*', '*K*', '*A*', '*C*', and '*E*'. The grammar of the calculus is specified as follows, where we may for the moment think of a "well-formed formula" as a formula expressing a proposition or sentence.

1. Any variable is a well-formed formula, and
2. if α and β are well-formed formulas, then so are $N\alpha$, $K\alpha\beta$, $A\alpha\beta$, $C\alpha\beta$, and $E\alpha\beta$.[10]

The class of well-formed formulas (abbreviated "wff" and, in the plural, "wffs") is the smallest class satisfying conditions 1 and 2. It follows that, for example, "*CKNpqq*" is a wff. The proof runs in stepwise fashion as follows.

(a) '*p*' is a wff, by clause 1.

(b) "*Np*" is a wff, by (a) and clause 2, choosing α as '*p*'.

(c) '*q*' is a wff, by clause 1.

(d) "*KNpq*" is a wff by (b), (c), and clause 2, choosing α as "*Np*," and β as '*q*'.

(e) "*CKNpqq*" is a wff by (d), (c), and clause 2, taking now α as "*KNpq*," and β, again, as '*q*'.

We interpret wffs as follows:

'*N*' is the negation operator: "*Np*" is called the *negation* or *denial* of '*p*', and may be read "not-*p*" or "it is not the case that *p*". The proposition expressed by "*Np*" is true if and only if the proposition expressed by '*p*' is false.

'*K*' is the conjunction operator: "*Kpq*" is called the *conjunction* of '*p*' and '*q*', and may be read "*p* and *q*." The proposition expressed by "*Kpq*" is true if both '*p*' and '*q*' are true, false if at least one of '*p*' and '*q*' is false (and,

---

[9] In the interest of expository simplicity, we ignore the (otherwise important) distinction frequently made between "sentence" and "proposition," for which see Church [26]. For further remarks on this point see the end of this section.

[10] This clause is to be understood in the following way. Given any well-formed formulas *a* and β (not necessarily distinct), say, for example, '*p*' and '*q*', then the result "*Np*" of writing '*N*' followed by *a* (namely '*p*') is a well-formed formula, and similarly the result "*Kpq*" of writing '*K*' followed by the well-formed formula *a* (namely '*p*') followed by the well-formed formula β (namely '*q*') is a well-formed formula; and so on for '*A*', '*C*', and '*E*'. In defining the class of well-formed formulas, we are defining a class of expressions, and we use familiar conventions concerning quotation marks to refer to expressions: '*p*' is the sixteenth letter of the English alphabet, '*q*' is the seventeenth, etc. Readers unfamiliar with this notation will find considerable help in Moore [58], which contains instructions designed for use with experimental subjects.

consequently, if both are false, since if both are false, at least one is, namely, either one you choose).

'*A*' is the disjunction operator: "*Apq*" is called the *disjunction* or *alternation* of '*p*' and '*q*', and may be read "*p* or *q*" in the sense of "*p* and/or *q*." The proposition expressed by "*Apq*" is true if at least one of '*p*' and '*q*' is true (and, consequently, if both are true), and false if both '*p*' and '*q*' are false.

'*C*' is the *material implication* operator: "*Cpq*" may be read "if *p* then *q*," or "*p* only if *q*." (Also, sometimes read "*p* implies *q*.") "*Cpq*" is true if and only if it is not the case that '*p*' is true and '*q*' is false. (The motivation for reading "*Cpq*" as "if *p* then *q*" is the following. Suppose that '*p*' and "*Cpq*" are both true. Then (1) '*p*' is true, but (2) it is *not* the case that '*p*' is true and '*q*' is false. In these circumstances '*q*' must be true, for if it were false, then by (1) '*p*' would be true and '*q*' false, contradicting (2). Hence from '*p*' and "*Cpq*" we can infer '*q*'; and this feature of the interpreted formal system reflects one important characteristic of "if *p* then *q*": from '*p*' and "if *p* then *q*" (i.e., "*Cpq*") we infer '*q*').

'*E*' is the *material equivalence* operator: "*Epq*" may be read "*p* if and only if *q*." "*Epq*" is true provided "*Cpq*" and "*Cqp*" are both true; i.e., provided '*p*' materially implies '*q*', and '*q*' materially implies '*p*'. Or what comes to the same thing, "*Epq*" is true if '*p*' and '*q*' are both true, or if '*p*' and '*q*' are both false, and "*Epq*" is false otherwise. In still other words, "*Epq*" is true if and only if '*p*' and '*q*' have the same truth-value.[11]

The interpretations suggested above for the five logical constants are only approximate, since the words "not," "and," etc., have a variety of more or less distinct uses in English, but are (with the help of the axioms and principles of inference to be mentioned presently) given precise and unambiguous meanings in the formal calculus.[12]

The foregoing account tells in some detail just which expressions are to be regarded as sentences (wffs) in the formalism of the propositional calculus (and incidentally, something about their intended interpretation as well). Notice that the wffs may be read unambiguously. For example, "*CCpqr*" may be read "if, if *p* then *q*, then *r*," whereas "*CpCqr*" is read "if *p*, then if *q* then *r*." The two expressions do not admit of confusion, since there is only one way of decomposing each into constituent wffs for the purpose of

[11] In the two-valued propositional calculus, *truth* and *falsity* are the two "values" or "truth-values" (hence the name "two-valued"). To say that a proposition or sentence is *true* is equivalent to saying that it has the value (or truth-value) *truth*; to say that it is false is equivalent to saying that it has the value (or truth-value) *falsity*. Thus to say that '*p*' and '*q*' have the same truth-value is to say that they are both true or both false. For a discussion of truth-values see, e.g., Lewis and Langford [48] ch. VII, or Church [26] Introduction.

[12] For a detailed discussion of the interpretations of the truth-functional constants see Strawson [75]. Less detailed discussions of this topic will be found in any of the texts mentioned in footnote 6. Church [26], pp. 15–31 has a general discussion of "functions," as the notion is currently used among mathematicians and logicians, and considers truth functions as a special case.

translation. To consider "*CCpqr*" in more detail, observe that the symbol 'C' (by clause 2 of the definition of wff) must be followed by two wffs if the resulting expression is to be a wff. Hence the initial occurrence of 'C' in "*CCpqr*" must be followed by two wffs. Now "*Cp*" is *not* a wff, since the occurrence of 'C' in "*Cp*" is followed by only one wff. Hence the first of the two wffs which follow the initial occurrence of 'C' in "*CCpqr*" must be "*Cpq*" (which is a wff), and the second must be '*r*' (which is also a wff). Thus the *antecedent* of "*CCpqr*" (i.e., the first wff following the initial occurrence of 'C') must be "*Cpq*," and the *consequent* (the second wff) must be '*r*', and we arrive at the interpretation "if *Cpq* then *r*," or "if, if *p* then *q*, then *r*." A similar argument shows that the only way of decomposing "*CpCqr*" results in the translation "if *p* then *Cqr*," or "if *p*, then if *q* then *r*."

The parenthesis-free notation can be read unambiguously, but in the case of more complicated formulas, it is still sometimes convenient to use parentheses simply to assist the eye in reading. We shall in consequence feel free to use parentheses where it is felt that they may make for easier reading, writing, e.g., "*C(CpCqr)(CCpqCpr)*" instead of "*CCpCqrCCpqCpr*," etc.[13] But parentheses are simply an informal aid, not to be confused with the primitive notation proper. (The reader should be warned that typographical considerations sometimes dictate splitting a long formula between two lines of type. Unless there are explicit indications to the contrary, such expressions should be read as one wff.)

Formulation of a system of symbolic logic requires[14] (a) a specification of the wffs, or sentences,[15] (b) a specification of the axioms (which constitute an initial stock of theorems from which other theorems are deducible), and (c) a specification of the principles of inference (i.e., the principles which

---

[13] In the future we shall omit quotation marks around wffs, since it will always be clear from context whether we are using, e.g.,

$$CKNpqq$$

to refer to the wff "*CKNpqq*", or to the propositions which the symbols are intended to express. For the point of using (and not using) quotation marks in such contexts, see Quine [72], pp. 23–33, or Church [26], pp. 61–63.

[14] The following requirements embody the essential ideas involved in formal logistic theories, but the list is not complete. For a more thorough discussion see Kemeny [46] or Church [26], pp. 47–58.

[15] Strictly speaking, the wffs of the propositional calculus are not "sentences" as that word is usually used, since, e.g., "*Kpq*" does not express any proposition which we are in a position to call true or false. What is meant rather is that the result of substituting meaningful expressions for the variables in "*Kpq*" is a sentence. For example choosing '*p*' as "George is at home" and '*q*' as "Tom is at work," we may render "*K*(George is at home)(Tom is at work)" as "George is at home and Tom is at work," or "George is at home but Tom is at work," or "George is at home although Tom is at work," or "George is at home; nevertheless, Tom is at work," etc. Note that any of the foregoing interpretations would be regarded as *true* provided *both* "George is at home" and "Tom is at work," are true, and false otherwise. (For further discussion of alternative interpretations see Strawson [75]. For an excellent non-technical account of "truth," as understood by contemporary logicians, see Tarski [77].)

We shall continue to use the word "sentence" interchangeably with "wff," but the reader should note that the word so used has only an analogical resemblance to its use in English grammar.

will count as valid in deducing new theorems from old ones).[16]   We have dealt with (a), and now turn to (b) and (c).

As axioms for the two-valued propositional calculus[17] we choose the following. This list of axioms is non-independent (in the sense that some are derivable as theorems from the others); they have been chosen primarily with a view to exhibiting as clearly as possible the intended interpretation of the formalism.

Axioms for material implication

Ax. 1.   *CpCqp*. If *p*, then if *q* then *p*. (Or *p* implies that *q* implies *p*.)[18]

Ax. 2.   *C(CpCqr)(CCpqCpr)*. If *p* implies that *q* implies *r*, then if *p* implies *q*, then *p* implies *r*.

Axioms for conjunction

Ax. 3.   *CKpqp*. If *p* and *q*, then *p*.

Ax. 4.   *CKpqq*. If *p* and *q*, then *q*.

Ax. 5.   *CpCqKpq*. If *p*, then if *q*, then (both) *p* and *q*.

Axioms for disjunction

Ax. 6.   *CpApq*. If *p*, then *p* or *q*.

Ax. 7.   *CqApq*. If *q*, then *p* or *q*.

Ax. 8.   *C(KCprCqr)(CApqr)*. If *p* implies *r* and *q* implies *r*, then *p* or *q* implies *r*.

Axioms for negation

Ax. 9.   *CpNNp*. If *p*, then it is not the case that not-*p*. (Or, if *p*, then not-not-*p*.)

---

[16] Notice that from the point of view of contemporary logic, most "formal theories" in the literature of the behavioral sciences are not formal theories at all. Although it is common to label certain propositions "postulates," "axioms," "theorems," "corollaries," and the like, one rarely finds an explicit discussion of what is to count as a sentence of the theory, or (more important) what principles are to be recognized as valid techniques of deduction. (A notable exception to this generalization is to be found in Hull *et al.* [44].)   In consequence, there is no satisfactory method for checking rigorously or formally the legitimacy of alleged "deductions." This is not, of course, to deny that such so-called "formal theories" may have great informal, heuristic, or suggestive value; but it *is* important to realize that no gain in logical or theoretical rigor is achieved simply by calling certain remarks "postulates," "corollaries," etc. It is not the use of these words that confers rigor on theories, but rather an explicit, unambiguous statement of axioms *and* principles for deducing consequences.

[17] The two-valued propositional calculus is perhaps the most thoroughly explored of modern logical systems. Numerous equivalent formulations are available, as are decision procedures, proofs of completeness, consistency, independence of axioms, etc. For an exhaustive account of this system, together with historical material see Church [26].

[18] The intuitive content of this axiom perhaps calls for remark. Recall that *Cpq* is to be regarded as true provided it is not the case that *p* is true and *q* is false. Thus we may read *CpCqp* as "if *p* is true, then it is not the case that *q* is true and *p* is false," and the latter is intuitively evident no matter what *q* may be. Alternatively, we may think of *CpCqp* as saying that if *p* is true, then *p* is true no matter what else (*q*) may be the case. For further discussion of this point see, e.g., Copi [27], pp. 251–252, or Prior [69], pp. 18–20.

Some readers may find the precise interpretation of *C* clearer if *Cpq* is read as *NKpNq*.

Ax. 10. *CNNpp*. If not-not-*p*, then *p*.

Ax. 11. *C(CpKqNq)(Np)*. If *p* implies *q* and not-*q* (i.e., if *p* implies a contradiction) then *p* is false (i.e., then not-*p*).

We shall not state any axioms for material equivalence, but rather treat '*E*' as defined, as follows.

Df. *E*. "*Eαβ*" is short for "*KCαβCβα*." ("*α* if and only if *β*" is defined as "if *α* then *β*, and if *β* then *α*.")

Theorems concerning '*E*' then turn out to be deducible from the other axioms, together with this definition.

The reader may verify that the axioms stated, and the definition of '*E*', accord with the statement of truth-conditions contained in the explanation above of the intended interpretation of logical constants '*N*', '*K*', etc.

We have now specified (a) the class of sentences and (b) the axioms of the formal system. It is important to note that (as yet) *nothing whatever* is deducible from the axioms stated, since no statement has yet been made regarding formal principles of proof. While it is true that one may argue informally, in English, from the intended interpretation of the logical constants, any such argument would depend not on formal or syntatical[19] properties of the calculus, but rather on our logical intuitions, which are notoriously fallible.[20] Formal treatment of the notion of deduction requires an explicit statement of the formal deductive procedures which are to be countenanced in the system.

The primitive formal principles of inference are the following:

I. *Substitution*. If *α* is a theorem, and if *β* results from *α* by replacing every occurrence of a variable *γ* in *α* by a wff *δ*, then *β* is a theorem.

II. *Detachment*. If *α* and *Cαβ* are both theorems, then *β* is a theorem.

These two rules enable us to deduce all theorems of the two-valued calculus of propositions from the axioms listed above. We append some sample deductions, together with an explanation of the notational conventions used in justifying steps of proofs.

	Theorem:	Justification:
1	*CpCqp*	Ax. 1
2	*C(CpCqp)(CCpqCpp)*	Ax. 2, *r/p*
3	*CCpqCpp*	1, 2, det
4	*CCpCqpCpp*	3, *q/Cqp*
5	*Cpp*	1, 4, det

Step 1 is simply a repetition of Ax. 1, which, being an axiom, is one of the initial stock of theorems from which further theorems may be deduced with the help of the principles of inference.

---

[19] We use this word in the sense of Morris [62] or [63], to which the reader is referred for a discussion of one current use of "syntax" and "semantics" in the literature on logic. See also Church [26], especially pp. 55–56.

[20] For a discussion of the contradictions which stem almost immediately from intuitively plausible logical assumptions, see, e.g., Lewis and Langford [48], ch. XIII.

Step 2 is derived from Ax. 2 by an application of *substitution*. The notation "*r/p*" (which we may read "for '*r*', write '*p*' ") means that step 2 results from Ax. 2 by replacing every occurrence of '*r*' in Ax. 2 by '*p*'. I.e., the principle of *substitution* says, relatively to this application of the principle: "If α (namely, in this case, Ax. 2: $C(CpCqr)(CCpqCpr)$) is a theorem, and if β (namely step 2: $C(CpCqp)(CCpqCpp)$) results from α by replacing every occurrence of a variable γ (in this case '*r*') in α by a wff δ (in this case '*p*'), then β (namely step 2) is a theorem."

Step 3 follows from steps 1 and 2 by *detachment* (abbreviated "det"). This principle states, relatively to this application: "If α (namely step 1: $CpCqp$) and Cαβ (namely step 2: $C(CpCqp)(CCpqCpp)$) are both theorems, then β (namely step 3: $CCpqCpp$) is a theorem.

Step 4 follows from step 3 by *substitution*, taking α as $CCpqCpp$, γ as *q*, δ as Cqp, and β as $CCpCqpCpp$. That is, we replace every occurrence of *q* in step 3 by Cqp.

Step 5 follows from steps 1 and 4 by *detachment*, taking α as $CpCqp$ (step 1), Cαβ as $CCpCqpCpp$ (step 4) and βas Cpp (step 5).

Each of the steps 1–5 is a theorem of the two-valued propositional calculus, since each is either (a) an axiom, or (b) a consequence of preceding steps by *substitution* or *detachment*. Notice that each theorem is justified by reference to axioms, or to preceding steps and a principle of inference; without such explicit justification we cannot legitimately regard any expression as a theorem.

Step 5 has the interpretation "if *p*, then *p*." It may seem odd that so simple and intuitively evident an assertion requires "proof," but it should be observed that it is "proved" only in the sense that it is shown to follow rigorously from the formal axioms with the help of the explicitly stated principles of inference. If one wished (for heuristic or other reasons), one could add Cpp to the collection of axioms, in which case it would be trivially a theorem, since all axioms are also theorems. But since it is provable on the basis of the other axioms assumed, there would be little point in doing so.

The two principles *substitution* and *detachment* are "primitive," in the sense that they have been stated as part of the definition of "theorem." (An expression is a *theorem* of the system, by definition, if it is either an axiom, or else follows from one or more theorems by applications of the primitive principles.) We shall find it convenient, however, to use additional *derived* principles of inference. As an example, we state the following:

Transitivity of material implication (hereafter referred to as "trans C"). If Cαβ and Cβγ are both theorems, then Cαγ is a theorem.

Since "trans C" is not one of the primitive principles of inference, it requires proof; that is, we require a general method of showing how to derive Cαγ from Cαβ and Cβγ, regardless of the particular α, β, and γ in question. Such a general method is provided by what follows.

1	$C\alpha\beta$	hypothesis
2	$C\beta\gamma$	hypothesis
3	$CC\beta\gamma C\alpha C\beta\gamma$	Ax. 1, $p/C\beta\gamma$, q/α
4	$C(C\alpha C\beta\gamma)(CC\alpha\beta C\alpha\gamma)$	Ax. 2, p/α, q/β, r/γ
5	$C\alpha C\beta\gamma$	2, 3, det
6	$CC\alpha\beta C\alpha\gamma$	4, 5, det
7	$C\alpha\gamma$	1, 6, det

Certain features of the foregoing proof call for remark.

First, as regards notational conventions, observe that step 3 involves two simultaneous applications of *substitution*. This is a simple extension of the principle originally stated; and in fact simultaneous substitution can always be dispensed with. We might, that is, replace step 3 above by the following two steps, each of which only involves a single substitution:

3a	$CpC\alpha p$	Ax. 1, q/α
3b	$C(C\beta\gamma)(C\alpha C\beta\gamma)$	3a, $p/C\beta\gamma$

But simultaneous substitutions, though unnecessary, serve to shorten proofs, and will be used freely in what follows.

Secondly, observe that the first two steps of the proof are *hypotheses*, to the effect, respectively, that $C\alpha\beta$ is a theorem, and $C\beta\gamma$ is a theorem. If α, β, and γ, have in fact been so chosen that $C\alpha\beta$ and $C\beta\gamma$ *are* theorems, then each of the following expressions in the proof will also be a theorem, since each follows from one or more theorems by one of the primitive principles. In particular, the last expression $C\alpha\gamma$ will be a theorem if $C\alpha\beta$ and $C\beta\gamma$ are. We may regard the proof, if we like, as a *proof-scheme*; that is, given any three wffs, we may put them in uniformly for α, β, and γ, in the proof above, and if the first two resulting expressions are theorems, the last will be also. These observations show that "trans C" is always avoidable. Instead of applying that principle, we can always fill in steps according to the recipe provided by the proof of "trans C." Still, "trans C" is a perfectly good derived principle of inference, and may be applied at our pleasure. An example application occurs in the proof of the following principle.

Transitivity of material equivalence (hereafter referred to as "trans E"). If $E\alpha\beta$ and $E\beta\gamma$ are theorems, so is $E\alpha\gamma$.

1	$E\alpha\beta$	hypothesis
2	$E\beta\gamma$	hypothesis
3	$KC\alpha\beta C\beta\alpha$	1, Df. E
4	$KC\beta\gamma C\gamma\beta$	2, Df. E
5	$C(KC\alpha\beta C\beta\alpha)(C\alpha\beta)$	Ax. 3, $p/C\alpha\beta$, $q/C\beta\alpha$
6	$C\alpha\beta$	3, 5, det
7	$C(KC\alpha\beta C\beta\alpha)(C\beta\alpha)$	Ax. 4, $p/C\alpha\beta$, $q/C\beta\alpha$
8	$C\beta\alpha$	3, 7, det
9	$C(KC\beta\gamma C\gamma\beta)(C\beta\gamma)$	Ax. 3, $p/C\beta\gamma$, $q/C\gamma\beta$

10 $C\beta\gamma$	4, 9, det
11 $C(KC\beta\gamma C\gamma\beta)(C\gamma\beta)$	Ax. 4, $pC/\beta\gamma$, $q/C\gamma\beta$
12 $C\gamma\beta$	4, 11, det
13 $C\alpha\gamma$	6, 10, trans C
14 $C\gamma\alpha$	8, 12, trans C
15 $C(C\alpha\gamma)(C(C\gamma\alpha)(KC\alpha\gamma C\gamma\alpha))$	Ax. 5, $p/C\alpha\gamma$, $q/C\gamma\alpha$
16 $C(C\gamma\alpha)(KC\alpha\gamma C\gamma\alpha)$	13, 15, det
17 $KC\alpha\gamma C\gamma\alpha$	14, 16, det
18 $E\alpha\gamma$	17, Df. E

Justifications follow previously established conventions, except for steps 3, 4, 13, 14, and 18.

In the case of 3, 4, and 18, we refer to "Df. E," i.e., to the definition of E, given previously. We regard "$E\alpha\beta$" as simply shorthand notation for "$KC\alpha\beta C\beta\alpha$," hence step 3, for example, simply amounts to rewriting step 1 in the primitive notation.[21]

In the case of step 13, we have applied "trans C." Notice (as remarked before) that instead of going directly from steps 6 and 10 to step 13 with the help of "trans C," we *could* have filled in intermediate steps, exactly like those of the proof of "trans C." The generality of the recipe provided by the proof of "trans C" is indicated in the application of that principle to get step 14 from steps 8 and 12. Here the steps to which the rule is applied are "$C\gamma\beta$" and "$C\beta\alpha$." These are evidently of the same form as "$C\alpha\beta$" and "$C\beta\gamma$" (writing α for γ and γ for α); hence we infer "$C\gamma\alpha$." Replacing α by γ and γ by α throughout, the statement and proof of "trans C" would yield the derived rule as thus applied.

In the sections that follow, familiarity with the two-valued propositional calculus (which we shall in the future refer to as "pc") will be assumed. Checking proofs in which theorems from pc are used does not require great facility in proof-construction on the part of the reader, since there is available a "truth-table decision procedure"[22] for pc, which provides a simple and elegant technique for determining of any wff of pc whether or not it is a theorem, without going to the trouble of constructing a proof from axioms. (The axiomatic approach is important, since for certain more complex systems no decision procedure is, or can be,[23] available; but for systems as simple as pc, the axiomatic approach is not the only way of determining theoremhood.) Theorems from this system will be used in proofs, and justified simply by reference to pc.

---

[21] For the role of such stipulative definitions in formal systems, see, e.g., Hempel [39] ch. I.

[22] An account of this procedure is to be found in any standard textbook; see, e.g., those mentioned in footnote 6. There are other algorithms, e.g., "Boolean normal forms" (Copi [28], pp. 31–39), as well as variants designed to facilitate computation.

[23] This is the essential point of very important theorems due to Gödel and Church, for an excellent non-technical account of which see Myhill [64].

The foregoing account has been intended to sketch some of the leading ideas behind the formalism, and to make it possible for readers unfamiliar with the logical notation to interpret formal expressions. Our discussion has lapsed in certain ways from extreme rigor, in the interests of simplicity of exposition; it is not to be taken as a substitute for the careful study of a good elementary textbook.

1.2. *Alethic modal propositional logic*

Systems of alethic modal (propositional) logic are designed to give an explication of *possibility, necessity, impossibility*, and related notions.[24] We shall be concerned here only with systems of alethic modal logic which contain the two-valued propositional calculus as a subsystem (which includes most of the systems familiar from the literature[25]).

We shall refer to any system X satisfying the following conditions as a "normal alethic modal logic."[26]

(a) X contains as theorems all the theorems of pc, and the two primitive principles of inference of pc are also valid principles of X;

(b) X has, in addition, a principle allowing for the intersubstitutability of materially equivalent expressions from pc; more specifically, if $Ea\beta$ is a theorem of pc, and if γ is a theorem of X, and if δ results from γ by writing α for one or more occurrences of β in γ, then δ is a theorem of X; and

(c) in addition to the primitive constants 'N', 'K', 'A', and 'C', of pc, X has logical constants (here symbolized 'M' and 'L') such that $CpMp$, $E(MApq)(AMpMq)$, $NMKpNp$, and $ELpNMNp$ are theorems of X, but $CMpp$ is not a theorem of X.

The intuitive intent behind this definition of *normal alethic modal logic* is the following.

We begin with (c). We wish to interpret "Mp" as "it is possible that p," and "Lp" as "it is necessary that p." The requirements stipulated under (c) then amount to the following:

$CpMp$ (If p, then it is possible that p) is a theorem of X.

---

[24] The first modern contributions to this field were made by Lewis [47]. Since that time, the systems S1–S5, proposed by Lewis (in [48]), and numerous other systems, have been extensively investigated. See for example, the following partial list of results: Parry [66] and [67], Gödel [37], McKinsey [52], [53], and [54], McKinsey and Tarski [55], Simons [73], A. R. Anderson [2], [3], [4], [7], and [8], Halldén [38], Łukasiewicz [50], Fitch [33] and [34], Feys [30], Wajsberg [78], and Prior [68].

[25] But not the systems of Fitch, cited in the preceding footnote. These systems are based on an underlying propositional calculus which is weaker than pc. The impact of the results of Sect. II and III on these systems has yet to be investigated.

[26] Our list of minimal requirements is different from that of Łukasiewicz [50], but this fact represents no disagreement; see in this connection footnote 28.

$E(MApq)(AMpMq)$ (It is possible that p-or-q[27] if and only if it is possible that p or it is possible that q) is a theorem of X.

$NMKpNp$ (It is impossible that p-and-not-p) is a theorem of X.

$ELpNMNp$ (It is necessary that p if and only if it is impossible that not-p) is a theorem of X.[28]

And finally, $CMpp$ (If it is possible that p, then p) is not a theorem of X (i.e., it is *not* provable that whatever is possible is true[29]).

The motivation for the stipulations under (a) are the same as the motivation for the corresponding rules of pc. As regards (b), the intent may be made clear with the help of an example. If $Ea\beta$ is a theorem of pc, then, on the intended interpretation, a is true if and only if β is true. The principle mentioned under (b) has the effect of then allowing us to infer $EMaM\beta$, i.e., it is possible that a if and only if it is possible that β. Intuitively, then, we may look at (b) as specifying that if a and β are true under exactly the same conditions, then Ma and $M\beta$ are true under exactly the same conditions.[30]

Most contemporary logicians would regard the requirements just listed as correctly characterizing virtually all reasonable concepts of *possibility*, but it is worth noting that these requirements do not uniquely characterize the sense of the word "possibility" in question. We are usually in the habit of distinguishing a number of senses of the word "possible." We distinguish, for example, "theoretical possibility" from "practical possibility." (E.g., it is theoretically possible to send a sociological questionnaire to every adult in the United States – nothing that we know of the "laws of nature" suggests that this is an impossibility; but from a "practical" point of view, such a procedure would be impossible, owing to limitations of time, cash, patience, etc.) And we usually distinguish "logical possibility" from both the other

---

[27] Here and in the future we shall from time to time hyphenate expressions, as in "it is possible that p-or-q," in order to emphasize the fact that the modal concept *possible* is intended to apply to the *disjunction* of p and q (and to obviate any inclination to confuse, e.g., "p or q is possible" with "p is possible or q is possible"; the latter two propositions, though intuitively equivalent, are not necessarily to be identified.)

[28] This equivalence fails for the system Q of Prior [71]. Q is therefore not "a normal alethic modal logic" by the criteria stated here. Our characterization of a "normal alethic modal logic" is proposed for the technical purposes of Sect. II and III, and is *not* intended as an explication of the corresponding intuitive notion. The fact that Prior's Q is obviously a system of alethic modal logic, in some reasonable sense, need therefore occasion no alarm. Similar remarks apply to the systems of Fitch cited in footnote 26. For a discussion of deontic logic (as considered in Sect. II) within the systems Q of Prior and Ł of Łukasiewicz [50], see Prior [71] Appendix D.

[29] To say that $CMpp$ is not provable is not equivalent to saying that its denial $NCMpp$ *is* provable. The latter condition can be shown (with the help of pc) to be equivalent to $KMpNp$, which says that every proposition is both possible and false, an assertion which has no intuitive plausibility. In any reasonable system of alethic modal logic, one would expect that both $CMpp$ and $NCMpp$ would be unprovable.

[30] It is not difficult to prove that the principle "If $Ea\beta$ is a theorem of pc, then $EMaM\beta$ is a theorem of X" is deductively equivalent to the principle stated under (b); so our "example" can in fact simply be taken as an alternative to (b). That is, in place of condition (b), we can require condition (b'): "X has a principle allowing inference of $EMaM\beta$ from $Ea\beta$, where the latter is a theorem of pc."

162

senses. (For example, it is "logically possible," no matter how improbable, that all the questionnaires would be returned promptly – at least, we cannot argue on purely logical grounds that this is an impossibility. But we have good empirical grounds, based on studies of apathy and ineptitude among human beings – grounds which may someday lead to an adequate formal theory – for considering this a "theoretical" impossibility.)

Our requirements are intended to be "minimal," in the sense that any (or almost any) reasonable sense of the word "possible" would be characterized by them. They are also "minimal" in the sense that a vast majority of systems of modal logic familiar from the literature satisfy the conditions of a *normal alethic modal logic*.

By way of introducing some new notational conventions, we give a sample proof which could be carried out in any normal alethic modal logic.

1	$E(EpKpq)(Cpq)$	pc
2	Cpp	pc
3	$C(LCpq)(LCpq)$	2, $p/LCpq$
4	$C(LCpq)(LEpKpq)$	3, $Cpq/EpKpq$-1

Steps 1 and 2 are theorems of pc, and are justified simply by reference to pc, in accordance with the convention mentioned at the end of I.1.

Step 3 results from step 2 by writing "$LCpq$" throughout for 'p', following conventions previously established.

Step 4 results from step 3 by writing "$EpKpq$" in place of the second occurrence of "Cpq" in step 3. This inference involves an application of the principle specified under (b), and the addition of "-1" to "$Cpq/EpKpq$" in the justification column indicates the step (step 1) which provides the material equivalence from pc required for application of the principle described under (b). Relatively to this application, we can treat the principle as stating: "If $Ea\beta$ (namely step 1: $E(EpKpq)(Cpq)$) is a theorem of pc, and if γ (namely step 3: $C(LCpq)(LCpq)$) is a theorem of X, and if δ (namely step 4: $C(LCpq)(LEpKpq)$) results from γ by writing a (namely $EpKpq$) for one or more occurrences of β (namely Cpq) in γ, then δ (namely step 4) is a theorem of X."

Notice that in getting step 3 from step 2, we substitute "$LCpq$" for *every* occurrence of 'p' in step 2; whereas in getting step 4 from step 3 we substitute "$EpKpq$" for *only one* of the two occurrences of "Cpq" in step 3. Substitutions of the latter sort must be justified by reference to some preceding material equivalence from pc in the list of theorems; in this case by reference to step 1. Our justification of step 4, that is to say, involves a new notational convention. The distinction between the two conventions is as follows: "n, p/β" means that we get the step in question by substituting the wff "β" for every occurrence of the *variable* 'p' in step n; whereas "n, a/β-m" means that we get the step in question by substituting the wff 'a' for *at least one* occurrence of the wff "β" in step n, and that the substitution in question is justified by the material equivalence $Ea\beta$ to be found in step m.

A minimal normal alethic modal logic (which we shall call "$X^\star$") may be constructed by expanding pc as follows.

(1) To the definition of "wff" for pc, add the clause:

3. If a is a wff, then Ma is a wff.

(2) To the axioms of pc add the following:

Axioms for possibility

Ax. 12. $CpMp$ If p, then it is possible that p.

Ax. 13. $E(MApq)(AMpMq)$. It is possible that p-or-q if and only if it is possible that p or it is possible that q.

Ax. 14. $NMKpNp$. It is impossible that p- and-not-p.

(3) To the primitive principles of inference for pc, add principles allowing for applications of *detachment* and *substitution* in $X^\star$ and allowing for substitutions as specified under (b).

We may then define "L" as follows.

Df. L. "La" is short for "$NMNa$." ("a is necessary" is defined as "not-a is impossible.")

Then we get $ELpNMNp$ (mentioned under (c)) as a theorem.

Proof:

1	Epp	pc
2	$ENMNpNMNp$	1, $p/NMNp$
3	$ELpNMNp$	2, Df. L

It can also be shown that in the system $X^\star$, $CMpp$ is not a theorem (the proof will be omitted[31]); hence $X^\star$ is a normal alethic modal logic.

An important relation, definable in any normal alethic modal logic, is the relation of "strict implication."[32] The definition is as follows:

Df. C'. "$C'a\beta$" is an abbreviation for "$LCa\beta$." ("a strictly implies β" is defined as "it is necessary that if a then β.")

This relation is stronger than that of material implication; i.e., $CLCpqCpq$ is provable in any normal alethic modal logic, but the converse $CCpqLCpq$ is not provable in any. We read "$C'pq$" as "p strictly implies q," or "p necessarily implies q," or "p entails q."[33] It is worth noting that "$C'pq$" is (materially) equivalent in $X^\star$ to "$NMKpNq$" (it is impossible that p is true and q is false). It may sometimes be convenient to use this equivalent interpretation of "$C'pq$."

It ought to be remarked again that the suggested interpretations of 'M', 'L', and 'C', like those for the constants of pc, are only approximate, and

---

[31] Proofs that certain expressions are *not* theorems of formal system require techniques distinct from any presented here; in many cases proofs of unprovability are extremely difficult (though not for the relatively simple systems discussed in this *Report*).

[32] This terminology was introduced by Lewis [47].

[33] For consequences of the definition of C' which appear (at first glance) to be counter-intuitive, see Lewis and Langford [48], pp. 248–251.

may well be misleading in certain cases, principally because of the vagueness and ambiguity of the ordinary English words in which the interpretations are customarily couched.[34]

Most of the interesting systems of alethic modal logic are stronger than the minimal system X^* just outlined. There are numerous ways of strengthening X^* by adding intuitively plausible axioms and rules. Among axioms, e.g., we might add any or all of the following:

$C'(C'pq)(CMpMq)$. p strictly implies q entails that if p is possible, then q is possible.

$C(C'pq)(C'MpMq)$. If p necessarily implies q then the possibility of p necessarily implies the possibility of q.

$C(Lp)(LLp)$. If p is necessary, then p is necessarily necessary.

There are also many other expressions one might add as axioms, some of which will be discussed later.

One might also strengthen the minimal system X^* by adding, e.g., the following principle of inference:

If a is a theorem, then La is a theorem. (This amounts to saying that whatever is provable in necessary.)

Detailed accounts of such extensions will be found among items listed in the bibliography.

*   *   *

The foregoing account of alethic modal logic has been intended (like that of I.1, for the two-valued propositional calculus) simply as a brief sketch of certain of the leading ideas behind the formal systems.

It should be emphasized that the main value of symbolic systems of the kind just described lies in the formalization of the notion of proof. The process of translating statements in informal English into the logical notation leads to some clarification, and to the revelation of unsuspected ambiguities in the common English idiom, but if this were the only value of a symbolic or mathematical treatment of logic, the subject would hardly have stimulated the intense probing which it has recently received. The point of the formal approach is to display in a clear and rigorous way the logical relations among groups of sentences, irrespective of their empirical content; for this purpose an unambiguous statement of (axioms and) principles of inference is essential.

For these reasons it is perhaps misleading to refer to the interpretations of the formal expressions as "translations." When we speak of a "translation" from English into German, for example, we generally have in mind two linguistic structures which are of the same strength, or in some appropriate

---

[34] On this point see again footnote 12. However, the difficulties attendant on the indefiniteness of natural languages cannot be entirely eliminated. For one thing, every formal system ever described has been discussed *in* some natural language. But it is to be hoped that the study of formal systems will illuminate the enormously complex structure of the natural languages in which they are discussed.

sense equivalent; roughly speaking anything we can say in English we can also say in German, and conversely. In the case of "translations" from our formal symbolic systems into English, or from English into the formalism, however, the situation is different. The logical structure of English (and natural languages generally) is vague, ambiguous, and in many respects confusing, whereas the logical structure of the formal systems is precise and clear. The point of "translating" ordinary English expressions into the formalism is *not*, therefore, simply to write familiar things in funny notation. It is rather to exhibit our ideas within a framework which has a well-defined and clearly specified logical structure, and which enables us to say accurately and in a way that minimizes the chance of disagreement, just what follows logically from what. It is only by considering theories formally that their deductive and explanatory power (or lack thereof) can be made manifest.

A final word of apology or warning is called for, concerning the neglect in informal discussions of interpretations (here and in what follows) of certain important but, from a common sense point of view, rather recondite distinctions.

Consider the expression "There are mountains on the other side of the moon is possible." This is clearly an ill-formed sentence according to the canons of English grammar; there is no way to parse it, since, like "John is running is singing," there are two verbs, unconnected by any of the usual relations of dependence. The presumed intent of such an expression is "It is possible that there are mountains on the other side of the moon," or the like. The point to note is that the rendering "p is possible" for the formal notation "Mp" makes no sense if for 'p' we write an ordinary English sentence. Similar remarks apply in the case of such expressions as "p is necessary," "p is obligatory," "p implies q," "p entails q," etc. "There are mountains on the other side of the moon entails there are mountains" is again an unparsible expression; the presumed intent being something like "If there are mountains on the other side of the moon, then there are mountains," or "That there are mountains on the other side of the moon entails that there are mountains."

It follows that we are lapsing from rigor in translating such formal expressions as Ax. 2; $C(CpCqr)(CCpqCpr)$, for example, as "if p implies that q implies r, then if p implies q, then p implies r." There is no way of consistently replacing variables in the quoted sentence by expressions from English in such a way as to arrive at a possible or parsible English sentence. (Consider the "if"-clause: "If John is running implies that John is exercising implies that John is bored, . . ." cannot be used as part of any grammatically well-formed English sentence.) To be consistent with the rendering of "if p then q" for "Cpq," we should translate Ax. 2 as "If if p then if q then r, then if if p then q then if p then r." This translation does remain well-formed if we put sentences in place of variables: "If if John is running then if John is exercising then John is bored, then if if John is running then John is exercising then if John is running then John is bored."

On the other hand, the last sentence mentioned, though grammatically well-formed, is unnatural and pedantic to the point of being unintelligible. It would be more in accord with common usage to render its content as something like "If John's running implies that if he's exercising he's bored, then if it's true that if he runs he's exercising, then if he runs he's bored." This sentence is not an exceptionally happy effort from the point of view of English style, but neither does it savor quite so strongly of the pedantry and obscurity characteristic of the last example in the preceding paragraph.

Now the extent of one's fussiness in observing fine distinctions[35] should surely be dictated in large part by the purpose of one's exposition. We are concerned here to make the intuitive content of certain formal systems available not to experts in symbolic logic (a task which would anyway be otiose), but rather to a reader not especially familiar with the techniques of modern mathematical logic. It is the writer's hope that this purpose justifies the rather cavalier handling of certain of the translations into English. In any event such laxity as may be found *need* occasion no confusion whatever; it is always a trivial matter to correct the translations, though the resulting corrections may be more arcane to common sense than the original. To make the required corrections one need only hew uniformly to the following interpretations:

"$N\alpha$": it is not the case that α.
"$A\alpha\beta$": α or β.
"$K\alpha\beta$": α and β.
"$C\alpha\beta$": if α then β.
"$E\alpha\beta$": α if and only if β.
"$M\alpha$": it is possible that α.
"$L\alpha$": it is necessary that α.
"$C'\alpha\beta$": it is necessary that if α then β.

It is to be hoped that the less rigorous translations of formal expressions in the following pages will have greater heuristic value than the result of a uniform adherence to the interpretations just listed.

II. Deontic Extensions of Alethic Modal Logic

Paralleling the definition of *normal alethic modal logic*, we now introduce a definition of *normal deontic logic*.

---

[35] A clear and more elaborate account of the distinction in question may be found in Quine [72], pp. 22–33. It is also discussed in Church [26], pp. 58–68, where the "autonymous" use of primitive symbols (a usage adopted in this *Report*) is explained.

We shall call D a *normal deontic logic*[36] if D satisfies the following conditions:

(a) D contains as theorems all the theorems of pc, and the two primitive principles of inference of pc are also valid principles of D;

(b) D has in addition a principle allowing for the intersubstitutability of materially equivalent expressions of pc (as in normal alethic modal logics); and

(c) in addition to the primitive constants of pc, D has logical constants (here symbolized 'P' and 'O') such that $COpPp$, $E(PApq)(APpPq)$, and $EOpNPNp$ are theorems of D, but neither $CPpp$ nor $CpPp$ is a theorem of D. (We add as a further condition, that if D should be an extension of a normal alethic modal logic X, then $CMpPp$ is not a theorem of D.)

Requirements (a) and (b) are motivated by considerations like those for normal alethic modal logics. As regards (c), the intent is to interpret "Pp" as meaning "it is permitted that p," or "p is permitted," and "Op" as "it is obligatory that p," or "p is obligatory." (c) then requires the following:

$COpPp$ (If it is obligatory that p, then it is permitted that p; or, whatever is obligatory is permitted) is a theorem of D.

$E(PApq)(APpPq)$ (It is permitted that p-or-q if and only if p is permitted or q is permitted) is a theorem of D.

$EOpNPNp$ (p is obligatory if and only if not-p is not permitted) is a theorem of D.

$CPpp$ (If p is permitted, then p; or, whatever is permitted is the case) is *not* a theorem of D.

$CpPp$ (If p, then p is permitted; or, whatever is the case is permitted) is *not* a theorem of D.

And, should D be an extension of a normal alethic modal logic, we also require that:

$CMpPp$ (Whatever is possible is permitted) is *not* a theorem of D.

---

[36] This definition of *normal deontic logic* embodies ideas due essentially to von Wright [79]. The chief difference between von Wright's system and those discussed in this *Report* is that von Wright takes "acts" (rather, "act-types"; see von Wright [79], or A. R. Anderson and Moore [13]) as arguments for the deontic operators P and O, rather than propositions. In von Wright's system, "Pa," for example, has the interpretation "Acts of type a are permitted"; in the systems to be discussed below "Pp" will have the interpretation "the state-of-affairs described by 'p' is permitted," or "it is permitted that p be the case," or "it is permitted that p." Since the variables in von Wright's system range over act-types rather than propositions, such expressions as "$CaPa$" are not well-formed, since 'a' is not a proposition. (An instance of "$CaPa$" would be "If smoking, then smoking is permitted," but this is not a sentence in English.) In systems D, on the other hand, "$CpPp$" *is* well-formed, an instance of which would be "If George is smoking then it is permitted that George is smoking," or (in better English) "If George is smoking, then it is permitted that George smoke." (Of course "$CaPa$" is not a theorem of von Wright's system, since it is not even a wff of that system; and "$CpPp$" is not a theorem of any systems D, in view of (c) below. The question at issue here is not what is provable, but what is to count as a wff, or sentence.)

The conditions (a)–(c) were suggested by Prior [69] pp. 220–221; the system $D*$, mentioned below is slightly weaker than that of Prior *loc. cit.*

In the same way that normal alethic modal systems fail to characterize the sense of "possibility" uniquely, so normal deontic systems fail to give us a unique sense of "permitted" and "obligatory." In most societies, people recognize distinctions among obligations, at least in the sense that the norms specify "obligations to" a variety of persons, groups, institutions, etc. The distinctness of these various obligations is most clearly recognized when they impose conflicting or incompatible demands, as in the case of so-called "role-conflicts". And in the same way that the requirements for normal alethic modal logics specify minimal features characteristic of all or most senses of the word "possible," so the requirements for normal deontic logics specify minimal features of the various senses of "permitted."

As an example of a normal deontic logic we may formulate a minimal system $D\star$ by expanding pc as follows.

(1) To the definition of "wff" for pc, add the clause:

3'. If a is a wff, then Pa and Oa are both wffs.

(2) To the axioms of pc add the following.

Axioms for permission

Ax. 12'. $APNpPp$. (Either it is permitted that not-p or it is permitted that p.)

Ax. 13'. $E(PApq)(APpPq)$. (It is permitted that p-or-q, if and only if it is permitted that p or it is permitted that q.)

(3) To the primitive principles of inference for pc, add principles allowing for applications of *detachment* and *substitution* in $D\star$, and allowing for substitutions as specified under (b), p. 161.

We may then define 'O' as follows.

Df. O. "Oa" is short for "$NPNa$." ("a is obligatory" is defined as "not-a is not permitted.")

The equivalence $EOpNPNp$ (mentioned in (c)) is provable as a theorem. The proof is similar to that of $ELpNMNp$ in Sect. I.2. It is also possible to prove $COpPp$, thus:

1	$CApqCNpq$	pc
2	$C(APNpPp)(CNPNpPp)$	1, p/PNp, q/Pp
3	$APNpPp$	Ax. 12'
4	$CNPNpPp$	2, 3, det
5	$COpPp$	4, Df. O

It may also be shown that neither $CPpp$ nor $CpPp$ are theorems of $D\star$ (we omit the proof); hence all the conditions (a)–(c) are satisfied by $D\star$, and $D\star$ is therefore normal.

It will be the object of this section to discuss an alternative method of formulating normal deontic logics by adding a propositional constant and an axiom to normal alethic modal logics. This procedure has the advantage of reducing the number of new primitive constants from two (for $D\star$) to one, and also of reducing the number of new axioms from two (for $D\star$) to one. The motivation for this new approach is as follows.

It is characteristic of normative systems to select from among the possible alternatives available to agents in a social group, certain possibilities as required or *obligatory*, others as *permitted* (but not obligatory), others as *forbidden*, others as *indifferent*, etc. From the point of view of the behavioral sciences, among the first questions that arise in considering any actual normative system, is the following: what penalties or sanctions does the social group use to enforce its norms? A similar question arises in positive law: in drafting a statute in which, e.g., some possible course of action is to be forbidden, an integral part of the statute is an explicit statement of the penalty or penalties to be incurred by those who fail to comply with the directive.

The intimate connection between obligations and sanctions in normative systems suggests that we might profitably begin by considering some penalty or sanction S,[37] and *define* the deontic or normative notions of obligation, etc., along the following lines: [38] a state-of-affairs p is obligatory if the falsity of p entails the sanction S; p is forbidden if p entails the sanction S; and p is permitted if it is possible that p is true without the sanction S being true.[39] It develops that formalization of these suggestions within a sufficiently strong alethic modal logic *does* lead to a system of deontic logic, provided an assumption is made concerning the sanction S, namely, that it is possibly false.[40] The rationale for such an additional assumption is that if the sanction

[37] The letter 'S' is to be taken as a constant proposition (not a connective), describing a situation which will count as a penalty or sanction, relatively to the normative system under investigation. In A. R. Anderson [6] (and in Prior [71] Appendix D) a script letter 'P' is used instead of the 'S' which we have here adopted for typographical reasons. We shall use the words "sanction" and "penalty" interchangeably in referring to the situation expressed by 'S'.

[38] This approach to deontic logic was suggested by a proposal of Bohnert [20]. Menger (in an article [57] containing criticisms of Mally [56] which also apply to Bohnert's [20]), also suggests definitions similar to these (Df. P, Df. O, and Df. F, below), using a three-valued underlying logic, in place of an alethic modal logic.

[39] It might be thought that this condition, as a definition of "permission", is too weak, and that permitted states-of-affairs should *guarantee* avoidance of the penalty, rather than simply be *possible* without the penalty. However, states-of-affairs which guarantee avoidance of the penalty may be more aptly characterized as "prudent," in the writer's opinion. In this connection see Sect. IX of this *Report*.

[40] A preliminary account of this approach was contained in the writer's unpublished lecture [6], a typescript of which was sent to Professor A. N. Prior. In that lecture, the assumption that the sanction S is possibly false (MNS) was replaced for reasons which will emerge in Sect. IX, by the assumption that the sanction is contingent ($KMSMNS$). It was noted independently by Prior that the clause MS in the axiom $KMSMNS$ makes no contribution to deontic logic proper. The writer's original plan for the present *Report* involved retaining $KMSMNS$ as an axiom; but subsequent investigations, which led to the results of Sect. III made this plan look less attractive.

It is worth remarking that in any empirically given normative system (formulable in any of the systems $XMNS$, or in any of the systems OX described in Sect. III)

were not possibly false (i.e., if it were necessary), then *no* behavior designed to avoid it could be successful. The point of choosing penalties in drafting laws (as well as the point of such penalties or sanctions as come to be associated with non-observance of unwritten social norms), is that the hope of avoiding the penalty might serve as a motivating factor in human behavior; a "sanction" would serve no such purpose if it were not avoidable[41] (i.e., possibly false).

To formulate a system of deontic logic as an extension of alethic modal logic, then, we add to the wffs of a normal alethic modal logic X[42] a propositional constant (symbolized 'S'), and a single axiom, as follows.

Ax. 15. *MNS*. (S is possibly false.)

We then add stipulative definitions of 'P' and 'O' as follows.

Df. P. "*Pa*" is short for "*MKaNS*." ("*a* is permitted" is defined as "it is possible that *a* and not-*S*," or "it is possible that *a* is true and the sanction is not invoked.")

Df. O. "*Oa*" is short for "*NPNa*." ("*a* is obligatory" is defined as "not-*a* is not permitted.")

We may also define operators 'F',[43] and 'I', such that "*Fp*" will have the interpretation "*p* is forbidden," and "*Ip*" will have the interpretation "*p* is indifferent."

Df. F. "*Fa*" is short for "*NPa*." ("*a* is forbidden" is defined as "*a* is not permitted.")

Df. I. "*Ia*" is short for "*KPaPNa*." ("*a* is indifferent" is defined as "*a* is permitted and not-*a* is permitted.")

The result of extending any normal alethic modal logic X by adding the propositional constant 'S' and Ax. 15, will be called "*XMNS*"; in particular, addition of Ax. 15 to $X^\star$ yields $X^\star MNS$. Before showing that all the systems *XMNS* are normal deontic logics, we shall prove four theorems concerning $X^\star MNS$. The first two indicate that the operators O and F have the effect mentioned in the informal discussion preceding the statement of Ax. 15.

---

which countenances states-of-affairs *p* such that *p* is both possible and forbidden (i.e., using the notation of this section, such that *Mp* and *Fp* are both the case), it is also the case that *MS* is true, since *CKMpFpMS* is a theorem of *XMNS* and all systems *OX*. (See Sect. VII). Hence *S* is contingent in any normative system which allows that "doing wrong" is a possibility – and surely any actual operative normative system satisfies this condition. But we leave it as a question to be decided empirically, whether or not the sanction is contingent. (In this connection see Prior [71] Appendix D.)

[41] Or at any rate if it were not *thought* to be avoidable. Questions concerning relations between what *is* avoidable and what is *thought* to be avoidable, which are exceedingly intricate and problematic vis-a-vis normative systems, will not be discussed here.

[42] I.e., we revise the definition of "wff" to read: "*S* is a wff, and any variable is a wff, [etc., as before]."

[43] Following von Wright [79].

1	$E(NCpq)(KpNq)$	pc
2	Epp	pc
3	$E(NMKpNq)(NMKpNq)$	2, $p/NMKpNq$
4	$E(NMKpNq)(NMNCpq)$	3, $KpNq/NCpq$-1
5	$E(NMKpNS)(NMNCpS)$	4, q/S
6	$E(NPp)(NMNCpS)$	5, Df. P
7	$E(NPp)(LCpS)$	6, Df. L
8	$E(NPp)(C'pS)$	7, Df. C'
9	$E(Fp)(C'pS)$	8, Df. F
10	$E(NPNp)(C'NpS)$	8, p/Np
11	$E(Op)(C'NpS)$	10, Df. O

The interesting theorems from the list above are step 9, $E(Fp)(C'pS)$, which says that p is forbidden if and only if p entails the sanction, and step 11, $E(Op)(C'NpS)$, which says that p is obligatory if and only if not-p (i.e., the failure of p to be the case) entails the sanction. These two theorems reflect the intentions described above.

We now derive two principles which will simplify subsequent proofs. These principles will be stated generally for X and will hence be available also in any systems $XMNS$.

Possibility. (Hereafter referred to as "poss.") If a is a theorem of X then Ma is a theorem of X. Proof:

1	a	hypothesis
2	$CaMa$	Ax. 12, p/a
3	Ma	1, 2, det

Distributivity of 'M'. (Hereafter referred to as "dist M".) (a) If $MAa\beta$ is a theorem of X, then $AMaM\beta$ is a theorem of X; and (b) if $AMaM\beta$ is a theorem of X, then $MAa\beta$ is a theorem of X. (We prove only (a); the proof of (b) is similar.)

1	$MAa\beta$	hypothesis
2	$E(MAa\beta)(AMaM\beta)$	Ax. 13, p/a, q/β
3	$KC(MAa\beta)(AMaM\beta)C(AMaM\beta)(MAa\beta)$	2, Df. E
4	$CK(C(MAa\beta)(AMaM\beta))(C(AMaM\beta)$ $(MAa\beta))(C(MAa\beta)(AMaM\beta))$	Ax.3,$p/C(MAa\beta)(AMaM\beta)$, $q/C(AMaM\beta)(MAa\beta)$
5	$C(MAa\beta)(AMaM\beta)$	3, 4, det
6	$AMaM\beta$	1, 5, det

Applications of "poss" and "dist M" will be found in this and the following section.

We now wish to show in general that the result of adding Ax. 15, MNS, to any normal alethic modal logic X yields a normal deontic logic $XMNS$. What is required is to show that the system $XMNS$ satisfies conditions (a)–(c) in the definition of "normal deontic logic."

It is trivial that conditions (a) and (b) are satisfied by any system $XMNS$, since they are satisfied by the underlying alethic systems X. The following list of theorems shows that $COpPp$, $E(PApq)(APpPq)$ and $EOpNPNp$ are theorems of $XMNS$.

1	Cpp	pc
2	$CMqMq$	1, p/Mq
3	$E(AKNpqKpq)q$	pc
4	$CMq(MAKNpqKpq)$	2, $q/AKNpqKpq$-3
5	$C(MNS)(MA(KNpNS)(KpNS))$	4, q/NS
6	MNS	Ax. 15
7	$MA(KNpNS)(KpNS)$	5, 6, det
8	$A(MKNpNS)(MKpNS)$	7, dist M
9	$APNpPp$	8, Df. P
10	$CApqCNpq$	pc
11	$C(APNpPp)(CNPNpPp)$	10, p/PNp, q/Pp
12	$CNPNpPp$	9, 11, det
13	$COpPp$	12, Df. O
14	Epp	pc
15	$E(MKApqr)(MKApqr)$	14, $p/MKApqr$
16	$E(AKprKqr)(KApqr)$	pc
17	$E(MKApqr)(MAKprKqr)$	15, $KApqr/AKprKqr$-16
18	$E(MApq)(AMpMq)$	Ax. 13
19	$E(MAKprKqr)(A(MKpr)(MKqr))$	18, p/Kpr, q/Kqr
20	$E(MKApqr)(A(MKpr)(MKqr))$	17, 19, Trans E
21	$E(MKApqNS)(A(MKpNS)(MKqNS))$	20, r/NS
22	$E(PApq)(APpPq)$	21, Df. P
23	$E(NPNp)(NPNp)$	14, $p/NPNp$
24	$EOpNPNp$	23, Df. O

The theorems required for (c) are those numbered 13, 22, and 24.

We require finally to prove that neither $CPpp$ nor $CpPp$ nor (since $XMNS$ is an extension of a normal alethic modal logic X) $CMpPp$ is a theorem of X. Such results can in fact be obtained, and will be proved at the end of the next section. It will follow that $XMNS$ is a normal deontic logic.

The foregoing results mean that a system of deontic logic arises by the addition of Ax. 15 (MNS) to any normal alethic system X. The device of adding MNS as an axiom to standard alethic modal systems therefore provides a rich source of systems of deontic logic and facilitates a comparative study of deontic principles. As remarked before, it also furnishes a simplification of deontic systems, in the sense that a single axiom with deontic content can replace the two specifically deontic assumptions of, e.g., von Wright's deontic logic. Finally, this approach offers a rationale for the deontic concepts *obligatory*, *permitted*, etc., which may assist decisions about the plausibility of various deontic propositions.[44]

[44] For instances of this sort of application see A. R. Anderson [11], and Prior's remarks on the Kantian principle $COpMp$, in [71] Appendix D.

However, these advantages still depend on the specifically deontic assumption embodied in Ax. 15, and the results mentioned above are still subject to whatever objections may attend that axiom; in particular, the fact that an assumption regarding the "value-term" S is made in $XMNS$, makes it look as if we are dealing with "applied" rather than "pure" logic. It will be shown in the next section that even this axiom is not required, and that with appropriate definitions, any normal alethic modal logic X can be shown to have a normal deontic logic as a subsystem.

III. Reduction of Deontic Logic to Alethic Modal Logic[45]

We have seen that normal systems of deontic logic may be formulated either (a) by adding constants 'P' and 'O' directly to pc, with appropriate axioms and principles of inference, or (b) by adding MNS as an axiom to a normal alethic modal logic, and defining 'P' and 'O' in terms of 'S' and alethic modal constants.[46] The motivation for choosing the axiom MNS is that we *intend to interpret* S as a "sanction"; and penalties or sanctions, if they are to function effectively in enforcing norms, must be avoidable, i.e., possibly false.

The intended interpretation of formal systems always functions as a partial guide in their construction. Nevertheless, it is frequently fruitful to consider certain symbols (perhaps all of them) as uninterpreted, and ask how, from a purely formal point of view, they function in the system. For example, we can prove generally concerning pc that $Ka\beta$ is a theorem if and only if a and β are both theorems – and this feature of the formal system, which is a consequence of the formulation of pc, will be true of pc no matter how we interpret 'K'. We have in fact formulated pc with the express purpose of interpreting 'K' as "and"; but no matter *how* we interpret 'K', it will still be the case that $Ka\beta$ is a theorem of pc if and only if a and β are both theorems of pc.[47]

Looking at the constant S in the systems $XMNS$, from a purely formal point of view, we notice that in these systems MNS is a theorem, but neither S nor NS is a theorem.[48] That is, the definitions of obligation and permission in $XMNS$ require a proposition S, the denial NS of which is demonstrably

---

[45] A more condensed version of the results of this section is contained in A. R. Anderson [9], an abstract of which appears in [10].

[46] Equivalently, we may use the definitions and take $COpPp$ as an additional axiom instead of MNS (as pointed out by Prior [71], Appendix D).

[47] This remark is not meant to suggest, of course, that we can place alternative interpretations on the constants of pc *ad libitum*; any correct interpretation must be such as to make the axioms true and the principles of inference preserve truth. Still, the literature on logic is rife with examples of alternative and perfectly adequate interpretations of the same formal system. For a relevant example, see the interpretation of the alethic modal system S4 as an algebra of topology, McKinsey [52].

[48] Apparently, at least; we shall prove this remark later.

possible, though neither S nor NS is demonstrably true.[49] And observe that from a purely formal point of view, this is virtually all we can say about 'S', since the only axiom mentioning 'S' says that it is possibly false.

Again, inspection of the definitions and theorems of the previous section shows that so long as S meets the conditions just mentioned, it is immaterial *how* S is chosen. In addition to trivial typographical changes (such as choosing 'p' instead of 'S', etc.), we might also, if we wished, choose S as some more complicated expression, involving a number of the constants C, K, etc., provided only that the expression chosen as S be such that its denial is demonstrably possible, but neither S nor its denial is demonstrable.

These considerations lead us quite naturally to ask whether or not there is some expression of X, not involving S, but satisfying the conditions required for S, which we might choose to function like S in $XMNS$. I.e., is there an expression a of X satisfying the conditions required for S, such that we might *define* S as a, and thereby eliminate the necessity of adding Ax. 15? It develops that such an expression is available,[50] as the following indicates.

We add to the primitive vocabulary of any normal alethic modal logic X, a primitive propositional constant 'B', to which, for the time being, we shall give no interpretation at all. Then we prove the following.

1	$ANpp$	pc
2	$ANMNpMNp$	1, p/MNp
3	$C(Apq)(CCprArq)$	pc
4	$C(ANMNpMNp)(C(CNMNpMNMNp)$ $(AMNMNpMNp))$	3, $p/NMNp$, q/MNp, $r/MNMNp$
5	$C(CNMNpMNMNp)(AMNMNpMNp)$	2, 4, det
6	$CpMp$	Ax. 12
7	$CNMNpMNMNp$	6, $p/NMNp$
8	$AMNMNpMNp$	5, 7, det
9	$MANMNpNp$	8, dist M
10	Cpp	pc
11	$C(MANpNq)(MANpNq)$	10, $p/MANpNq$

---

[49] Reverting for a moment to the intended interpretation of S, we can easily see why neither S nor NS should be a theorem, if S is to bear the interpretation we wish to give it. If S were a theorem, then the situation described by the penalty-clause S would be the case on (presumably) purely logical grounds; hence *no* behavior designed to avoid S could be successful, and the hope of avoiding S would consequently lose its motivating force. Similarly, if NS were a theorem, then it would be pointless to plot to avoid S, since S would in any case not eventuate; again the hope of avoiding S would lose such motivating force as it has. So the intended interpretation of S requires not only that its denial be possible, but also that neither it nor its denial be demonstrably true.

Prior has shown that the effect of adding NMS as an axiom to the systems $XMNS$ is to identify P and M; i.e., $EPpMp$ becomes a theorem, which vitiates P. See [71], Appendix D.

[50] That there are such expressions a seems first to have been noticed by Parry; see his [67] theorem 22.8.

12	$E(ANpNq)(NKpq)$	pc
13	$C(MANpNq)(MNKpq)$	11, $ANpNq/NKpq$-12
14	$C(MANMNpNp)(MNKMNpp)$	13, p/MNp, q/p
15	$MNKMNpp$	9, 14, det
16	$MNKMNBB$	15, p/B

Theorem 16 provides us with a constant proposition (namely "$KMNBB$"), whose denial is demonstrably possible. $KMNBB$ therefore satisfies one of the requirements for S; we now show that it also satisfies the others.

Suppose that $NKMNBB$ were a theorem of X. Since none of the axioms of X mention 'B', $NKMNBB$ could be a theorem of X only if it can be regarded as a consequence by the principle of *substitution* of some theorem of the form $NKMNpp$.[51] But if $NKMNpp$ were a theorem, then we could construct a proof as follows:

1	$NKMNpp$	hypothesis
2	$NKMNNpNp$	1, p/Np
3	$ENNpp$	pc
4	$NKMpNp$	2, NNp/p-3
5	$C(NKpNq)(Cpq)$	pc
6	$C(NKMpNp)(CMpp)$	5, p/Mp, q/p
7	$CMpp$	4, 6, det

But $CMpp$ is not a theorem of X, by the definition of *normal alethic modal logic*; hence neither is $NKMNBB$. And if $KMNBB$ were a theorem, then again $KMNpp$ would be a theorem; in which case (using $CKqpp$ of pc) we could derive p, and ultimately (by substitution) $CMpp$, again contradicting the definition of *normal alethic modal logic*.

The constant proposition $KMNBB$ consequently satisfies all the formal requirements satisfied by S, and can therefore be used simply to replace S in the definitions of 'O', 'P', and 'F', of Sect. II. That is, we may now define S as follows:

Df. S. 'S' is an abbreviation for "$KMNBB$."

And since the axiom MNS of the systems $XMNS$ is now unnecessary it may be dropped. We shall use "OX" to refer to systems obtained by adding a propositional constant 'B' and the definitions of 'S', 'P', 'O', and 'F', to normal alethic modal logics X.

The results thus far indicate that a deontic logic of some sort is forthcoming by addition of a propositional constant 'B' to any normal alethic modal logic X, but we have yet to make certain that the resulting deontic logics are normal – i.e., that they satisfy conditions (a)–(c) of the definition of "normal deontic logic."

That the deontic logics OX satisfy conditions (a) and (b) is a trivial consequence of the fact that the underlying alethic modal logics X satisfy

---

[51] This assertion can be given a rigorous demonstration, omitted here.

those conditions. As regards condition (c), we have already in effect shown that $COpPp$ and $E(MApq)(AMpMq)$ are theorems of OX, since the proofs of Sect. II can all be simply repeated in OX (taking now 'S' as defined). It remains to show that neither $CpPp$ nor $CPpp$ nor $CMpPp$ is a theorem of OX.

Suppose first that $CpPp$ were a theorem. Using the definition of P, $CpPp$ is an abbreviation for $CpMKpNS$, which, using now the definition of S, comes to $Cp(MKpNKMNBB)$. Arguing as before, the last expression would be a theorem of OX only if $Cp(MKpNKMNqq)$ were also a theorem of OX, since none of the axioms of OX mentions 'B'. But if $Cp(MKpNKMNqq)$ were a theorem, then we could construct a proof as follows.[52]

1	$Cp(MKpNKMNqq)$	hypothesis
2	$C(Cpq)(CNqNp)$	pc
3	$C(Cp(MKpNKMNqq))(C(NMKpNKMNqq)Np)$	2, $q/MKpNKMNqq$
4	$C(NMKpNKMNqq)Np$	1, 3, det
5	$C(NMK(KMNqq)(NKMNqq))(NKMNqq)$	4, $p/KMNqq$
6	$NMKpNp$	Ax. 14
7	$NMK(KMNqq)(NKMNqq)$	6, $p/KMNqq$
8	$NKMNqq$	5, 7, det
9	$NKMNpp$	8, q/p

The foregoing proof shows that if $Cp(MKpNKMNqq)$ were a theorem of OX, then $NKMNpp$ would be a theorem of OX. But we have already shown that $NKMNpp$ is not a theorem of OX, (for if it were, then $CMPP$ would be a theorem of OX). Hence $Cp(MKpNKMNqq)$ is not a theorem of OX, and neither is $Cp(MKpNKMNBB)$, i.e., $CpMKpNS$, i.e., $CpPp$.

To see that neither $CPpp$ nor $CMpPp$ are theorems of OX, we observe that if either were, then $CpPp$ would be a theorem also, contrary to the result just established. For if $CPpp$ were a theorem, then we would have:

1	$CPpp$	hypothesis
2	$CPNpNp$	1, p/Np
3	$C(CpNq)(CqNp)$	pc
4	$C(CPNpNp)(CpNPNp)$	3, p/PNp, q/p
5	$CpNPNp$	2, 4, det
6	$CpOp$	5, Df. O
7	$COpPp$	(Proved in Sect. II)
8	$CpPp$	6, 7, trans C

Hence $CPpp$ is not a theorem of OX. And if $CMpPp$ were a theorem of OX, we would have:

1	$CMpPp$	hypothesis
2	$CpMp$	Ax. 12
3	$CpPp$	1, 2, trans C

---

[52] This derivation was suggested by a theorem of Prior's in [71], Appendix D.

Hence $CMpPp$ is not a theorem of OX. This completes the proof that OX is a normal deontic logic.

The foregoing argument also suffices to complete the proof that the systems $XMNS$ are normal deontic logics. It is easy to see that every theorem of $XMNS$ is also a theorem of OX; hence in particular if $CpPp$, $CPpp$, or $CMpPp$ were theorems of $XMNS$, they would also be theorems of OX, contrary to results just established. Hence the systems $XMNS$ are normal deontic logics.

To summarize: Addition of a propositional constant 'B' and definitions of 'S', 'P', 'O', (and 'F'), to any normal alethic modal logic X yields a normal deontic logic OX. Such systems arise *regardless* of the interpretation placed on 'B'; hence from a formal point of view we may regard deontic logic simply as a special branch of alethic modal logic.

It is easy to find an interpretation for 'B' which is consonant with the intended interpretation of 'S' and the deontic constants. Namely, we take 'B' again as expressing a sanction, or penalty of some sort. Then our original sanction 'S' (now defined as "$KMNBB$") is to be understood as saying that the sanction expressed by 'B' is true, but possibly false. And if the sanction expressed by 'B' is true, though possibly false, this situation can obviously itself count as a sanction 'S'. This makes 'S', if anything, even more poignant than as originally construed, since in the systems $XMNS$ we cannot say of 'S' that it is avoidable without a special assumption (Ax. 15) to that effect; whereas 'S' as now construed says that the bad state-of-affairs 'B' obtains, and adds the information (without extra assumptions) that 'B' could have been avoided.

In the sections to follow, we shall discuss in detail three normal deontic logics, namely OM, OM', and OM'' (got respectively by adding 'B' and the appropriate definitions to the alethic modal systems M, M', M'').

IV. The System OM

The normal deontic logic OM results from the addition of the constant 'B' to the system M of alethic modal logic.[53] We shall here summarize the axioms, principles of inference, and definitions for the system OM. (To distinguish the following discussion from that of previous sections, we use "A1," "A2," etc., to number axioms, "P1," "P2," etc., to number primitive

---

[53] The name 'M' was given to the system by von Wright [80], p. 85. An earlier formulation of the system by Feys [30] (labelled "tt") was shown equivalent to von Wright's M by Sobociński [74]. Addition of P4 below, to the system S2 of Lewis and Langford [48] also yields a system equivalent to M, as is remarked in A. R. Anderson [1]; and we take this occasion to note that addition of P3 to S2 has the same effect. Other formulations of M are discussed in Sobociński [74] and in A. R. Anderson [4]. Von Wright provided a decision procedure for M [80], an improved version of which may be found in A. R. Anderson [2]. Independent axioms are also available for M; see A. R. Anderson [8].

principles of inference, "D1," D2," etc., to number definitions, and "OM1," "OM2," etc., to number theorems of OM.)

Axioms:

A1. $CpCqp$
A2. $CCpCqrCCpqCpr$
A3. $CCNqNpCpq$
A4. $CpMp$
A5. $EMApqAMpMq$

Principles of inference:

P1. *Detachment*. If α and $C\alpha\beta$ are theorems of M, so is β.

P2. *Substitution*. If a is a theorem of M, and if β results from a by replacing every occurrence of a variable γ in a by a wff δ, then β is a theorem of M.

P3. *Extensionality*. If $C\alpha\beta$ is a theorem of M, then $CM\alpha M\beta$ is a theorem of M.

P4. *Necessitation*. If a is a theorem of M, then so is $NMN\alpha$.

Definitions:

D1. "La" is short for "$NMN\alpha$".
D2. "$C'\alpha\beta$" is short for "$LC\alpha\beta$".
D3. "S" is short for "$KMNBB$".
D4. "Pa" is short for "$MK\alpha NS$".
D5. "Oa" is short for "$NPN\alpha$".
D6. "Fa" is short for "NPa".
D7. "$K\alpha\beta$" is short for "$NC\alpha N\beta$."
D8. "$A\alpha\beta$" is short for "$NKN\alpha N\beta$."
D9. "$E\alpha\beta$" is short for "$KC\alpha\beta C\beta a$."

Axioms A1–A3 in this formulation of OM are due to Łukasiewicz;[54] together with the principles P1 and P2 they generate the whole of the two-valued propositional calculus. Axioms A4 and A5 should by this time be familiar. Principle P3 is somewhat stronger than the intersubstitutability principle required for normal alethic modal logics. As a direct consequence of P3 we have the following derived principle: if $Ea\beta$ and γ are theorems of OM, and if δ results from γ by writing a for one or more occurrences of β in γ, then δ is a theorem of OM. The difference between the principle just stated and the intersubstitutability (b) of Sect. I is that the latter demands that the equivalence $Ea\beta$ be a theorem of pc, whereas the former allows that the equivalence $Ea\beta$ might be a theorem of OM, and not of pc. In adding P3, we are therefore extending the minimal normal alethic modal logic $X^\star$; and the same remark holds for P4. The intuitive content of P4 is that every provable expression in OM is a necessary truth. The definitions have been discussed previously.

---

[54] See Łukasiewicz and Tarski [51].

The remainder of this section consists of a catalogue of elementary theorems provable in *OM*, together with occasional animadversions on their meanings. Proofs will for the most part be omitted, here and in following sections.

IV.1. *Relations among P, O, F, and S*

Most of these theorems are trivial, but are included here simply by way of summarizing remarks in Sect. I–III.

OM1. *EOpNPNp*. *p* is obligatory if and only if not-*p* is not permitted.

OM2. *EOpFNp*. *p* is obligatory if and only if not-*p* is forbidden.

OM3. *EFpNPp*. *p* is forbidden if and only if *p* is not permitted.

OM4. *EFpONp*. *p* is forbidden if and only if not-*p* is obligatory.

OM5. *EPpNONp*. *p* is permitted if and only if not-*p* is not obligatory.

OM6. *EPpNFp*. *p* is permitted if and only if *p* is not forbidden.

OM7. *EOpC'NpS*. *p* is obligatory if and only if not-*p* entails the sanction.

OM8. *EFpC'pS*. *p* is forbidden if and only if *p* entails the sanction.

OM9. *EPpMKpNS*. *p* is permitted if and only if it is possible that *p* is true and the sanction is false.

OM10. *COpPp*. If *p* is obligatory, then *p* is permitted.

OM11. *CFNpPp*. If not-*p* is forbidden, then *p* is permitted.

OM12. *CFpPNp*. If *p* is forbidden, then not-*p* is permitted.

IV.2. *Relations among A, K, and the deontic constants*

OM13. *CPpPApq*. If *p* is permitted then *p*-or-*q* is permitted.

Ordinary usage of the word "or" in such contexts may make OM13 appear counterintuitive, since we are not likely to give immediate assent to the proposition "if smoking is permitted then smoking or murder is permitted." The counterintuitive appearance is specious, however; it stems from the fact that "or" in ordinary English contexts of the form "*p* or *q* is permitted" is usually used in a sense more closely approximating the truth-functional sense of "and". When one says, for example, "You are permitted to go or stay, as you like," what is meant is that you are permitted to go *and* you are permitted to stay. Such a statement would be of the form *KPpPq*, rather than of the form *PApq*. Expressions of the form *PApq* have the interpretation "it is permitted that *at least one* of *p* and *q* be the case"; and if it is permitted that *p* be the case, then it is permitted that at least one of *p* and *q* be the case (namely *p*) – which is the intuitive content of OM13. Similar remarks apply to OM14.

OM14. *COpOApq*. If *p* is obligatory then *p*-or-*q* is obligatory.

A similar theorem is not forthcoming with '*F*' in place of '*O*', however. *FApq* has the interpretation "it is forbidden that at least one of *p* and *q* should be the case"; from which it follows that it is forbidden that *p* should be the case (for if *p* were permitted, then at least one of *p* and *q* would be permitted (OM13)). This is the intuitive content of OM15 and OM16.

OM15. $CFApqFp$. If p-or-q is forbidden then p is forbidden.

OM16. $E(FApq)(KFpFq)$. p-or-q is forbidden if and only if p is forbidden and q is forbidden.

OM17. $C(OApq)(APpPq)$. If p-or-q is obligatory, then p is permitted or q is permitted.

OM18. $C(PKpq)(KPpPq)$. If p-and-q is permitted then p is permitted and q is permitted.

The converse of OM18 is not provable; and this situation is intuitively satisfactory, since a normative system may well permit p and permit q, but fail to permit p-and-q. E.g., one may be permitted to promise to execute act X, and one may be permitted not to execute act X, but *not* permitted to promise to execute act X *and* not execute act X.

OM19. $E(OKpq)(KOpOq)$. p-and-q is obligatory if and only if p is obligatory and q is obligatory.

OM20. $CFpFKpq$. If p is forbidden then p-and-q is forbidden.

V. The Deontic Status of Impossible and Necessary Propositions

Questions as to the deontic status of impossible and necessary propositions rarely if ever arise in the course of normative deliberations, in large part, perhaps, because they are "academic," in the sense of leading to no practical conclusions. Reflections on the permissibility or obligatoriness of an impossible state-of-affairs are fruitless, since in the nature of the case nothing can be done toward realizing such states-of-affairs, and that not for empirical or practical reasons, but for purely logical ones. It is accordingly difficult, when faced with the question "Is $KpNp$ permitted, or forbidden, or obligatory, or none of these?" to decide what sort of answer to give.

Still, the propositions $PKpNp$, $FKpNp$, and $OKpNp$, all have an assignable sense in deontic systems, and it may well be that the systems thus far discussed may give us indications as to whether such statements should be regarded as true or false. Further, we may conjecture that what some writers have in mind in discussing the "consistency" of sets of norms has been, in part, at least, something like this: a set of norms is to be regarded as inconsistent if it specifies some state-of-affairs p such that $OKpNp$, i.e., such that p-and-not-p is obligatory. The latter suggestion requires qualification, perhaps, for reasons which will be discussed later (see OM35 in Sect. VI); but it serves for the moment to connect the apparently odd question "Can a contradictory state-of-affairs be obligatory?" with some more familiar considerations.

Now it develops that even in the minimal system $D^\star$ of Sect. II, enough assumptions have been made to eliminate *certain* answers to the question "Is $KpNp$ permitted, or forbidden, or obligatory, or none of these?" In particular, it follows from the assumptions of $D\star$ that $KpNp$ may *not* be consistently regarded as obligatory. For in $D\star$ it may be shown that if a is a theorem, then Pa is also a theorem;[55] i.e., all the "logically true" propositions of the system are permitted. Hence we may not hold that any "logically true" propositions are forbidden, nor (equivalently) that any "logically false" propositions are obligatory; and this view seems, at least, to coincide with intuitive feelings about the "consistency" of sets of norms.

Logically true propositions are at least permitted; should we say in addition that they are obligatory? A. N. Prior finds "no evident reasonableness"[56] in this assertion, and von Wright proposes, perhaps in the interests of paucity of assumptions, a principle of Deontic Contingency;[57] "A tautologous act is not necessarily obligatory, and a contradictory act is not necessarily forbidden." Such a principle may be held consistently vis-a-vis $D\star$, but the logical structure of OM definitely commits us to rejecting this principle, as the following theorems indicate:

OM21. $CLpOp$. Whatever is necessary is obligatory.

OM22. $CLpPp$. Whatever is necessary is permitted.

OM23. $CNMpFp$. Whatever is impossible is forbidden.

These theorems force us to change, or at least extend, our interpretations of the deontic modes as formalized in OM. We should understand "Oa," that is, as asserting that a is *either* obligatory (relatively to the sanction S), *or* necessary.[58] Similarly, "Pa" says that a is either permitted or necessary, and "Fa" says that a is either forbidden or impossible. Whether or not these interpretations accord with the usual usage of the English words "obligatory," "permitted," etc., it is difficult to say, since, as remarked before, questions as to the obligatory character of logically true propositions rarely if ever arise. But it is of interest to note that "ought," "must," and some other similar words *are* ambiguous in just the way that 'O' is ambiguous as between necessity and "pure" obligation: it is not uncommon to say "it ought to be the case" that something-or-other, meaning thereby that the something-or-other follows logically from propositions accepted as true. In any event we shall continue to interpret "Oa" as "a is obligatory," but we shall use the word "obligatory" in such a way as to allow for the possibility that what is said to be obligatory might also be necessary.

We take this tack at the moment for the sake of convenience, but it is not the only alternative. In Sect. IX we shall discuss the properties of an operator 'O'' such that "$O'a$" will have the interpretation "a is obligatory,

---

[55] This fact was pointed out by Prior ([69], p. 223), following up an observation of Jaakko Hintikka (in von Wright [80], p. 39).

[56] See Prior [69], p. 222.

[57] Von Wright [79], p. 11. This principle is of course consistent with the other two principles assumed by von Wright, though it is not consistent with OM.

[58] 'O' has just the interpretation proposed for his systems SX_m by Feys [31]. For further discussion of Feys's interpretation see Prior [70], Feys [32], and A. R. Anderson [12].

but not necessary." So we have (or will have) available in systems OX two operators, 'O' ("obligatory," in the sense of "obligatory or necessary") and 'O'' ("obligatory," in the sense of "obligatory but not necessary"). Which of these more adequately represents the ordinary English usage of "obligatory" is a linguistic question on which we shall not enter.

Theorems OM21–23 enable us to derive the following principle of inference for OM and all stronger systems:

If α is a theorem, then $O\alpha$, $P\alpha$, and $FN\alpha$ are all theorems.

Repeated applications of this principle, and the principle of necessitation, lead to theorems involving iterated modal notions; e.g., $OApNp$, $OOApNp$, $PApNp$, $OPApNp$, etc., as well as $OLApNp$, $PMApNp$, etc. For discussion of the sense of these expressions see Sect. VIII.

As regards further relations among the deontic and alethic modes we may mention the following theorems.

OM24. $COpMp$. Whatever is obligatory is possible.[59]

OM25. $CPpMp$. Whatever is permitted is possible.

OM26. $C(KOpC'pq)(Oq)$. If p is obligatory, and p entails q, then q is obligatory.[60]

OM27. $C(KPpC'pq)(Pq)$. If p is permitted, and p entails q, then q is permitted.

OM28. $C(KFpC'qp)(Fq)$. If p is forbidden, and q entails p, then q is forbidden.

VI. Commitment

In OM we are able to represent at least two distinct senses of the word "commitment." Neither of these will be chosen as *the* sense of the word for our purposes; both $OCpq$ and $C'pOq$ have similarities with certain uses of "p commits one to q."

The expression $OCpq$ was proposed by von Wright, who stated a number of theorems concerning "commitment" in this sense. We repeat here some of his theorems,[61] together with his interpretations of them (verbatim).

OM29. $C(KOpOCpq)(Oq)$. If doing what we ought to do commits us to do something else, then this new act is also something which we ought to do.

OM30. $C(KPpOCpq)(Pq)$. If doing what we are free to do commits us to do something else, then this new act is also something which we are free to do. In other words: doing the permitted can never commit us to do the forbidden.

---

[59] This is the Kantian principle, "What I ought, I can." It is also discussed in connection with deontic logic by Prior, [69], p. 224, and [71], Appendix D.

[60] Prior, [69], p. 228, discusses further the interpretation of OM26.

[61] OM29–OM34 are von Wright's theorems 1–6 [80], pp. 39–40.

OM31. $C(KFqOCpq)(Fp)$.   If doing something commits us to do the forbidden, then we are forbidden to do the first thing.

OM32. $C(K(OCpAqr)(KFqFr))(Fp)$.   An act which commits us to a choice between forbidden alternatives is forbidden.

OM33. $NK(OApq)(KFpFq)$.   It is logically impossible to be obliged to choose between forbidden alternatives.[62]

OM34. $C(KOpOCKpqr)(OCqr)$.   If doing two things, the first of which we ought to do, commits us to do a third thing, then doing the second thing alone commits us to do the third thing.   Our commitments, we might say, are not affected by our (other) obligations.

OM29–34, being theorems of von Wright's system, are also theorems of the systems OX, in particular of OM.   Some similar theorems arise in OM by replacing certain occurrences of F by NM, for example:

OM35. $C(KOCpqNMq)(Fp)$.   If doing p commits us to doing the impossible, then p is forbidden.

OM35 concerns cases where one might be committed by a previous action to do the impossible (as opposed to cases of being obligated outright to do the impossible; see sect. V).   An instance of OM35 in most societies would be that one should not contract debts one cannot repay.   I.e., if borrowing money commits one to repay it, and it is impossible to repay it, then it is forbidden to borrow it.   It seems to be a feature of most normative systems, or anyhow of those we would want to call "consistent," that though one cannot be obligated outright to do the impossible, one can, through doing something forbidden, be committed to doing the impossible. Similarly, though one cannot be obligated outright to choose between forbidden alternatives (OM33), one can be committed to a choice between forbidden alternatives (OM32) by a forbidden action.[63]   These features of OM seem to be in accord with the usual practice in existing normative systems.

It is well-known that the definitions of 'C'' lead to consequences which, according to some authors, have a counterintuitive character.[64]   In his exposition of von Wright's system, Prior suggests looking for "paradoxes" concerning $OCpq$, analogous to the so-called "paradoxes" of strict implication.[65]   As Prior points out, certain (possibly) *prima facie* counterintuitive results are forthcoming (in particular he mentions OM36–37 below).

---

[62] The English would be more appropriately rendered as $NMK(OApq)$ $(KFpFq)$, which is also a theorem of OM.

[63] As was pointed out by P. T. Geach, these theorems reflect a distinction discussed by St. Thomas; see von Wright [80], p. 40.

[64] For examples, see the citation in footnote 33.   It is the writer's view that the so-called "paradoxical" features of strict implication are intuitively acceptable; but the point will not be argued here.   These "paradoxes" have received considerable discussion in the literature; see for example Prior [69], pp. 193–198, and references there given.

[65] Prior [69], p. 224.

OM36. *COqOCpq*. If it is obligatory that *q*, then it is obligatory that if *p* then *q*.

We may interpret OM36 as indicating that the obligations considered in OM are such that *all* actions commit us to obligatory actions; i.e., if *q* is obligatory, then any act *p* commits us to *q* (not necessarily because of any hook-up between *p* and *q*, but rather because *q* is obligatory outright).

OM37. *CFpOCpq*. If it is forbidden that *p*, then it is obligatory that if *p* then *q*.

The intuitive content of OM37 may be more readily appreciated if we recast it in the following equivalent form.

OM38. *CFpOANpq*. If it is forbidden that *p* (i.e., if it is obligatory to realize not-*p*) then it is obligatory to realize not-*p* or *q* (namely, in this case, not-*p*).

In the form of OM38, the theorem is clearly unobjectionable. Such *prima facie* counterintuitive force as OM37 may have probably stems from a tendency to confuse it with *CFpC'pOq*, or with *CFpCpOq*. The former says that if *p* is forbidden, then *p* entails that *q* is obligatory; and the latter says that if *p* is forbidden then if *p*, then *q* is obligatory.[66] Both principles in effect say that the execution of a forbidden act makes *anything* obligatory; i.e., it completely destroys the normative structure – an unreasonable principle, surely, and not characteristic of any actual normative system known to the writer. Neither principle is provable in any of the deontic systems *OX*.

Still another way of viewing OM37, designed to deprive it of its counterintuitive appearance, is the following (suggested by Prior):

OM39. *C(Fp)(ONKpNq)*. If *p* is forbidden, then "we are obliged not to do *p* in conjunction with the omission of *q*."[67]

And the quoted clause, as Prior points out, "follows naturally enough from *Fp*, i.e., from our being obliged not to do *p* at all."

While OM37 need not itself be regarded as counterintuitive, it does suggest that we should be wary in interpreting *OCpq* as meaning "*p* commits us to *q*." An alternative candidate for the formal analogue of commitment is *C'pOq*: "*p* entails that *q* is obligatory." That this assertion is stronger than *OCpq* is expressed by the following.

OM40. *C(C'pOq)(OCpq)*. If *p* entails that *q* is obligatory, then it is obligatory that if *p* then *q*.

The converse of OM40 is not provable in any of the deontic systems.[68]

---

[66] For further remarks on *CFpCpOq*, see Prior [69], p. 225, and A. R. Anderson [11].

[67] Quoted, in effect, from Prior [69], p. 224.

[68] This and other statements concerning non-provability of formal expressions can be demonstrated with the help of various decision procedures available for the underlying alethic modal logics; see footnotes 53, 80, and 85. We omit the demonstrations.

Corresponding to OM29–32 we have the following theorems OM41–44, with $C'pOq$ in place of $OCpq$.

OM41. $C(KOpC'pOq)(Oq)$. If p is obligatory and p entails that q is obligatory, then q is obligatory.

OM42. $C(KPpC'pOq)(Pq)$. If p is permitted and p entails that q is obligatory, then q is permitted.

OM43. $C(KC'pOqFq)(Fp)$. If p entails that q is obligatory, and q is forbidden, then p is forbidden.

OM44. $C(K(C'pOAPr)(KFqFr))(Fp)$. If p entails that q-or-r is obligatory, and q and r are both forbidden, then p is forbidden.

The formula $COqC'pOq$, corresponding to OM36 with $C'pOq$ for $OCpq$, is not a theorem of OM, though it is a theorem of OM' and OM'' (see Sect. VIII below). The corresponding analogue of OM37, however, is not a theorem of any of the deontic systems. $CFpC'pOq$ suffers from the same intuitive objections as $CFpCpOq$, mentioned above. If $CFpC'pOq$ were a theorem of any of the deontic systems, so would be $CFpCpOq$, and since the latter fails, the former does also. The fact that $CFpC'pOq$ fails in deontic logics may be taken as supporting the view that $C'pOq$ (rather than $OCpq$) should be regarded as reflecting the notion of "commitment" in formal deontic logic.

We should perhaps add a word about $CpOq$, which expresses a notion of commitment, if at all, only in a very weak sense. For example, it is intuitively true of "commitment" that if p is obligatory, and p commits us to q, then q is obligatory (see OM29 and OM41). But the formula $C(KOpCpOq)(Oq)$ is not provable in any of the systems OM, OM', or OM''. The content of $C(KOpCpOq)(Oq)$ is: if it is obligatory that p, and if p then it is obligatory that q, then it is obligatory that q. That this formula is not intuitively true may be seen from the following considerations. Suppose that p is obligatory but false. Then the antecedent $KOpCpOq$ of $C(KOpCpOq)(Oq)$ is true, and we infer the consequent Oq, which says that anything is obligatory. Thus $C(KOpCpOq)(Oq)$ amounts to saying that if any obligatory proposition is false, then every proposition is obligatory; which is again not generally characteristic of normative systems.[69]

VII. Miscellaneous Theorems

As was remarked in Sect. V, if a is a theorem of OM, then Oa, OOa, etc., are theorems as well. Thus far, however, the only theorems of the form Oa we have considered have been such that a is also a theorem. We may very naturally ask, then, whether there are any theorems of the form Oa where a is not itself a theorem.

---

[69] $C(KOpCpOq)(Oq)$ is in fact deductively equivalent to $CFpCpOq$; see Prior [69], p. 225.

Prior[70] has suggested a candidate for this position which does turn out to be a theorem of OM (though it is not provable in von Wright's system[71] M or the systems SX_m proposed by Feys[72]):

OM45. $OCOpp$. It is obligatory that if p is obligatory then p.

We might more easily appreciate the intuitive significance of OM45 if we read it "It ought to be the case that whatever ought to be the case is the case." It is easy to show, with the help of the results of Sect. III, that $COpp$ is not a theorem of OM; hence OM45 satisfies the condition mentioned above.

$OCpOp$ is, however, not a theorem. $OCpOp$ is interdeducible with $CKpPNpS$, which says that the penalty follows from any (true) state-of-affairs, the denial of which is permitted. Such a principle would in effect require that every state-of-affairs be either obligatory or forbidden – surely too stringent a requirement for most normative systems. But we do have the following weaker principles:

OM46. $OCpPp$. It ought to be the case that whatever is the case is permitted.

OM47. $OCFpNp$. It ought to be the case that whatever is forbidden is not the case.

Among states-of-affairs which are forbidden outright, as one might expect, is the sanction itself:

OM48. FS. S is forbidden.

The sanction is forbidden, and, in view of remarks in Sect. III, possibly false. Whether or not the sanction is possible is not decided by the formal system OM; i.e., MS is not a theorem. But, as was remarked before, the sanction *is* possible in any normative system which allows that contravening the norms is a possibility – and this surely includes any normative system worth the name. This fact is expressed formally as:

OM49. $C(KFpMp)(MS)$. If the forbidden state-of-affairs p is possible, then the sanction is possible.

From OM49 and the theorem MNS, it follows that the sanction is contingent in any normative system which allows that wrongdoing is a possibility.

Various other relations between the alethic and deontic modes are provable, among them the following.

OM50. $COpOMp$. If p ought to be true, then it ought to be possible.

OM51. $CFpFLp$. If p ought not be true, then it ought not be necessary.

OM52. $CPpPMp$. If it is permitted that p be true, then it is permitted that p be possible.

Concerning iterated deontic modes we have the following:

---

[70] Prior [69], p. 225. For further discussion of the interpretation of OM45 see Prior [70], Feys [32], and A. R. Anderson [12].
[71] Von Wright [79] and [80], pp. 36–41.
[72] Feys [31].

OM53. $CPpPPp$. If p is permitted, then it is permitted that p be permitted.

Proof:

1	$C(KpNS)(MKpNS)$	A4, $p/KpNS$
2	$CKpqq$	pc
3	$CKpNSNS$	2, q/NS
4	$C(Cpq)(CCprCpKqr)$	pc
5	$C(CKpNSMKpNS)(C(CKpNSNS)$ $(C(KpNS)(KMKpNSNS))$	4, $p/KpNS$, $q/MKpNS$, r/NS
6	$C(CKpNSNS)(C(KpNS)(KMKpNSNS))$	1, 5, det
7	$C(KpNS)(KMKpNSNS)$	3, 6, det
8	$C(MKpNS)(MKMKpNSNS)$	7, extensionality
9	$C(Pp)(MKPpNS)$	8, Df. P
10	$CPpPPp$	9, Df. P

The intuitive content of OM53 may lead to confusion, unless we bear in mind that 'P' is always to be understood as relative to the (same) sanction S. For we sometimes have occasion to say things like "p is permitted, but ought not be permitted." Now *prima facie* this fact makes OM53 look counter-intuitive, but it only looks so if we fail to distinguish different senses of "permitted" and "ought" in the quoted sentence. If we say that a given practice is permitted in a given society, then we mean[73] (on the analysis here suggested) that in that society it is possible to adhere to the practice without incurring such sanctions or penalties as are effective in the society. When we go on to say that in spite of this the practice *ought not* be permitted, we mean that the practice is forbidden relatively to some *other* set of sanctions or penalties. For example, the assertion "infanticide, though permitted in Sparta, ought not to be permitted," would be taken as meaning that relatively to the sanctions effective in Sparta, infanticide was permitted, but that relatively to some other set of sanctions (perhaps those effective in our society, perhaps some sanctions arrived at by philosophical reflection), infanticide is not permitted. We would clearly *not* take the quoted remark as meaning that the Spartans permitted infanticide, but did not permit permitting it. Such an assertion *would* contradict OM53, but it is extremely doubtful whether anyone would ever want to hold such a view – indeed OM53 gives good ground for saying that such a view would be logically inconsistent. In other words, if a practice ought not be permitted (i.e., if it is forbidden, relatively to a sanction, that it be permitted, relatively to the *same* sanction), then it is forbidden (relatively, again, to the same sanction).[74] This is the content of OM54.

---

[73] It is important to note that the analysis suggested need not *exhaust* the meaning of "p is permitted," nor need the "sanction" S be one of the customary social sanctions. The writer wishes to make no such claim. On this point see Sect. X.

[74] For a discussion of the artificiality involved in having just one sanction S, see Sect. X.

OM54. $CFPpFp$. If it is forbidden that p be permitted, then p is forbidden.

Similar remarks apply to the following theorem.

OM55. $COOpOp$. If p ought to be obligatory, then p is obligatory.

Again, such slight counterintuitive appearance as OM55 may have is no doubt due to a tendency to think of "ought" and "obligatory," in the interpretation above, as relative to different sanctions, instead of to the same sanction.

We can also prove another group of theorems, stemming from OM56, below.

OM56. $CPNPNpPp$. (I.e., $CPOpPp$, if it is permitted that p be obligatory, then it is permitted that p be true.)

Proof:

1	$C(KNMKNpqq)(Kpq)$	M^{75}
2	$C(K(NMKNpNS)NS)(KpNS)$	1, q/NS
3	$C(MK(NMKNpNS)NS)(MKpNS)$	2, extensionality
4	$CPNPNpPp$	3, Df. P

From OM56 we readily get:

OM57. $C(NPp)(NPNPNp)$. (I.e., $CFpFOp$, if p is forbidden, then it is forbidden that p be obligatory.)

OM58. $CPNPpPNp$. (I.e., $CPFpNp$, if it is permitted that p be forbidden, then it is permitted that p be false.)

OM59. $C(NPNp)(NPNPp)$. (I.e., $COpOPp$, if p is obligatory, then p ought to be permitted.)

Finally, we state without proof the following two derivable principles of inference, which will be of use in the section to follow:

P-extensionality. If $Ca\beta$ is a theorem of OM, then $CPaP\beta$ is a theorem of OM.

O-extensionality. If $Ca\beta$ is a theorem of OM, then $COaO\beta$ is a theorem of OM.

These two principles are also available in the systems OM' and OM'' of the following section.

VIII. Iterated Deontic Modalities

Parry[76] gives what amounts to the following recursive definition of (alethic) *modalities*:

1. Any propositional variable is a modality;
2. if a is a modality, then Ma and Na are modalities;
3. an expression is a modality only if it is so in virtue of clause 1 or 2.

---

[75] In the future we shall use this notation to refer to easily proved theorems of M, and similarly for M' and M'' in the next section. In the interest of further compressing proofs, we shall sometimes justify steps simply by reference to preceding steps from which they can be shown to follow by elementary techniques.

[76] Parry [67].

For example, p, Np, Mp, NMp, MNp, MMp, NNp, etc., are all modalities. In virtue of the equivalence $EpNNp$ of pc and the derivable rule for the intersubstitutability of material equivalents in M, any modality in M can be proved equivalent to a modality in which there are no two consecutive occurrences of N. But further than this no reduction is possible. M, that is to say, distinguishes infinitely many modalities.[77]

This fact leaves us with the problem of distinguishing among the meanings of, for example, Mp, MMp, $MMMp$, etc., all of which are distinguished (by failure of intersubstitutability) in M. We may be able to distinguish intuitively between "it is possible that p," and "it is possible that it is possible that p"; but as modalities grow more complex, logical intuitions seem to flag. What difference are we to make between "it is false that it is possible that it is false that it is possible that it is false that it is possible that p" ($NMNMNMp$) and "it is false that it is possible that it is false that it is possible that it is false that it is possible that it is possible that p" ($NMNMNMMp$)?

A similar situation faces us vis-a-vis the deontic modalities in OM. We define *deontic modalities* in the following way:

1. Any propositional variable is a deontic modality;

2. if a is a deontic modality, then Pa and Na are deontic modalities;

3. an expression is a deontic modality if and only if it is so in virtue of clause 1 or 2.

It is then possible to show that OM distinguishes infinitely many deontic modalities, and that in particular Pp, PPp, $PPPp$, etc., are all distinct. But again it is difficult to distinguish between the meanings of, e.g., "it is permitted that p" and "it is permitted that it is permitted that p."

The difficulty of distinguishing the meanings of complex alethic modalities has led certain authors to propose additional axioms[78] which have the effect of identifying some of the modalities. Among the more important of these is the following.

A7. $CMMpMp$. If it is possible that it is possible that p, then it is possible that p.

This axiom, due originally to Becker,[79] when added to the alethic system M leads to the M' of von Wright (equivalent to Lewis's system S4.[80]) Parry[81] has shown that M', unlike M, distinguishes just fourteen modalities, namely, the following seven, together with their denials:

---

[77] Proved by Sobociński [74].

[78] For a discussion of these see Lewis and Langford [48], and Parry [67].

[79] See Becker [17].

[80] This system has been extensively investigated. For independent axioms see Simons [73]; for decision procedures see McKinsey [52], von Wright [80], and A. R. Anderson [2].

[81] Parry [67].

1. p
2. Mp
3. MNp
4. $MNMp$
5. $MNMNp$ (i.e., MLp)
6. $MNMNMp$ (i.e., $MLMp$)
7. $MNMNMNp$ (i.e., $MLMNp$)

Every (alethic) modality in M' is equivalent to one of these fourteen modalities: i.e., it is equivalent to (and intersubstitutable with) one of the seven listed, or the denial of one of the seven listed. The implication relations holding among the fourteen alethic modalities of M' are summarized as follows (where if there is an arrow leading from α to β, then $C\alpha\beta$ is a theorem of M'):

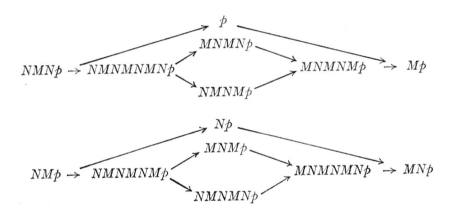

Adapting methods used by Parry to reduce alethic modalities in M', we can also show that the deontic modalities in OM' reduce to at most fourteen. We require the following theorems of OM':

OM'60.[82] $CPPpPp$. If it is permitted that p be permitted, then p is permitted.

Proof:

1	$CMKpqMp$	M
2	$C(MK(MKpNS)NS)(MMKpNS)$	1, $p/MKpNS$, q/NS
3	$C(MMKpNS)(MKpNS)$	A7, $p/KpNS$
4	$C(MK(MKpNS)NS)(MKpNS)$	2, 3, trans C
5	$CPPpPp$	4, Df. P

[82] Theorems of OM' (and OM'', below) will be so numbered. Since OM is a subsystem of OM', we may use theorems of OM in carrying out proofs in OM'. Similar remarks apply to OM'' (of which OM', and consequently also OM, are subsystems).

Taken together with OM53, OM'60 yields $EPPpPp$, and in view of the intersubstitutability of material equivalents in OM', this means that OM' fails to distinguish between "it is permitted that p" and "it is permitted that it is permitted that p." Moreover, since $ENNpNp$ is a theorem of pc, and hence of OM', all modalities in OM' reduce to modalities consisting of a string of alternating N's and P's. The following theorems show that no such string need contain more than three P's.

OM'61. $E(PNPNPNPp)(PNPp)$. (This is difficult to interpret. We may write it equivalently $E(PFFFp)(PFp)$, indicating that under certain circumstances two F's may be struck out, or as $E(POPFp)(PFp)$ which says of the proposition PFp that it is true if and only if it is permitted that it be obligatory. The strain on one's logical intuitions occasioned by such modalities as $PNPNPNPp$ may be regarded as one reason for identifying longer ones with shorter ones, where feasible, and in particular for identifying $PNPNPNPp$ with $PNPp$, which is the sense of OM'61.)

Proof:

1	$C(K(NMKNpq)q)p$	M
2	$C(K(NMKNPpNS)NS)Pp$	1, p/Pp, q/NS
3	$C(MK(NMKNPpNS)NS)MPp$	2, extensionality
4	$C(PNPNPp)MPp$	3, Df. P
5	$CMPpPp$	A7, $p/KpNS$, Df. P
6	$C(PNPNPp)Pp$	4, 5, trans C
7	$C(NPp)(NPNPNPp)$	6 PC
8	$C(NPp)(PNPNPNPp)$	7, P-extensionality
9	$C(PNPNPNPp)(PNPp)$	6, p/NPp

The result required follows from steps 8 and 9. OM'61 guarantees that any modality consisting of alternating N and P collapses to a modality with not more than three P's. OM' therefore distinguishes at most fourteen modalities, which (if we replace 'M' by 'P') are formally similar to the alethic modalities distinguished by M'. They are as follows, using definitions of F and O:

1	p	8	Np
2	Pp	9	Fp
3	PNp	10	Op
4	PFp	11	OPp
5	POp	12	FOp
6	$POPp$	13	$OPFp$
7	$PFOp$	14	$OPOp$

Every deontic modality in OM' is demonstrably equivalent to one of those mentioned above. Implication relations among deontic modalities are as follows.

192

$$a \qquad c\ POp\ b \qquad a$$
$$Op \to OPOp \diagdown\diagup POPp \to Pp$$
$$b\ OPp\ c$$

$$a \qquad c\ PFp\ b \qquad a$$
$$Fp \to OPFp \diagdown\diagup PFOp \to PNp$$
$$b\ FOp\ c$$

The implications marked 'a' follow readily from step 6 of the proof of OM'61. Implications marked 'b' follow from OM'62.

OM'62. $C(PNPp)(PNPNPNp)$. (I.e., $CPFpPFOp$, if it is permitted that it is forbidden that p, then it is permitted that it is forbidden that p be obligatory.)

Proof:

1	$C(NPp)(NPNPNp)$	OM57
2	$C(PNPp)(PNPNPNp)$	1, P-extensionality

And implications marked 'c' follow from OM'63.

OM'63. $C(NPNPNPNp)(PNPNp)$. (I.e., $COPOpPOp$, if it is obligatory that it is permitted that p be obligatory, then it is permitted that p be obligatory.)

Proof:

1	$C(NPNPNPNp)(PPNPNp)$	OM10, $p/PNPNp$
2	$C(PPNPNp)(PNPNp)$	OM'60, $p/NPNp$
3	$C(NPNPNPNp)(PNPNp)$	1, 2, trans C

It will be noticed that the structure of deontic modalities in OM' is the same[83] as the structure of alethic modalities in M', save for the lack of connection between deontic modalities and truth or falsity. The failure of implications between proper deontic modalities and truth or falsity reflects the lack of connection between "is" and "ought," so often stressed by moral philosophers. It is no doubt true that a sharp distinction is made by most normative systems between what *is* the case and what *ought* to be the case, but it is doubtful whether the distinction need drive us to the view that

[83] (*Added in 1966*) In the original (1956) version of this paper, the question as to whether or not further reduction of deontic modalities could be obtained was left open. The problem was solved by Saul Kripke, who wrote me on August 1, 1958: "Add to OM' the axiom NMS; in the resulting system Mp and Pp are equivalent, so that the deontic modalities reduce to their alethic counterparts. Now in the augmented system 'S' (or 'B') can be taken to be any demonstrably impossible proposition, so that we do not obtain any alethic theorems beyond those of M' (and we can still define 'S' within M'). In M' it is known that the fourteen alethic modalities are irreducible; hence no further reduction of deontic modalities is possible in OM'."

normative statements and factual statements are somehow irreducibly different in kind, having no logical connection whatever. On this point see Sect. X.

The number of distinct deontic modalities is reduced, in OM', to a manageable number, but they still present a rather bewildering variety, and it is doubtful whether any actual normative system in fact makes as many distinctions as are available in OM' (though of course this is a question for empirical investigation). Moreover, if any normative system were found in which just fourteen deontic modalities were distinguished, there would be no reason *a priori* to suppose that the fourteen distinguished were just the fourteen distinguished by OM'. A further reduction of the number of distinct deontic modalities might be achieved in either of two ways.

(a) We might add further axioms concerning the deontic modalities themselves, for example, $COPFpFp$.[84] (And, of course, it would be possible also to add axioms concerning deontic modalities directly to OM as well; this alternative will not be discussed here.) Just what effect the addition of reduction axioms concerning the deontic modalities has on the systems OM and OM' has yet to be investigated.

(b) We might repeat the procedure which led from OM to OM'; that is, we might add further reduction axioms for alethic modalities directly to the underlying alethic modal logic, leaving the definitions of P, O, F, etc., the same. We shall conclude this section by mentioning one such system.

The result of adding the following axiom to the system M' yields a system known as M''.[85]

A8. $CMNMpNMp$. If it is possible that p is impossible, then p is impossible.

Since all the implication relations available in M' are also available in M'', the latter will distinguish no more modalities than the former. And in view of the theorems $EMMpMp$ (provable in M') and $EMNMpNMp$ (provable in M''), every modality in M'' reduces to a modality containing at most one occurrence of 'M' and one occurrence of 'N'. These reductions lead to a total of six modalities distinguished by M'', namely:

1	p		4	Np
2	Mp		5	NMp
3	MNp		6	$NMNp$

---

[84] This is the deontic analogue of an alethic modal axiom discussed by Parry [67], pp. 150–151.

[85] The name M'' is due to von Wright [80], p. 85. M'' is equivalent to the system S5 of Lewis and Langford [48]. This system has also been much discussed in the literature on modal logic. For decision procedures see Wajsberg [78], Carnap [23], and von Wright [80]. For alternative formulations see the writers just cited and Parry [67]. For independent axioms see A. R. Anderson [7].

Every (alethic) modality in M'' is equivalent to one of the six listed. The implication relations among these modalities are the following:

$$NMNp \to p \to Mp$$
$$NMp \to Np \to MNp$$

OM'' also reduces deontic modalities to six, as shown by the following theorem.

OM''64. $EPNPpNPp$. (I.e., $EPFpFp$, it is permitted that p be forbidden, if and only if p is forbidden.)

Proof:

1	$CMKpqMp$	M
2	$C(MK(NMKpNS)NS)(MNMKpNS)$	1, $p/NMKpNS$, q/NS
3	$C(MNMKpNS)(NMKpNS)$	A8, $p/KpNS$
4	$CPNPpNPp$	2, 3, trans C, Df. P

From the table of implications for deontic modalities in OM', we see that $CFpOPFp$ (i.e., $CNPpOPFp$) and $COPFpPFp$ (i.e., $COPFpPNPp$) are both theorems of OM' (and therefore of OM''); hence by trans C we have $CNPpPNPp$, and OM''64 then follows with the help of step 4 above.

The three theorems $CNNpp$, $EPPpPp$, and $EPNPpNPp$ of OM'' enable us to collapse all deontic modalities in OM'' to deontic modalities with no consecutive occurrence of N or P, and with no more than one occurrence of P; i.e., to the six listed below.

1	p		4	Np
2	Pp		5	NPp (i.e., Fp)
3	PNp		6	$NPNp$ (i.e., Op)

And the implication relations among these are just the following.

$$NPNp \to Pp$$
$$NPp \to PNp$$

These relations among modalities in OM'' are particularly simple, and the writer would conjecture that as a matter of fact no actual normative systems distinguish more deontic modalities than the six distinguished by OM'' (though, of course, this would again be a matter for empirical investigation). The situation vis-a-vis combined alethic and deontic modalities is also especially simple in OM'', since if a is a proper deontic modality (i.e., one of $NPNp$, NPp, Pp, PNp), then $EaLa$ and $EaMa$ are both theorems of OM''. That is, OM'' makes no distinction between "p is obligatory," "p is necessarily obligatory," and "p is possibly obligatory," and similarly with other proper modalities.

The simplicity of OM'' recommends it as a system with which to initiate the empirical study of the logic of actual normative systems. If it should develop that there are normative structures which make distinctions among deontic modalities not reflected by OM, OM', or OM'', then it would be a task for logicians to construct (if it is possible consistently to do so) deontic systems which accurately reflect the distinctions in fact made by the structures in question. The systems OM, OM', and OM'' represent three alternative ways of handling questions concerning iterated deontic operators; but these are not the only ways, since, as the results of Sect. III indicate, a normal deontic logic can be constructed by adding appropriate definitions to *any* normal alethic modal logic, and there are many logics of the latter kind.

IX. RESTRICTION OF DEONTIC MODES TO CONTINGENT PROPOSITIONS

It was suggested in Sect. V that one approach to the deontic status of necessary and impossible propositions would involve defining obligation, permission, and prohibition in such a way as to apply only to contingent propositions, i.e., to those which are neither necessary nor impossible. Such a course would be dictated in part by our discomfort when faced with such questions as "Are necessary states-or-affairs obligatory?"[86] It will be remembered that in the systems OM, OM', and OM'', the expression "Op" has the interpretation "p is obligatory or necessary," or "it ought to be the case (for either normative or logical reasons) that p." The operator 'O''', defined below, has the interpretation "it ought to be the case, for normative, but not for logical reasons, that p." Similarly for P' and F'.

D7. "$O'a$" is short for "$KOaMNa$". ("$O'a$" is short for "a is obligatory, but possibly false (i.e., not necessary).")

D8. "$F'a$" is short for "$KFaMa$." ("$F'a$" is short for "a is forbidden, but possible.")

D9. "$P'a$" is short for "$KPaMNa$". ("$P'a$" is short for "a is permitted, but possibly false.")

In informal discussion, we shall read "$O'a$" as "*obligatory*" (i.e., *underlined*, with a "prime" sign added), and similarly for 'F'' and 'P'', in order to distinguish the senses of these operators from those of 'O', 'F', and 'P'. The systems obtained from OM, OM', and OM'' by the addition of D7–D9 will be referred to as "$O'M$," "$O'M'$," and "$O'M''$," respectively.

If we read "$KMpMNp$" as "p is contingent," the intent to restrict O', F', and P', to contingent propositions is reflected in the following three theorems.

O'M65. $C(O'p)(KMpMNp)$. If p is *obligatory'*, then p is contingent.

O'M66. $C(P'p)(KMpMNp)$. If p is *permitted'*, then p is contingent.

O'M67. $C(F'p)(KMpMNp)$. If p is *forbidden'*, then p is contingent.

[86] Compare Menger [57], pp. 58–59: "No normal man wishes that tomorrow it may either rain or not rain, nor that tomorrow it may neither rain nor not rain. It is likewise unreasonable to command another man that he should either pay nor not pay a certain sum, or that he should neither pay nor not pay a sum. . . . In general we can say: *The objects of our wishes and commands are neither necessities nor impossibilities.*" Such a view might very reasonably be extended to statements of obligation.

One result of construing deontic modes in this way is that the logical relations among them become conspicuously less tidy than among O, P, and F. For example, "p is not obligatory" is equivalent to "not-p is permitted"; but "p is not *obligatory*'" is not equivalent to "not-p is *permitted*'." The point is that if p is not *obligatory*', this might be true for either of two reasons: p might be necessary (in which case it would not be *obligatory*' since only contingent propositions are *obligatory*'), or p might fail to be obligatory (in which case it would not be *obligatory*' either, since only obligatory propositions are *obligatory*'). As a consequence, many of the simple equivalence relations of Sect. IV.1 fail to hold for O', P', and F'. For example OM1 (which was $EOpNPNp$) gives way to:

O'M68. $CO'pNP'Np$. If p is *obligatory*', then not-p is not *permitted*'.

The converse $CNP'NpO'p$ of O'M68 fails for reasons similar to those just discussed. The failure of the equivalence relations of OM1–6 means that many substitutions used in proofs in OM, OM', and OM'', are not available for the modes O', P', and F', with the result that the latter modes have a more cumbersome set of interrelations. The situation can to a certain extent be improved, however, by requiring antecedently that the states-of-affairs governed by the deontic modes O', P', and F', be contingent. By adding such stipulations, the relatively simple relations among O, P, and F, can be retained for O', P', and F'. For example, corresponding to OM1, we have

O'M69. $C(KMpMNp)(EO'pNP'Np)$. If p is contingent, then p is *obligatory*' and if and only if not-p is not *permitted*'.

Similarly with OM2–12: corresponding to each of these theorems there is a theorem concerning O', P', and F', obtained by adding the antecedent condition $KMpMNp$, and changing O to O', etc. From OM2 we get $C(KMpMNp)(EO'pF'Np)$; from OM3, $C(KMpMNp)(EF'pNP'p)$; and so on.

We can obviate the necessity of stipulating contingency of the states-of-affairs to which the deontic operators O', P', and F' are to be applied, by the device of adopting a new style of variable, together with suitable notational conventions. Let us agree that any formula a containing as variables 'a', 'b', 'c', etc., in place of 'p', 'q', 'r', etc., is to be understood as shorthand notation for a formula β containing the usual variables, together with an antecedent stipulation to the effect that all expressions governed by O', P', or F' in a are contingent. I.e., let us take "$EO'aNP'Na$" as short for "$C(KMpMNp)(EO'pNP'Np)$," "$EO'aF'Na$" as short for "$C(KMpMNp)(EO'pF'Np)$," "$E(P'Aab)(AP'aP'b)$" for "$C(K(K(KMpMNp)$ $(KMqMNq))(K(MApq)(MNApq)))(E(P'Apq)(AP'pP'q))$," and so on. Using these conventions (for which we shall not bother to give a rigorous statement), some of the relations among O', P', and F', may be perspicuously expressed as follows:

197

O'M70. $EO'aNP'Na$. For contingent propositions a, a is *obligatory'* if and only if not-a is not *permitted'*.

O'M71. $EF'aNP'a$. For contingent propositions a, a is *forbidden'* if and only if it is not *permitted'*.

O'M72. $CO'aP'a$. For contingent propositions a, if a is *obligatory'*, then a is *permitted'*.

O'M73. $E(P'Aab)(AP'aP'b)$. For contingent propositions a and b, such that a-or-b is also contingent, a-or-b is *permitted'* if and only if a is *permitted'* or b is *permitted'*.

It is not difficult to show that the system $O'M$, together with the conventions governing the special variables 'a', 'b', etc., constitutes a normal deontic logic in the sense of Sect. II. That is, if in the statement of the conditions defining a normal deontic logic, we take O as O', P as P', and variables as 'a', 'b', etc., then $O'M$ can be shown to satisfy the three defining conditions (a), (b), and (c), of normal deontic logics. This is, of course, hardly surprising, but it is of interest in indicating that the defining conditions for normal deontic logics are sufficiently general so as to admit either "obligatory" or "*obligatory'*" as interpretations for operator 'O'.

In the systems $O'X$ it is possible also to define and prove plausible theorems about additional deontic concepts. It was remarked in Sect. II (footnote 39) that, in effect, there is perhaps an alternative sense of the English word "permitted," in which a state-of-affairs p is regarded as "permitted" if p *guarantees* avoidance of the penalty. That this is probably not the most usual sense of "permitted" may be seen from such considerations as the following. In a railroad car bearing the sign "smoking forbidden," it is usually understood (and sometimes explicitly stated) that smoking is punishable in some way by some authority, say by being fined five dollars by appropriate legal action. But the sign "smoking permitted," appearing in a smoking car, is not understood to mean that smoking guarantees that the five dollar fine will not be levied, since one might well be fined five dollars for another activity compatible with smoking, say spitting, or committing some other public nuisance. Pretty clearly "smoking permitted" is taken to mean that it is *possible* to smoke without incurring the penalty, not that smoking *guarantees* avoidance of the penalty.

Still, we are interested in states-of-affairs which guarantee escape from penalties, and a review of the fundamental theorems of our deontic systems indicates that thus far such states-of-affairs have not been explicitly considered. For we have said that a state-of-affairs p is obligatory if not-p leads to the sanction (and *obligatory'* if in addition p is contingent), forbidden if p leads to the sanction (and *forbidden'* if p is also contingent), and permitted if not-p does not lead to the sanction (and *permitted'* if p is contingent). That is, we have not explicitly considered states-of-affairs which lead (or fail to lead) to the *denial* of the sanction.

States-of-affairs which entail the denial of the sanction might, for example, be regarded as *prudent*, and those which do not may be regarded as *imprudent*, or *risky*, or *rash*. We shall not discuss such notions extensively here, beyond noting that in normative systems in which the sanction is possible,[87] the logic of "rash" and related concepts is strictly isomorphic with the logic of "permitted" and related concepts. I.e., the resulting systems are normal deontic logics in the sense of Sect. II, with 'P' interpreted as "rash," and 'O' interpreted as "not-rash-not." Moreover, in such systems the expected relations among the various deontic concepts hold, at least among contingent propositions.[88] For example, any contingency that is forbidden is rash, any that is obligatory is prudent, and so on. And it is of interest to note that these concepts provide a third interpretation of *normal deontic logics*: we may read 'P' equally well as "permitted," "*permitted'*," or "rash," and in each case have an intuitively plausible interpretation of the syntactical system.

We have seen that it is possible to define deontic operators which accord more closely with ordinary usage (perhaps) in being restricted in application to contingent propositions. Adopting this device also enables us to define in a plausible way certain other deontic concepts. But in the writer's opinion it is doubtful whether these gains are adequate compensation for the additional complications which ensue. In the first place, if the intended interpretation of 'O' as "obligatory for logical or normative reasons" is borne carefully in mind, no confusion need occur as a consequence of the fact that, e.g., $OApNp$ is a theorem. Secondly, the complications involved in requiring contingency of propositions characterized as *obligatory'*, *permitted'*, and *forbidden'* make it considerably less easy to get an intuitive insight into the formal relations. And thirdly (a point which illustrates the second remark), in the stronger systems, some intuitively unpalatable results arise. For example, one is able to prove in $O'M''$ that for any p, it is *forbidden'* that p be *permitted'*; i.e., $NP'P'p$.[89] This certainly does not accord with our intuitive intent, and may be regarded as a reason for considering 'O' as closer to our usual sense of "obligatory" than 'O'''. For these reasons we shall postpone further discussion of the systems $O'M$, $O'M'$, and $O'M''$ until such time as subsequent investigations may show them to be of more interest.

---

[87] It will be recalled that this is no very great requirement, since in any normative system which allows that wrong-doing is a possibility, the sanction will be contingent.

[88] But not in general. For example, impossible states-of-affairs are forbidden in the systems OX, but they are not rash, under this construction, since p is rash only if it is possible that p and the sanction are both the case, hence only if it is possible that p. Still, common usage would incline us to say that whatever is forbidden is rash (or imprudent, or risky), and this fact may be considered as an argument in favor of considering F' as more adequately reflecting the common-sense notion than F.

[89] This fact was pointed out to me by Professor Prior, in correspondence.

IX. Adequacy of the Systems OX

The systems *OX* discussed in this *Report* have been proposed for two purposes. (1) They are intended to explicate a group of concepts which are familiar to investigators in the behavioral sciences, and to provide a way of formulating rigorously logical relations among these concepts; and (2) they are intended to serve as a vehicle for the formulation and study of other normative systems, for example, systems of positive law, sets of rules for games, or substantive ethical and moral theories as proposed by philosophers. The success or failure of the systems *OX* must accordingly be judged by their success or failure in providing conceptual tools for the analysis of normative systems generally. And inasmuch as no such applications have yet been attempted, we can say nothing very conclusive about the adequacy of these formalisms. Still, it is possible to give some indication of the direction that further investigations might take, and to answer certain *prima facie* plausible objections to the approach presented here. It is to these topics that the present section will be devoted.

But before discussing considerations in favor of the adequacy of the formal analysis, it will be well to consider some limitations of the systems *OX*, and ways in which more extensive logics may be constructed.

In the first place, the systems *OX* are concerned solely with the *propositional* content of normative systems. No machinery is available within these systems for the explicit formal consideration of acts, agents, or the like. In this respect the systems are analogous to the two-valued propositional calculus, and alethic modal propositional logics. All these systems, in order to be of value in the analysis of most problems, must be supplemented with a theory of quantification.[90] Quantificational extensions of systems *OX* will be discussed in a sequel to this *Report*. In these extensions it will be possible to formalize statements mentioning individual agents in a society, such as "*A* has a duty toward *B*", where *A* and *B* are persons (or institutions, in the generalized legal sense of "person"). We can also characterize legal relations as analyzed, for example, by Hohfeld.[91]

The fact that the systems *OX* are calculi of propositions, however, does not constitute a defect (though it is a limitation). A propositional calculus of some sort is always required as a foundation for any theory at all, since the content of any theory is expressed in (or by) propositions. In presenting a calculus for deontic propositions, considered in abstraction from any particular content, we are laying such foundations for more extensive systems.

---

[90] The theory of quantification deals with notions of existence ("there is an x such that x has the property ϕ") and universality ("for all x, x has the property ϕ"). For discussion of this theory see any standard textbook on logic; for the extended propositional calculus, mentioned below, see Church [26], pp. 151 ff.

[91] See Hohfeld [42], and the application of Hohfeld's ideas in Hoebel [40].

A second limitation of the present system stems from the fact that a single sanction S is taken as the basis for definitions of the deontic concepts. This again is not a defect; it is a deliberate simplification characteristic of the mathematical approach in general. In Euclidean geometry, for example, it is customary to consider dimensionless points, and one-dimensional lines. The fact that the points and lines we draw (on blackboards or on paper) are three-dimensional blobs of chalk or graphite is not taken as an objection to Euclidean geometry; it is simply recognized that the points and lines we draw are different from (but a model of) the corresponding geometrical concepts. Similarly, the fact that there are no frictionless pulleys is not taken as showing the worthlessness of Newtonian mechanics. And in the case of the systems OX, the fact that there are probably no normative systems in which one single proposition is taken as *the* sanction, need not deter us from studying the logic of such a system. It is frequently fruitful as a heuristic device to consider the simplest possible case, not because any such case is actualized, but because it is easiest to "see one's way around" in the simpler cases.

And having seen how the simplest case looks, it is then not so difficult to generalize to more complex ones. For example in the extended propositional calculus, with axioms for alethic modal logic, it is possible to consider a class of propositions, any one of which might function as a sanction. In such a system, we can define obligation in the following way: a state-of-affairs p is obligatory if and only if there is a proposition q such that q is a sanction, and not-p entails q. This approach allows for a variety of penalizing states-of-affairs some of which may be more severe than others.[92] Alternatively, one can consider several classes of penalizing states-of-affairs of varying severity (e.g., as in many legal codes, fining, imprisonment, execution), and define a variety of senses of obligation. It is also possible to define obligations in such a way that an agent might be obligated (relatively to one set of sanctions) to realize a certain state-of-affairs, and obligated (relatively to a different set of sanctions) *not* to realize the same state-of-affairs. Systems of this type would enable us to deal formally with the familiar notion of "rôle-conflict" ("conflict of obligations"). The point we wish to emphasize is that the limitations characteristic of the systems OX are accidental to these systems, and *not* characteristic of the logical approach. Techniques of symbolic logic are sufficiently flexible and general to allow for the construction of formal systems of virtually any complexity.

But granting that the limitations of the systems OX are due to their simplicity, and that sufficiently elaborate structures involving the same

---

[92] For techniques which can be used to measure the "severity" of sanctions see Davidson, McKinsey, and Suppes [29], von Neumann and Morgenstern [65], pp. 24 ff, and *passim*, and Suppes and Winet [76]. For a suggestive application of the theory of games to problems of measuring value, see Braithwaite [21].

leading ideas can be built, one may still ask whether construing obligations in terms of sanctions adequately reflects our intuitive ideas of obligation. In favor of the view that our definitions of the deontic operators do little or no damage to the usual sense of obligation, we can offer evidence from several quarters.

(a) In the first place, it has been customary among social scientists to speak as if obligations in a given society are precisely those acts the omission of which is punished. The view that norms are always related to sanctions is sufficiently common in sociological and anthropological literature as to make citation of supporting references otiose.

It will perhaps be charged in philosophical quarters, however, that the formalisms presented here commit one to a teleological[93] form of ethical or moral theory, and that, accordingly, the systems OX are not "neutral" to important issues in ethics or morals in the same way that, for example, the two-valued propositional calculus is "neutral" to various scientific theories. For it is usually admitted that the two-valued propositional calculus, alethic modal logics, and quantificational extensions thereof are "neutral," in the sense that their acceptance does not commit us to any empirically verifiable conclusions. They are designed simply to show the logical relations among propositions, but not to tell us which empirical propositions are in fact true. It is of course important to know what logical relations various propositions bear to each other, and such knowledge is useful and influential in, for example, deciding what experiments to carry out. Still, competing scientific theories can both be formalized in these calculi, without commitment to one or the other.

We would require similarly of a system of logic designed to handle normative concepts that it not predispose the investigation in favor of one or another of various theories about norms. Such predisposition would in effect be a serious limitation on the calculi, since the purpose of the calculi is to enable us to deal rigorously with *any* normative structure, and perhaps on the basis of such rigorous formalization enable us more easily to decide between competing theories. Now if it is correct that the systems OX predispose the case in favor of teleological as opposed to deontological theories of norms, this is a serious charge.

It is important to see, therefore, that the systems OX do not suffer such limitations. And that they do not can most easily be seen by reflecting on the fact that the formal systems proper are purely syntactical. Nothing whatever in the formalism dictates the particular choice of an interpretation

---

[93] We use a distinction due to Broad [22], pp. 206–207. "Deontological theories hold that there are ethical propositions of the form 'Such and such a kind of action would always be right (or wrong) in such and such circumstances, no matter what its consequences might be' . . . Teleological theories hold that the rightness or wrongness of an action is always determined by its tendency to produce certain consequences which are intrinsically good or bad."

for 'S'. In particular, the "sanction" might be the disapproval of God, or pain (on a hedonistic theory of ethics), or simply the statement that something wrong has been done. The latter would presumably be the "sanction" for certain intuitionistic ethical philosophers, who claim that we have a special faculty which enables us to "see," without further argument, that certain acts are right and others wrong. For such a philosopher, an act would be obligatory if failure to execute it would entail that something wrong (namely, the wrong act in question) had been done. Whatever we may think of this way of interpreting 'S', it is at least clear that the systems OX provide ways of formalizing the resulting logic of obligation, permission, prohibition, etc. Presumably on *any* account of obligation, if an obligation is not executed, there is some way in which things are worse off than if the obligation had been executed – and this "way in which things are worse off," no matter how vague, can function as an interpretation of 'S' for the relevant account of obligation. (The aim of this remark is not to recommend that 'S' be given a vague interpretation, but rather to dispel the notion that we are committed by the formalism to some *particular* choice of an interpretation for 'S'.)

But to return to the point: it is certainly customary for specialists in the behavioral sciences to construe norms in the way recommended by the systems OX, and this fact may be urged as evidence that the systems OX adequately fulfill their intended function, namely, to serve as a tool for the analysis of normative systems.

(b) It is customary also in drafting legal obligations to specify explicitly the sanction which is to accompany non-observance of the obligation. So common is this view of positive law, that statutes expressing legal obligations may fail to refer to the "obligatory" or "forbidden" character of actions at all. The Connecticut State regulations concerning elections, for example, read in part as follows:

Sec. 1029. Fraudulent Registration. Any person who fraudulently procures himself or another to be registered as an elector shall be fined not more than five hundred dollars or imprisoned not more than one year or both.

Here, at least, we have one important class of cases, namely, explicit formulations of positive legal obligations, where obligations are in fact construed in the idiom recommended in systems OX.

(c) Our usual ways of supporting statements of obligation involve reference to what is entailed by non-observance. We talk and act as if our obligations were "reasonable" in the sense that reasons can be given for them, though of course, the reasons that *are* given vary widely. Still, if one asks "Why ought I to do X," the answer is very likely to be something like "If you don't, you'll get sick," or "If you don't, the law will catch up with you," or "If you don't, then people won't like you," or "If you don't, then God will disapprove," etc. That is, we try to specify some situation which will be

203

recognizably a penalty or sanction, and which will follow from failure to fulfill the alleged obligation. And indeed it is difficult to see what other kind of justification could be offered. It is true that certain philosophers have talked as if the only reason for saying "A ought to do X" is simply that he ought – nothing more can be said. And this doctrine may have some attractiveness, when persuasively argued. But most of us recognize that to say "you ought because you ought" is an unsatisfactory answer to the question "Why ought I?" Unless some appeal is made to a state-of-affairs which can be regarded as a sanction, however vague or nebulous, we do not ordinarily regard a person as having offered a reason for his statement of an obligation.

Two further points should be made regarding (b) and (c).

In the first place, though it is true that we are sometimes motivated to observe our obligations by considering the sanction attached to non-observance, this is by no means always the case. An agent's habitual failure to indulge in wanton murder, for example, may have nothing to do with the contemplation of social sanctions. He may simply not want to murder anyone. But if his society imposes a penalty on murderers, he is nonetheless "under an obligation" (relatively to the penalty) not to murder. The point to be made is that the systems OX are designed to handle obligations proper, and not motivations (though of course the two are closely related, and the systems may be of some use in studying motivations as well).

A second misunderstanding might arise through the claim (sometimes made) that "people do not act logically." It might be supposed, in consequence of this allegation, that it would be erroneous to attempt to use formal logic to characterize the normative assertions mentioned above. But it is difficult to know what is meant by "acting illogically" (unless it means simply acting in a way which seems unreasonable to the investigator). And in any event, the use of formal logic in the analysis of behavior and norms of behavior does not in any way make any presupposition about the actual behavior of human beings. In this respect the use of formal logic is like the use of statistics; we use the latter, not because it is habitually used by the subjects studied, but rather because it is helpful in the analysis of data.

(d) And finally, not only is it possible and plausible to construe statements of obligation in the idiom recommended by the systems OX, it is as a matter of fact the standard way of construing such assertions in certain natural languages. In Japanese,[94] for example, the standard way of rendering "X ought to be done," is "X wo shinakereba, narimaseng." The clause before the comma may be literally translated "if X is not done," and the clause after the comma means something like "it won't do," or "things will go wrong" (literally, "it won't become"). "Narimaseng," in short, is standardly

---

[94] See Bloch and Jorden [19], pp. 399 and 415.

taken in Japanese as the interpretation of what we have called the sanction 'S'. The fact that obligations are expressed in a natural language by means of locutions paralleling so exactly those of the systems OX, should be sufficient to dispel any notion that the locutions of OX are somehow arbitrary or artificial or unnatural. And Japanese is not the only example; comparable modes of expression are also found in Korean.[95]

*   *   *

To recapitulate these brief remarks concerning the adequacy of the systems OX: It appears that the analysis of the deontic notions offered here accords well with the practice of behavioral scientists, drafters of legal statutes, and with our usual methods of attempting to justify normative assertions. Our suggested analysis is also closely paralleled in certain natural languages. The remarks in this section have been intended to be persuasive, rather than conclusive. The ultimate test of the value of the analyses proposed here lies in possible fruitfulness in the analysis and empirical study of normative systems.

[95] See Horne and Yun [43], pp. 198 and 332. I am indebted to Professor Rulon S. Wells for the references given here and in the preceding footnote.

BIBLIOGRAPHY

ANDERSON, ALAN ROSS
  [1] Review of von Wright [80]. *The journal of symbolic logic*, vol. 18 (1953), pp. 174–176.
  [2] "Improved decision procedures for Lewis's calculus S4 and von Wright's calculus M." *The journal of symbolic logic*, vol. 19 (1954), pp. 201–214. (See also [5].)
  [3] "On the interpretation of a modal system of Łukasiewicz." *The journal of computing systems*, vol. 1 (1954), pp. 209–210.
  [4] "Alternative formulations of a modal system of Feys–von Wright." *The journal of computing systems*, vol. 1 (1954), pp. 211–212.
  [5] "Correction to a paper on modal logic." *The journal of symbolic logic*, vol. 20 (1955), p. 150.
  [6] "A formal system of deontic logic." Lecture delivered at the Philosophy Seminar, Johns Hopkins University, May 1956; unpublished.
  [7] "Independent axiom schemata for S5." *The journal of symbolic logic*, vol. 21 (1956), pp. 255–256.
  [8] "Independent axiom schemata for von Wright's M." *The journal of symbolic logic*, vol. 22 (1957), pp. 241–244.
  [9] "A reduction of deontic logic to alethic modal logic." *Mind*, vol. 67 n.s. (1958), pp. 100–103.
  [10] Abstract of [9]. *The journal of symbolic logic*, vol. 22 (1957), p. 105.
  [11] "On the logic of 'Commitment'." *Philosophical studies*, vol. 10 (1959), pp. 23–27.
  [12] Review of Prior [70] and Feys [32]. *The journal of symbolic logic*, vol. 21 (1956), p. 379.
ANDERSON, ALAN ROSS, and MOORE, OMAR KHAYYAM
  [13] "The formal analysis of normative concepts." *American sociological review*, vol. 22 (1957), pp. 1–17.
ANDERSON, SCARVIA B.
  [14] *Problem solving in multiple-goal situations*. Ph.D. thesis, University of Maryland, 1955.
  [15] "Shift in problem solving." *Naval Research Laboratory memorandum report No. 458*, Washington, 1955.
  [16] "Analysis of responses in a task drawn from the calculus of propositions." *Naval Research Laboratory memorandum report No. 608*, Washington, 1956.
ANDERSON, SCARVIA B., and MOORE, OMAR KHAYYAM. See [59], [60] and [61].
BARRY, GLADYS and FITCH, FREDERIC B. See [35].
BECKER, OSKAR
  [17] "Zur Logik der Modalitäten." *Jahrbuch für Philosophie und phänoenomlogische Forschung*, vol. 11 (1930), pp. 497–548.
  [18] *Untersuchungen über den Modalkalkül*. Westkulturverlag Anton Hain, Meisenheim am Glan, 1952.
BLOCH, BERNARD, and JORDEN, ELEANOR HARZ
  [19] *SpokenJapanese*. War Department Education Manual, EM 561.
BOHNERT, HERBERT GAYLORD
  [20] "The semiotic status of commands." *Philosophy of science*, vol. 12 (1945), pp. 302–315.
BRAITHWAITE, RICHARD BEVAN
  [21] *Theory of games as a tool for the moral philosopher*. New York, 1955.
BROAD, CHARLIE DUNBAR
  [22] *Five types of ethical theory*. London, 1930.
CARNAP, RUDOLF
  [23] "Modalities and quantification." *The journal of symbolic logic*, vol. 11 (1946), pp. 33–64.
  [24] *Logical foundations of probability*. Chicago, 1950.

CASTAÑEDA, HÉCTOR NERI
[25] "La lógica general de las normas y la ética." *Universidad de San Carlos* (Guatamala), no. 30 (1955), pp. 129–196.
CHURCH, ALONZO
[26] *Introduction to mathematical logic*, vol. 1. Princeton, 1956.
COPI, IRVING MARMER
[27] *Introduction to logic.* New York, 1953.
[28] *Symbolic logic.* New York, 1954.
DAVIDSON, DONALD, MCKINSEY, J. C. C. and SUPPES, PATRICK
[29] *Outlines of a formal theory of value, I.* Stanford, 1954.
FEYS, ROBERT
[30] "Les logiques nouvelles des modalités." *Revue néo-scholastique de philosophie*, vol. 40 (1937), pp. 517–553, and vol. 41 (1938), pp. 217–252.
[31] "Expression modale du 'devoir-être'." *The journal of symbolic logic*, vol. 20 (1955), pp. 91–92.
[32] Reply (untitled) to A. N. Prior [70]. *Revue philosophique de Louvain*, vol. 54 (1956), pp. 88–89.
FITCH, FREDERIC B.
[33] "Intuitionistic modal logic with quantifiers." *Portugaliae mathematica*, vol. 7 (1948), pp. 113–118.
[34] *Symbolic logic.* New York, 1952.
FITCH, FREDERIC B. and BARRY, GLADYS
[35] "Towards a formalization of Hull's behavior theory." *Philosophy of science*, vol. 17 (1950), pp. 260–265.
FITCH, FREDERIC B., HULL, CLARK L., *et al.* See [44].
GALANTER, EUGENE H.
[36] "An axiomatic and experimental study of sensory order and measure." *Psychological review*, vol. 63 (1956), pp. 16–28.
GÖDEL, KURT
[37] "Eine Interpretation des intuitionistischen Aussagenkalküls." *Ergebnisse eines mathematischen Kolloquiums*, vol. 4 (1933), pp. 39–40.
HALL, MARSHALL, HULL, CLARK L., *et al.* See [44].
HALLDÉN, SÖREN
[38] "Results concerning the decision problem of Lewis's calculi S3 and S6." *The journal of symbolic logic*, vol. 14 (1950), pp. 230–236.
HEMPEL, CARL G.
[39] *Fundamentals of concept formation in empirical science.* International encyclopedia of unified science, Chicago, 1952.
HOEBEL, E. ADAMSON
[40] *The law of primitive man.* Cambridge, 1954.
HOFSTADTER, ALBERT and MCKINSEY, J. C. C.
[41] "On the logic of imperatives." *Philosophy of science*, vol. 6 (1939), pp. 446–457.
HOHFELD, WESLEY NEWCOMB
[42] *Fundamental legal conceptions as applied in judicial reasoning, and other essays.* New Haven, 1919.
HORNE, ELINOR CLARK and YUN, SANG SOON
[43] *Introduction to spoken Korean.* New Haven, 1951.
HOVLAND, CARL I., HULL, CLARK L., *et al.* See [44].
HULL, CLARK L., HOVLAND, CARL I., ROSS, ROBERT T., HALL, MARSHALL, PERKINS, DONALD T., and FITCH, FREDERIC B.
[44] *Mathematico-deductive theory of rote learning.* New Haven, 1940.
JORDEN, ELEANOR HARZ and BLOCH, BERNARD. See [19].
KALINOWSKI, JERZY
[45] "Théorie des propositions normatives." *Studia logica*, vol. 1 (1953), pp. 147–182.

Kemeny, John G.
[46] "Models of logical systems." *The journal of symbolic logic*, vol. 13 (1948), pp. 16–30.
Langford, Cooper H. and Lewis, Clarence I. See [48].
Lewis, Clarence I.
[47] *Survey of symbolic logic.* Berkeley, 1918.
Lewis, Clarence I. and Langford, Cooper H.
[48] *Symbolic logic.* New York, 1932.
Łukasiewicz, Jan
[49] *Aristotle's syllogistic.* Oxford, 1951.
[50] "A system of modal logic." *The journal of computing systems*, vol. 1 (1953), pp. 111–149.
Łukasiewicz, Jan and Tarski, Alfred
[51] "Untersuchungen über den Aussagenkalkül." *Comptes rendus des séances de la Société des Sciences et des Lettres de Varsovie*, Classe III, vol. 23 (1930), pp. 30–50.
McKinsey, J. C. C.
[52] "A solution to the decision problem for the Lewis systems S2 and S4, with an application to topology." *The journal of symbolic logic*, vol. 6 (1941), pp. 117–134.
[53] "On the number of complete extensions of the Lewis systems of sentential calculus." *The journal of symbolic logic*, vol. 9 (1944), pp. 42–46.
[54] "On the syntactical construction of systems of modal logic." *The journal of symbolic logic*, vol. 10 (1945), pp. 83–94.
McKinsey, J. C. C., Davidson, Donald and Suppes, Patrick. See [29].
McKinsey, J. C. C. and Hofstadter, Albert. See [41].
McKinsey, J. C. C. and Tarski, Alfred
[55] "Some theorems about the sentential calculi of Lewis and Heyting." *The journal of symbolic logic*, vol. 13 (1948), pp. 1–15.
Mally, Ernst
[56] *Grundgesetz des Sollens*, Graz, 1926.
Menger, Karl
[57] "A logic of the doubtful; on optative and imperative logic." *Reports of a mathematical colloquium* (Notre Dame), 2nd series, vol. 1 (1939), pp. 53–64.
Moore, Omar Khayyam
[58] *Language Ł.* Technical Report No. 3, Office of Naval Research, Contract No. SAR/Nonr-609(16), New Haven, 1956.
Moore, Omar Khayyam and Anderson, Alan Ross. See [13].
Moore, Omar Khayyam and Anderson, Scarvia B.
[59] "Search behavior in individual and group problem solving." *American sociological review*, vol. 19 (1954), pp. 702–714.
[60] "Modern logic and tasks for experiments on problem solving behavior." *The journal of psychology*, vol. 38 (1954), pp. 151–160.
[61] "Experimental study of problem solving." *Report of Naval Research Laboratory progress*, August, 1954.
Morgenstern, Oskar and von Neumann, John. See [65].
Morris, Charles
[62] *Foundations of the theory of signs.* International encyclopedia of unified science, Chicago, 1938.
[63] *Signs, language and behavior.* New York, 1946.
Myhill, John
[64] "Some philosophical implications of mathematical logic." *Review of metaphysics*, vol. 6 (1953), pp. 165–198.
von Neumann, John and Morgenstern, Oskar
[65] *Theory of games and economic behavior.* Princeton, 1953.

PARRY, WILLIAM TUTHILL
[66] "Zum Lewisschen Aussagenkalkül." *Ergebnisse eines mathematischen Kolloquiums*, vol. 4 (1933), pp. 15–16.
[67] "Modalities in the *Survey* system of strict implication." *The journal of symbolic logic*, vol. 4 (1939), pp. 137–154.
PERKINS, DONALD T., HULL, CLARK L., *et al.* See [44].
PRIOR, A. N.
[68] "The interpretation of two systems of modal logic." *The journal of computing systems*, vol. 1 (1954), pp. 201–208.
[69] *Formal logic.* Oxford, 1955.
[70] "A note on the logic of obligation." *Revue philosophique de Louvain*, vol. 54 (1956), pp. 86–87.
[71] *Time and modality.* Oxford. Clarendon Press, 1957.
QUINE, WILLARD V.
[72] *Mathematical logic.* Cambridge, 1951.
ROSS, ROBERT T., HULL, CLARK L., *et al.* See [44].
SIMONS, LEO
[73] "New axiomatizations of S3 and S4." *The journal of symbolic logic*, vol. 18 (1953), pp. 309–316.
SOBOCIŃSKI, BOLESLAW
[74] "Note on a modal system of Feys–von Wright." *The journal of computing systems*, vol. 1 (1953), pp. 171–178.
STRAWSON, P. F.
[75] *Introduction to logical theory*, London, 1952.
SUPPES, PATRICK, DAVIDSON, DONALD, and MCKINSEY, J. C. C. See [29].
SUPPES, PATRICK and WINET, MURIEL
[76] *Axiomatization and representation of difference structures.* Stanford, 1954.
TARSKI, ALFRED
[77] "The semantic conception of truth." *Philosophy and phenomenological research*, vol. 4 (1944), pp. 341–376. (Reprinted in Feigl, Herbert, and Sellars, Wilfrid, *Readings in philosophical analysis*, New York, 1949.)
TARSKI, ALFRED and ŁUKASIEWICZ, JAN. See [51].
TARSKI, ALFRED and MCKINSEY, J. C. C. See [55].
WAJSBERG, MORDECAI
[78] "Ein erweiterter Klassenkalkül." *Monatshefte für Mathematik und Physik*, vol. 40 (1933), pp. 113–126.
WINET, MURIEL, and SUPPES, PATRICK. See [76].
VON WRIGHT, GEORG H.
[79] "Deontic logic." *Mind*, vol. 60 (1951), pp. 1–15.
[80] *An essay in modal logic.* Amsterdam, 1951.
YUN, SANG SOON and HORNE, ELINOR CLARK. See [43].

SUPPLEMENTARY BIBLIOGRAPHY (1966)

THE LIST below is intended to cover works on deontic logic published since 1956 (supplemented by a few earlier items of which the writer was ignorant in 1955, when the monograph above was written). My intent has been to include only articles or books in which modern mathematical logic has been applied to such notions as obligation, permission, and the like, or such items as have a clear bearing on the formal treatment of these ideas. I have consequently omitted material dealing solely with imperatives, commands, and prescriptions; a comprehensive bibliography on these topics can be found in Rescher 1966. Limitations of space have also made it necessary to exclude informal discussions of rights, duties, responsibilities, actions, and the like. All of these notions are of course germane to deontic logic, broadly conceived; but anything like a complete bibliography of recent writings on these topics would be a volume all by itself.

ACKERMANN, WILHELM
> 1956. "Begründung einer strengen Implikation." *The journal of symbolic logic,* vol. 21, pp. 113–128.

ADAMS, E. M.
> 1958. "Hall's analysis of 'ought'." *The journal of philosophy,* vol. 55, pp. 73–75.

AJDUKIEWICZ, KAZIMIERZ
> 1943. *Logiczne podstawy nauczania.* Warszawa.

ALLEN, LAYMAN EDWARD
> 1957. "Symbolic logic: a razor-edged tool for drafting and interpreting legal documents." *The Yale law journal,* vol. 66, pp. 833–879.
> 1959. "Logic, law and dreams." *Law library journal,* vol. 52, pp. 131–144.
> 1960. "Deontic logic." *Modern uses of logic in law,* pp. 13–27.

ANDERSON, ALAN ROSS
> 1958. "The logic of norms." *Logique et analyse,* vol. 1 n.s., pp. 84–91.
> 1959. "On the logic of 'commitment'." *Philosophical studies,* vol. 10, pp. 23–27.
> 1962. "Reply to Mr. Rescher." *Philosophical studies,* vol. 13, pp. 6–8.
> 1963. "Some open problems concerning the system E of entailment." *Acta philisophica Fennica,* Fasc. XVI.

APOSTEL, LEO
> 1960. "Game theory and the interpretation of deontic logic." *Logique et analyse,* vol. 3 n.s., pp. 70–90.

ÅQVIST, LENNART
> 1963. "A note on commitment." *Philosophical studies,* vol. 14, pp. 22–25.
> 1963a. "Postulate sets and decision procedures for some systems of deontic logic." *Theoria,* vol. 29, pp. 154–175.
> 1964. "Interpretations of deontic logic." *Mind,* vol. 73, pp. 246–253.

BERG, JAN
> 1960. "A note on deontic logic." *Mind,* vol. 69 n.s., pp. 566–567.

BOBBIO, NORBERTO
> 1954. "Considerations introductives sur le raisonnement des juristes." *Revue internationale de philosophie,* vol. 8, pp. 67–83.
> 1954a. "La logica giuridica di Eduardo Garcia Maynez." *Rivista internationale de filosofia del diritto,* vol. 31 3rd s., pp. 644–669.

BRUSIIN, OTTO
> 1950–51. "Das Deduktive im juristischen Denken." *Archiv für Rechts- und Sozialphilosophie,* vol. 39, pp. 324–337.

CASTAÑEDA, HECTOR NERI
1956. "Nota sobre la logica de los fines y medios." *Universidad de San Carlos*, vol. 39, pp. 63–75.
1957. "Un sistema general de logica normativa." *Dianoia*, vol. 3, pp. 303–333.
1957a. "On the logic of norms." *Methodos*, vol. 9, pp. 207–216.
1957b. "A theory of morality." *Philosophy and phenomenological research*, vol. 17, no. 3, pp. 339–352.
1958. "Imperatives and deontic logic." *Analysis*, vol. 19, pp. 42–48.
1959. "The logic of obligation." *Philosophical studies*, vol. 10, pp. 17–23.
1960. "Obligation and modal logic." *Logique et analyse*, vol. 3 n.s., pp. 40–48.
1960a. " 'Ought' and assumption in moral philosophy." *The journal of philosophy*, vol. 57, pp. 791–804.
CHISHOLM, RODERICK
1963. "Contrary-to-duty imperatives and deontic logic." *Analysis*, vol. 24, pp. 33–36.
CHURCH, ALONZO
1951. "The weak theory of implication." *Kontrolliertes Denken*, Munich.
CLARK, ROMANE L.
1955–56. "On Mr. Tammelo's conception of juristic logic." *Journal of legal education*, vol. 8, pp. 491–496.
COHEN, JONATHAN
1951. "Three-valued ethics." *Philosophy*, vol. 26, pp. 208–227.
CONTE, AMEDEO G.
1961. "Bibliografia di logica giuridica." *Rivista internationale de filosofia del diritto*, vol. 38, pp. 119–144.
1962. *Saggio sulla completezza degli ordinamenti giuridici.* Torino, Giappichelli.
DAWSON, EDWARD
1959. "A model for deontic logic." *Analysis*, vol. 19, pp. 73–78.
ENGLIS, KARL
1956. *Einfuhrung in das Juristische Denken.* Stuttgart, Kohlhammer Verlag.
1959. "Aufgaben einer Logik und Methodik der juristichen Denkens." *Studium Generale*, vol. 12, pp. 76–87.
FABREGUETTES, POLYDORE
1962. *La logique judiciare et l'art de juger.* Paris, Librairie générale de droit et de jurisprudence.
FENSTAD, JENS ERIK
1959. "Notes on normative logic." *Avhandlinger utgitt av det norske videnskaps-akademi i Oslo. 2. Historisk-filosofisk klasse*, vol. 1, pp. 1–25.
FEYS, ROBERT and MOTTE, MARIE-THÉRÈSE
1959. "Logique juridique, systèmes juridiques." *Logique et analyse*, vol. 2 n.s., pp. 143–147.
FISHER, MARK
1961. "A three-valued calculus for deontic logic." *Theoria*, vol. 27, pp. 107–118.
1962. "A system of deontic-alethic modal logic." *Mind*, vol. 71 n.s., pp. 72–78.
1964. "A contradiction in deontic logic?" *Analysis*, vol. 25, pp. 12–13.
FREY, G.
1965. "Imperativ-kalküle." *The foundation of statements and decisions*, ed. Kasimierz Ajukiewicz, Warszawa.
FRUTIGER, P.
1949. "Logique neccesaire et logique obligatoire." *Proceedings of the tenth international congress.* Amsterdam, North Holland Publishing Co., pp. 33–41.
GEACH, PETER
1958. "Imperative and deontic logic." *Analysis*, vol. 18, pp. 49–56.
GIORGIANNI, VIRGILIO
1953. "Logica matematica e logica guiridica." *Revista internazionale di filosofia del diritto*, vol. 30 3rd s., pp. 462–486.

GRELLING, KURT
1939. "Zur logik der sollsätze." *Unity of science forum*, January, pp. 44–47.

HALLDEN, SÖREN
1957. *On the logic of 'better'*. Lund, C. W. K. Gleerup. Kobenhavn, E. Musks-gaard. Library of theoria, 2.

HARE, R. M.
1952. *The language of morals*. Oxford, Clarendon press; reprinted in 1961.

HINTIKKA, J. JAAKKO K.
1958. "Quantifiers in deontic logic." *Sociatas scientiarum fennica*, commenta-tiones humanarum litterarum, vol. 23, pp. 1–23.

KALINOWSKI, JERZY
1959. "Y a-t-il une logique juridique?" *Logique et analyse*, vol. 2 n.s., pp. 48–53.
1959a. "Interpretation juridique et logique des propositions normatives." *Logique et analyse*, vol. 2 n.s., pp. 128–142.
1965. *Introduction a la logique juridique*. Bibliotheque de philosophie du droit, vol. III.

KLUG, ULRICH
1951. *Juristische logik*. Berlin, Springer Verlag. Second edition, augmented, 1959.

KOTARBINSKI, TADEUZ
1951. *Kurs logiki dla prawnikou*. [Course in logic for lawyers.] Warszawa, Gebethner i Woeff. Second, third, fourth editions, Warszawa, Panstwowe wydawnictwo naukowe, 1953, 1955, 1960.

LEMMON, E. J. and NOWELL-SMITH, P. H.
1960. "Escapism: the logical basis of ethics." *Mind*, vol. 69 n.s., pp. 289–300.

MARTIN, R. M.
1959. *Toward a systematic pragmatics*. Amsterdam, North Holland Publishing Company.

MCLAUGHLIN, R.N.
1955. "Further problems of derived obligation." *Mind*, vol. 64 n.s., pp. 400–402.

MEREDITH, DAVID
1956. "A correction to von Wright's decision procedure for the deontic system P." *Mind*, vol. 65 n.s., pp. 548–550.

MOSTOWSKI, ANDRZEJ
1948. *Logika matematyczna*. Warszawa-Wroclaw, monografie matematyczane, t. XVIII.

NAESS, ARNE
1958. "La validité des normes fondamentales." *Logique et analyse*, vol. 1 n.s., pp. 4–13.
1959. "Do we know that basic norms cannot be true or false?" *Theoria*, vol. 25, pp. 31–53.
1962. "We still do know that norms cannot be true or false. A reply to Dag Oesterberg." *Theoria*, vol. 28, pp. 205–209.

OESTERBERG, DAG
1962. "We know that norms cannot be true or false. Critical comments on Arne Naess: Do we know that basic norms cannot be true or false?" *Theoria*, vol. 28, pp. 200–204.

PRIOR, ARTHUR N.
1954. "The paradoxes of derived obligation." *Mind*, vol. 63 n.s., pp. 64–65.
1958. "Escapism: the logical basis of ethics." *Essays in moral philosophy*, edited by A. J. Melden, Seattle, University of Washington Press, pp. 135–146.

RESCHER, NICHOLAS
    1958. "An axiom system for deontic logic." *Philosophical studies*, vol. 9, pp. 24–30.
    1962. "Conditional permission in deontic logic." *Philosophical studies*, vol. 13, pp. 1–6.
    1966. *The logic of commands*. London, Routledge and Kegan Paul.

SELLARS, WILFRID
    1956. "Imperatives, intentions, and the logic of 'ought'." *Methodos*, vol. 8, pp. 227–268.

TRANØY, KNUT ERIK
    1957. "An important aspect of humanism." *Theoria*, vol. 23, pp. 37–52.
    1958. "Reply to Erik Ryding. A note on E. Ryding's 'The Sense of "Smoking Permitted"'." *Theoria*, vol. 24, pp. 190–191.

TURNBULL, ROBERT G.
    1960. "Imperatives, logic and moral obligation." *Philosophy of science*, vol. 27, pp. 374–390.

WEDBERG, ANDERS
    1951. "Some problems in the logical analysis of legal science." *Theoria*, vol. 17, pp. 246–275.

WEINBERGER, OTA
    1958. *Die Sollsatzproblematik in der modernen Logik.* *Können Sollsätze (imperative) als wahr bezeichnet werden?* Praha.
    1960. "Theorie des propositions normatives. Quelques remarques au sujet de l'interprétation normative des systèmes K₁ et K₂ de M. Kalinowski." *Studia logica*, vol. 9, pp. 7–21.

WRIGHT, GEORG HENRIK von
    1956. "A note on deontic logic and derived obligation." *Mind*, vol. 65 n.s., pp. 507–509.
    1957. *Logical studies*. London, Routledge and Kegan Paul.
    1963. *Norm and action*. London, Routledge and Kegan Paul.

ZIEMBINSKI, ZYGMUT
    1962. "Le caractère sémantique des normes juridiques." *Logique et analyse*, vol. 5 n.s., pp. 54–65.

ZINOV'EV, A. A.
    1958. "O logike normativnyi predlozenii." [On the logic of normative propositions.] *Voprosy filozofii*, no. 11, pp. 156–159.

APPENDIX II

ASPECTS OF ACTION

Nicholas Rescher

As the rapidly growing literature on the subject attests, the problem of action is at this writing an active and fertile field of philosophical inquiry. However, because most of this literature concerns itself with points of detail, the generic concept of "an action" as such, in its full and ramified generality, has not been explored as fully as one might wish. In this brief Appendix, I shall approach this question of *What is an action?* obliquely, from the angle of the question *How is an action to be described?*

My aim will be to develop the tools for what might be called the *canonical description* of an action. The object is to give an essentially exhaustive *catalogue of the key generic elements of actions,* so as to provide a classificatory matrix of rubrics under which the essential features of actions can be classed. The following tabulation represents an attempt at the compilation of such a catalogue:

The Descriptive Elements of an Action

(1) *Agent* (WHO did it?)

(2) *Act-type* (WHAT did he do?)[1]

(3) *Modality of Action* (HOW did he do it?)
    a. Modality of manner (IN WHAT MANNER did he do it?)
    b. Modality of means (BY WHAT MEANS did he do it?)

(4) *Setting of Action* (IN WHAT CONTEXT did he do it?)
    a. Temporal aspect (WHEN did he do it?)[2]
    b. Spatial aspect (WHERE did he do it?)
    c. Circumstantial aspect (UNDER WHAT CIRCUMSTANCES did he do it?)

(5) *Rationale of Action* (WHY did he do it?)
    a. Causality (WHAT CAUSED him to do it?)
    b. Finality (WITH WHAT AIM did he do it?)
    c. Intentionality (IN WHAT STATE OF MIND did he do it?)

---

[1] Note that this is the fundamental item in the specification of an action, and that the "it" that occurs in the wording of all the other questions refers to *the relevant instance of the act-type in question.*

[2] To individuate a (concrete) action it is sufficient to specify the agent, the act-type, and the occasion (time) of acting. But to say this is not, of course, to say that the adequate *description* of an action does not require a good deal more.

Each of these elements of the canonical description of an action must be discussed briefly.[3]

(1) *The Agent*

The agent of an action may be an individual or a group (crowds, boards of directors, parliaments, etc., all being capable of action). Groups can act distributively, as single individuals (as when the audience applauds), or collectively, as a corporate whole (as when the Congress overrides a Presidential veto).

(2) *The Act-Type*

An act-type can be specified at varying levels of concreteness. It can be a *fully generic act-type* (e.g., "the opening of a window," "the sharpening of a pencil"). Such a generic act-type characterization can be rendered more specific ("the opening of this window" "the sharpening of that pencil") whenever a concrete object involved in the action is indicated (*this* window, *that* pencil). Such a *specific act-type* is one which, though still a general type, involves a concrete particular. And it goes without saying that any particular action can be described (i.e., placed within types) at varying levels of generality. In a particular case we might say "He raised *a* hand" or "He raised *his* right hand." Those items that correspond to the question "Upon what did the agent act?" – i.e., that deal with the recipients or the grammarian's *objects* of action – are to be viewed as definite parts of what we call the "act type." Thus if Bob hands a book to Jim, the act-type is not *a handing*, but either the specific "handing a book to Jim" or the generic "handing a book to someone."

(3) *The Modality of Action*

Modality of manner is a straightforward conception. Suppose an action to be done – say that Jones shook hands with Smith. Did he do it firmly or weakly, rapidly or slowly, energetically or placidly, gently or roughly? All of these – endlessly variant – characterizations of the *way* in which the action was accomplished relate to the modality of manner.

White opened the curtains. Did he do so with the pull-rope, or with his hands or with a stick? Such characterizations of the means (instruments) by which the action was done relate to the modality of means. The means can be generic ("He killed the man with *a* revolver") or specific ("He killed the man with *this* revolver").

Of course if Robinson breathed or twiddled his thumbs, it makes little sense to ask about the means by which he did so (though we could, of course, inquire about the manner). Normal bodily movements are accomplished

---

[3] I am not unmindful of the similarities between the questions presented in the tabulations and those inherent in Aristotle's *Categories*. But the relationships, though real, are too intricate to warrant setting out here.

without overt means. And many other types of actions are such that – barring exotic cases – the means of action is implicitly specified within the action-type itself.

(4) *The Setting of Action*

Suppose an act of a certain type to be done by a certain agent in a certain manner with a certain means ("He opened the can of soup smoothly with a can opener"). The question still remains as to the specific setting of the action that fixes its position in time, and space, and in the course of events (his doing so in the kitchen yesterday afternoon while the radio was playing). Every action must have a chronological occasion in occurring at a certain time or times, a positional location in occurring at a certain place or places, and a circumstantial setting fitting it among other things going on within its relevant environment. The ensemble of these three elements constitutes what we have termed the *setting* of the action.

(5) *The Rationale of Action*

Suppose an action to be performed – say that Smith strikes his fist upon the table. An explanation of this fact may well proceed in caused terms: he acted "out of rage," or "out of drunkenness," or "by an irrepressible urge," or even "due to post-hypnotic suggestion." All these act-characterizations represent answers (i.e., partial answers) to the question *Why did he do it?*, and they all answer this question in the mode of *causality*. Bypassing the issue of Smith's wishes and desires, there act-explanations proceed, not in terms of the agent's choices, but in terms of the impersonal "forces" that are at work. Denying – or ignoring – that the act was a matter of the agent's deliberate choices, they address themselves to the question of what *caused* him to do it.[4]

When an agent's action was a matter of choice – i.e., was something he "chose" rather than something he "was caused" to do – the aspect of finality comes upon the scene, and we can ask "*With what aim* did he do it?" Although both causes and motives provide answers to the question "What led him to do it?" the latter alone answers the question "What *considerations* led him to do it?" (Both causal and motivational explanations can in many cases be given of one of the same action – e.g., Smith's sitting down when he feels his knees giving way because of dizziness.) We can, in short, inquire into the agent's purposes, wishes, goals, and objectives: his reasons, motives, and intentions. Now we may have such things as that he did it "out of ambition," or "out of concern for her feelings," or "out of avarice" (i.e., for reasons of

---

[4] In common parlance "to cause" and "to motivate" do not contrast neatly in the way philosophers would wish to draw the contrast. Compare the locutions: "Her hesitancy caused him to persevere" or "My importunity caused him to reconsider the decision."

prestige, advancement, gain, etc.). Such act-characterizations tell us, in the case of an act that was a matter of the agent's voluntary choice,[5] what *motivated* him in doing it.

Consider the following group of contrasts:

voluntarily/involuntarily
deliberately/inadvertently (or accidentally)
intentionally/unintentionally (or by mistake)
consciously/out of habit (or automatically)
knowingly/unwittingly
willingly/unwillingly

All these[6] relate to what may in the aggregate be called the intentionality of action – the considerations having to do with generic features of the agent's state of mind and train of thought with respect to the action. They set a general frame of reference within which the specific issue of causal vs. motivational explanation can be posed. Clearly if X did A unwittingly and involuntarily, out of habit, an explanation along causal lines is called for,[7] while if he did it consciously and deliberately we would require a motivational explanation.

The dichotomy of the *rationale* of action on the one hand and its *type-modality-setting* upon the other reflects the amphibious nature of the concept of action. Like the concept of a *person* in general, in which physical and mental aspects are inseparably united, the concept of action has both *overt*, physical and observable, and *covert*, mental and unobservable involvements. The overt side relates to the issue of *what* he did and its ramifications into *how-and-in what context* he did it. The covert side relates to the issue of his *state of mind* (thoughts, intentions, motives, awareness, etc.) at the time of action. All this latter aspect of action is comprehended under our rubric of the *rationale* of action.

It might be said that one ought to separate these issues of explicability from the other perhaps more strictly descriptive aspects of the characterization of an action. "Keep" (so the advice might run) "*what* the agent did sharply apart from the issue of *why* he did it." This course is infeasible. The language of human action is everywhere permeated by the coloration of intentionality and purposiveness. Even in such simple locutions as "He gave her the book," "He turned on the light," or "He flourished his cane," we find not simply behavioristically overt descriptions of matter in motion but fertile

---

[5] Or rather, simply "choice": voluntary choice is a pleonasm.
[6] And there are of course a great many others, e.g., gladly/reluctantly and confidently/ hesitantly.
[7] As with items of behavior best not called actions, though in many ways related to them, such as reflex *reactions*, or such "automatic" behavior as sneezing. In the interests of clarity such items, with respect to which the issues of finality and intentionality do not arise at all, should be excluded from the rubric of *actions*.

clues and suggestions as to the intentional aspects of the transaction ("gave" vs. "handed," "turned on" vs. "caused to go on," "flourished" vs. "moved about").

* * *

It is, however, in principle feasible and in practice desirable to maintain a a line of separation between the *description* of action and its *evaluation*. There are a vast host of act-characterizing terms bearing upon the evaluative assessment of actions: Was the act prudent or rash, considerate or thoughtless, courteous or rude, appropriate or inappropriate, etc.? Such issues relate to the evaluation of the action, not to its actual depiction. They are thus not a proper part of our survey of the descriptive elements of an action.

Certain act-characterizations are descriptive not so much of the action itself as of the relationship it bears to other actions of the agent himself or of people in general. Was the act typical or atypical, normal or abnormal, characteristic or unusual, expected or unexpected, etc. Such considerations, while indeed descriptive rather than evaluative in nature, have their primary orientation directed away from the action itself.

* * *

If adequate, our survey of the descriptive elements of an action has a significant bearing upon Kenny's problem of the "variable polyadicity" of actions.[8] For it suggests that, while the description of an action can indeed be elaborated more and more (perhaps indefinitely so), this can be viewed as the increasingly detailed presentation of a limited and manageable number of distinctive characteristic aspects of action.[9]

---

[8] Anthony Kenny, *Action, Emotion and the Will* (London, 1963), ch. VII. Cf. Donald Davidson's discussion on pp. 81–84 above.

[9] So far as I can see, our discussion has relatively little bearing on Davidson's problem of "the logical form of action sentences." We have been concerned to urge that the items called *actions* have certain significantly distinguishable aspects. But nothing we have said bears on the question of how the linguistic characterization of these aspects is to be accomplished with maximal exactness, comprehensiveness, elegance, and precision.

INDEX OF NAMES

Ackermann, R., 71–79, 147
Ackermann, W., 210
Adams, E. M., 210
Ajdukiewicz, K., 210
Allen, L. E., 210
Anderson, A. R., 28, 63–70, 77, 147–213
Anderson, S. B., 151, 206, 208
Apostel, L., 210
Aquinas, St. T., 184
Aqvist, L., 38, 62, 210
Aristotle, 38, 62, 214
Arrow, K. J., 5, 33, 62
Austin, J., 84, 115

Barry, G., 151, 206, 207
Bayes, S., 73–75, 78
Baylis, C., 62
Becker, O., 152, 190, 206
Belnap, N. D., Jr., 27–35, 66, 70, 147
Bennett, D., 81
Berg, J., 210
Binkley, R., 21–26, 32–33
Bloch, B., 204, 206, 207
Bobbio, N., 210
Bohnert, H. G., 152, 170, 206
Braithwaite, R. B., 201, 206
Braybrooke, D., 39
Brentano, F. C., 38
Broad, C. D., 152, 202, 206
Brogan, A. P., 62
Brusiin, O., 210

Carnap, R., 43, 151, 194, 206
Castaneda, H. N., 104–112, 117–119, 152, 207, 211
Chisholm, R. M., 38, 43, 52–63, 70, 86–89, 97, 113–114, 119–120, 137–139, 144–145, 211
Church, A., 147, 152, 153, 154, 155, 157, 160, 167, 200, 207, 211
Clark, R. L., 211
Cohen, J., 211
Conte, A. G., 211
Copi, I. M., 152, 157, 160, 207

Davidson, D., 30, 81–120, 201, 207, 208, 209, 219
Dawson, E., 211

Englis, K., 211
Emery, D. W., 22

Fabreguettes, P., 211
Fenstad, J. E., 211
Feys, R., 128, 152, 161, 178, 182, 187, 207, 211
de Finetti, 33
Fisher, M., 211
Fitch, F. B., 151, 152, 161, 162, 206
Frege, G., 28, 63, 66
Frey, H., 211
Frutiger, P., 211

Galanter, E. H., 151, 207
Geach, P. T., 184, 211
Gentzen, G., 65
Giorgianni, V., 211
Gödel, K., 28, 29, 63, 70, 160, 161, 207
Goodman, N., 64
Grelling, K., 212
Grice, P., 81

Hailperin, T., 64, 70
Hall, M., 207
Halldén, S., 38, 43, 62, 161, 207, 212
Hare, R. M., 212
Harris, T., 5
Hempel, C. G., 151, 160, 207
Herbrand, J., 28
Hintikka, J., 182, 212
Hoebel, E. A., 200, 207
Hofstadter, A., 152, 207, 208
Hohfeld, W. N., 200, 207
Horne, E. C., 205, 207, 209
Hovland, C. I., 207
Houthakker, H. S., 62
Hull, C. L., 156, 207, 209

Jeffrey, R. C., 39, 44, 62, 73, 74
Jespersen, O., 101
Jorden, E. H., 204, 206, 207
Jörgensen, J., 32

Kalinowski, J., 147, 152, 207, 212
Kant, I., 173, 183
Katkov, G., 38, 62
Kenny, A., 83–104, 219
Kemeny, J. G., 155, 208

Klug, U., 212
Kotarbinski, T., 212
Kraus, O., 38, 62
Kripke, S., 193

Langford, C. L., 152, 154, 157, 164, 178, 190, 194, 208
Larson, S., 81
Lemmon, E. J., 96–103, 115, 118, 147, 212
Lewis, C. I., 152, 154, 157, 161, 164, 178, 190, 194, 208
Lowe, V., 148
Luce, R. D., 33, 39
Lukasiewicz, J., 152, 161, 162, 179, 208, 209

McCarthy, J., 8
McKinsey, J. C. C., 152, 161, 174, 190, 201, 207, 208, 209
McLaughlin, R. N., 212
Mally, E., 152, 170, 208
Martin, R. M., 38, 43, 52–59, 62, 64, 212
Marschak, J., 2, 5
Marshall, A., 39, 207
Menger, K., 152, 170, 196, 208
Meno, 7, 8
Meredith, D., 212
Moore, G. E., 62, 149, 151, 152, 153, 168
Moore, O. K., 147, 148, 206, 208
Moore, R. G., 149
Morgenstern, O., 201, 208
Morris, C., 157, 208
Mostowski, A., 212
Motte, M. T., 211
Myhill, J., 160, 208

Naess, A., 212
Nakhnikian, G., 112
Nassau, M., 147
von Neumann, 33, 201, 208
Nowell-Smith, P. H., 147, 212

Oesterberg, D., 212

Parry, W. T., 161, 175, 177, 189, 190, 191, 194, 209
Pears, D., 81
Pelon, A., 37
Pence, R. W., 22
Perkins, D. T., 207, 209
Post, E. L., 70

Prior, A. N., 147, 148, 152, 156, 161, 162, 168, 170, 171, 173, 175, 182, 183, 184, 185, 186, 187, 199, 209, 212
Provence, M., 81

Quine, W. V., 64, 152, 155, 167, 209

Raiffa, H., 39
Ransey, F. P., 33
Reichenbach, H., 90, 91–93, 97, 105
Rescher, N., 30, 32, 37–79, 147, 210, 213, 215–219
Robison, J., 37, 140–143, 145–146
Ross, R. T., 207, 209
Russell, B., 28, 63

Savage, L. J., 33
Scheffler, I., 89, 90
Scheler, M., 38, 62
Schwarz, H., 38, 62
Sellars, W., 112, 213
Simon, H. A., 1–35
Simons, L., 101, 209
Sobocinski, B., 178, 190, 209
Socrates, 7, 8
Sosa, E., 38, 43, 52–63, 70, 147
Strawson, P. F., 154, 155, 209
Suppes, P., 33, 201, 207, 208, 209
Synge, J. M., 27

Tarski, A., 92, 155, 161, 179, 208, 209
Tranoy, K. E., 213
Turnbull, R. E., 213

Wajsberg, M., 161, 194, 209
Wald, A., 33
Wallace, J., 81
Wedberg, A., 213
Weinberger, O., 213
Wells, R. S., 205
Whitehead, A. N., 63
Wiggins, D., 81
Winet, M., 201, 209
Wittgenstein, L., 63, 122
von Wright, G. H., 1, 30, 38, 43–63, 75, 77, 87–91, 97, 113, 121–147, 152, 168, 171, 178, 182, 183, 184, 187, 190, 194, 209, 213

Yun, S. S., 205, 207, 209

Ziembinski, Z., 213
Zinov'ev, A. A., 213

SUBJECT INDEX

Absolute permission (see Permission, unconditional)

Action, canonical description of, 214–218

Act-characterizations, 214–218

Acting situation, 124, 127–132, 134, 136, 142

Action, aspects of, 214–220

Action, course of, 1, 7, 125, 136

Action, covert aspects of, 218–219

Action description (see also Action, canonical description of) 85, 93, 127, 134, 214–220

Action, evaluation of, 219

Action, intentional (& intentions), 82, 83, 84, 85, 87–90, 94–95, 102, 103, 105, 110–112, 113, 118–119, 121, 124, 130, 144, 216, 218, 219

Action, logic of, 1, 2, 5, 15, 27–30, 121–146

Action, modality of, 214–215

Action, nature of, 124

Action, overt aspects of, 218–219

Action, preventive, 121, 127–129, 138, 139

Action, productive, 121, 125

Action, quantification over, 84–91

Action, rationale of, 214–216

Action-sentences, 81–120

Action sentences, analysis of (acc. to Chisholm), 86–87, 88, 89, 97, 113–114, 119–120

Action sentences, analysis of (acc. to Kenny), 83–86, 88, 89, 91, 96, 97, 219

Action sentences, analysis of (acc. to Reichenbach), 90–92, 93, 97

Action sentences, analysis of (acc. to Scheffler), 89–90

Action sentences, analysis of (acc. to von Wright), 87–89, 91, 97

Action sentences & tense logic, 96–103, 115–116

Action sentences, logical form of, 81–120

Action sentences, predicate analysis of, 83, 92–93, 104

Action, setting of, 215–216

Action space, 7–11, 20, 29

Action verbs, 83, 84, 91, 93, 95, 117

Action verbs, variable polyadicity of, 84, 91, 93, 101–102, 104, 105, 107, 117, 219

Act-type, 215

Act-type, generic, 215

Act-type, specific, 215

Afferent channels, 9

Agency and agent, 24, 72, 83, 86, 88, 93–95, 105–107, 109–111, 113, 117–118, 120, 123–125, 126–134, 137, 141, 142, 144–146, 170, 200, 201, 215, 217–219

Alethic logic, 152, 161, 165, 170, 171, 173, 174, 176, 178, 194, 200–202

Alethic logic, minimal normal (X*), 164–165, 179

Alethic logic, normal (X), 161, 163–165, 167, 169, 171, 173–176, 178, 179, 196

Alethic modalities (see Modalities, alethic)

Aspectival preference (see Preference, aspectival)

Attention-directing decisions, 4, 6, 20

Badness (see Goodness)

Basic implication (B), 66–69

Basic implication with propositional constants (B*), 68–70

Bayesian decision theory, 73, 74, 75, 78

B-constant (bad state of affairs), 175–179

Belief, rational, 23

Biography, 126–127, 132

Breadth first rule, 14–15

Canonical description of action (see Action, canonical description of)

Change, 97, 116–117, 121–123, 125, 127, 130, 132, 138–142

Change-description (see History)

Change, logic of, 88, 121–123, 140

Command (or action) variables, 3, 10, 15–16, 20, 24, 29, 34

Commands (see Imperatives)

Commitment, 151, 183–186

Comparative preference (see Preference, comparative)

Comparative value (see Value, comparative)

Compulsion, 130

Conclusive verbs, 101

Conditional permission (see Permissions, conditional)

Connections, table of, 13, 15

Control, 130–131

Counterfactuals, 124, 137, 142, 144

Course of action (see Action, course of)

Decision making, 1–35

Decision, rational, 23–24

Degree of freedom (see Freedom, degree of)

Deontic contingency, principle of, 182
Deontic logic, 1, 30, 35, 134–135, 138, 144, 147, 152, 170, 171, 173, 174, 176, 178, 181, 185, 186
Deontic logic, minimal normal (D*), 169–170, 181
Deontic logic, normal (D), 167–169, 171–174, 178, 196, 198, 199
Deontic modalities (see Modalities, deontic)
Depth first rule, 14–15
Descriptive discourse (see Discourse, descriptive)
Design decisions & problems, 7–20
Determinism, 128, 129, 131, 136
Differential goodness (see Goodness, differential)
Differential preference (see Preference, differential)
Directly undertaking (see Undertaking, directly)
Discourse, descriptive, 1, 22, 27
Discourse, prescriptive, 22

Efferent channels, 9
End state (see State, end)
Entailment, system of (E), 147
Environment variables, 3, 20, 24, 29
Epistemic indeterminism (see Indeterminism, epistemic)
Erotetic logic, 30–31, 35
Evaluation of action (see Action, evaluation of)
Event-sentences, 96–97, 99, 101
Events, identity of, 84–87, 92, 98–100, 104, 116–117
Events, quantification over, 86–87, 92–93, 98–100, 105

First-order goodness (see Goodness, first-order)
First-order preference (see Preference, first-order)
First-person intentions (see Intentions, first person)
Forbearance (see also Inaction), 121, 123, 125, 138, 139, 151, 170–172, 180–189, 193, 195, 196, 198, 199, 203
Freedom, degree of, 130

General Problem Solver (GPS), 12–15, 20, 27, 29
Generic act-type (see Act-type, generic)
Generic propositions (see Propositions, generic)
Generic state of affairs (see State of affairs, generic)

Goal-state (see State, end)
Goodness, differential, 40, 41, 44
Goodness, first-order, 40, 41, 44
Ground-floor preference (see Preference, ground floor)

"He" of self-consciousness (he*), 111
Heuristic power, 17–19, 20
Heuristics, 1–35
History (change-description), 122, 126, 131
Hypothetical permission (see Permission, conditional)

I-connective, 124–125, 146
Identity of events (see Events, identity of)
Imperatives (commands, injunctions), 5–6, 20, 21–24, 32
Imperatives, logic of, 1, 2, 21, 23–24, 27, 30–32, 35, 152
Imperatives, reduction to declaratives, 2, 5–6, 15, 21, 27–31, 34–35
Impotence, 130
Inaction (see also Forbearance), 3–4, 6, 125, 130, 131
Independence of propositions, 49–51, 59–70
Indeterminism, 132, 133, 135
Indeterminism, epistemic, 131–132
Index of merit (see Merit measure)
Indifference, 171
Individual state of affairs (see State of affairs, individual)
Initial state (see State, initial)
Injunctions (see Imperatives)
Intentional action (see Action, intentional)
Intentionality, 90, 94–95, 96, 102, 105, 216, 218
Intentions, first person, 110–111
Intentions, team, 112
Intrinsic preferences (see Preference, intrinsic)
Intrinsic value (see Value, intrinsic)

Life, 126, 127, 131, 132, 134–136
Life, length of, 126
Life-plan, 136
Life-situation, 126–128
Life-tree, 128–129, 132–133, 135–136
Logical form of action sentences (see Action sentences, logical form of)
Logic of action (see Action, logic of)
Logic of change (see Change, logic of)
Logic of preference (see Preference, logic of)

Manner, modality of, 214–218
Means-end, 7, 12, 13, 15, 20, 21–24, 25, 32, 215, 217
Measures of merit (see Merit measure)
Merit measure ♯, 44–46, 48–50, 55–58, 60–62, 74, 75, 78
Merit measure ★, 44–45, 57, 58, 61, 74, 75
Minimal normal alethic logic (see Alethic logic, minimal normal)
Minimal normal deontic logic (see Deontic logic, minimal normal)
Modalities, 189–192, 194, 195, 197
Modalities, alethic, 187, 189–195
Modalities, deontic, 30, 187, 190–197
Modalities, reiterated deontic, 187, 189–196
Modality of action (see Action, modality of)
Modality of manner (see Manner, modality of)

Non-conclusive verbs, 101
Normal alethic logic (see Alethic logic, normal)
Normal deontic logic (see Deontic logic, normal)
Normative logic (systems), 1, 28, 32, 34, 148, 151, 170, 181, 184–187, 193, 194, 200, 201, 203, 205
Normative systems, analysis of, 147–205

Obligation, 151, 152, 168–174, 180–187, 189, 192, 193, 195–199, 201–205
Omnipotence, 129, 130

Passivity, 130
Performance-actions, 4–5, 15, 16, 25–26, 32
Performance verbs, 101–102
Permission, 133, 134–136, 151, 152, 168–171, 173, 174, 180–183, 186–190, 192, 193, 195–199, 203
Permission, conditional, 135, 142–143
Permission, unconditional, 135
Planning-actions, 7, 15, 16, 25–26, 32, 33
Possible histories (see Possible worlds)
Possible worlds, 3, 6, 11, 43–44, 46–48, 55, 58, 59, 74–75, 78, 122
Practical reason (see Reason, practical)
Preferability, other things being equal, 45
Preference, aspectival, 42
Preference, comparative, 46–47, 74–75
Preference, differential, 42, 44

Preference, first-order, 41, 44, 55
Preference, ground floor, 48
Preference, intrinsic, 55–56, 74–75, 145
Preference, logic of, 37–79, 135, 138, 144
Preference, modes of, 41–42
Preference, P♯, 44–45, 47, 49–54, 56–61, 63, 67, 69, 70, 74, 75, 78
Preference, P★, 44–45, 47–54, 56–59, 61–63, 67, 74, 75, 78
Preference, P^w, 48–49, 53, 54, 55
Preference-principles, semantic vs. axiomatic approach to, 52–54
Preference, principles of (acc. to Chisholm-Sosa), 52–56, 58
Preference, principles of (acc. to R. M. Martin), 52–54, 59
Preference, principles of (acc. to von Wright), 52–54, 56, 75, 77
Preference, semantics of, 37–39, 47–49
Preference, synoptic, 42
Preference-tautologies, 49–51, 52, 58
Preference-tautologies, restricted, 50, 52–55
Preference-tautologies, unrestricted, 50, 52–55
Prescriptive discourse (see Discourse, prescriptive)
Preventive action (see Action, preventive)
Problem-space, 8–11, 13, 15, 17
Productive action (see Action, productive)
Progress test, 14, 15
Prohairetic logic (see Preference, logic of)
Prohibition (see Forbearance)
Propositions, generic, 88–89
Propositions, individual, 88–89

Quantification over actions (see Action, quantification over)
Quantification over events (see Events, quantification over)
Quantification over space-time zones (see Space-time zones, quantification over)
Quantification, restricted (A), 51, 53, 59–62, 64–65, 67–78, 77
Quantification, unrestricted (∀), 51, 53, 59–62, 64–65, 67–68, 77
Quasi indicators, 111–112

Rationality, 23
Rational belief (see Belief, rational)
Rational decision (see Decision, rational)

Realizability measure (R), 136
Reason, practical, 21–24
Reason, theoretical, 22–23
Reiterated deontic modalities (see Modalities, reiterated deontic)
Relevant implication, system of (R), 147
Restricted preference tautologies (see Preference tautologies, restricted)
Restricted quantification (see Quantification, restricted)
Role-conflict, 169–201

Sanction, 151, 170–172, 178, 187–189, 198, 199, 201–204
Satisficing, 19, 20
Scan & search rule, 14–15
S-constant (sanction), 170–175, 178–180, 187–189, 191, 195, 203
Semantics of preference (see Preference, semantics of)
Setting of action (see Action, setting of)
Space-time zones, 99–100, 116–117
Specific act-type (see Act-type, specific)
State description, 43, 48, 74, 77, 122, 125–132, 141, 142, 144
State, end, 15–16, 85, 88, 97, 123–124, 127, 138, 142
State, initial, 15, 19, 88, 97, 123–124, 132, 137
State of affairs, 74, 86, 89, 121, 135, 140, 144, 145, 170, 178, 187, 196–199, 201, 204
State of affairs, generic, 121–122, 124, 140–141, 145
State of affairs, individual, 121–122, 140, 145
State space, 7–11, 14, 16, 20, 29
Static verbs, 101
Synoptic preference (see Preference, synoptic)

Table of connections (see Connections, table of)
T-calculus, 123–146
T-connective (and next), 122–123, 125–132, 134–135, 141, 142
Team intentions (see Intentions, team)
Tense logic (see Action sentences and tense logic)
Terminal state (see State, end)
Termination-statement, 30
Theoretical reason (see Reason, Theoretical)
TI-calculus, 125, 131
Time moments, 97, 100
Time stretches, 97
Total value, 136

Unconditional permission (see Permission, unconditional)
Undertaking, directly, 113
Undertaking, indirectly, 113
Unrestricted preference tautologies (see Preference tautologies, unrestricted)
Unrestricted quantification (see Quantification, unrestricted)
Utility, concept of, 38, 39
Utility function, 3

Valuation, concept of, 39
Value, comparative, 40–42, 46, 75
Value-intrinsic, 46, 55, 74–75
Value, total, 136
Variable polyadicity (see Action verbs, variable polyadicity of)

We-intentions, 112
Wittgenstein-world, 122
Worlds, possible (see Possible worlds)